RHETORIC
Essays in Invention
and Discovery

RHETORIC
Essays in Invention and Discovery

Richard McKeon

Edited with an introduction by
Mark Backman

Ox Bow Press

"The Uses of Rhetoric in a Technological Age: Architectonic Productive Arts" in *The Prospect of Rhetoric:* Report of the National Development Project, edited by Lloyd F. Bitzer and Edwin Black, © 1971, pp. 44–63. Reprinted by permission of Prentice-Hall, Inc., Englewood Cliffs, NJ.

"Creativity and the Commonplace" from *Philosophy and Rhetoric*, vol. 6 (1973): 199–210. Reprinted by permission of Penn State Press, University Park, PA.

"Discourse, Demonstration, Verification, and Justification" from *Démonstration, Vérification, Justification* (Louvain: Nauwelaerts, 1969), pp. 37–55.

"The Methods of Rhetoric and Philosophy: Invention and Judgment" from *The Classical Tradition: Literary and Historical Studies in Honor of Harry Caplan*, edited by Luitpold Wallach, pp. 365–373. © 1966 by Cornell University. Used by permission of the publisher, Cornell University Press.

"Symbols, Myths, and Arguments" from *Symbols and Values: An Initial Study*, edited by Lyman Bryson, Louis Finkelstein, R. M. MacIver and Richard McKeon, pp. 13–38. © 1955 by the Conference on Science, Philosophy and Religion in their Relation to the Democratic Way of Life, Inc. Reprinted by permission of Harper & Row, Publishers, Inc.

"Philosophy of Communications and the Arts" reprinted from *Perspectives in Education, Religion and the Arts* edited by H. Keifer and M. Munitz by permission of the State University of New York Press. © 1970 State University of New York.

"Rhetoric in the Middle Ages" reprinted, by permission, from *Speculum: A Journal of Medieval Studies* 17/1 (1942), 1–32.

"Poetry and Philosophy in the Twelfth Century: The Renaissance of Rhetoric" from *Modern Philology* 43, no. 4 (May 1946): 217–34. © The University of Chicago.

"A Philosopher Meditates on Discovery" from *Moments of Personal Discovery*, edited by Robert M. MacIver. © 1952 by the Institute for Religious and Social Studies. Reprinted by permission of Harper & Row, Publishers, Inc.

Published by
Ox Bow Press
P.O. Box 4045
Woodbridge, CT 06525

Library of Congress Cataloging-in-Publication Data

McKeon, Richard Peter, 1900–1985
Rhetoric: essays in invention and discovery.
1. Rhetoric. I. Backman, Mark. II. Title.
PN175.M3 1987 808 86–28574

ISBN 0–918024–49–8

Printed in the United States of America

Contents

Introduction: Richard McKeon and the Renaissance of Rhetoric vii

1. The Uses of Rhetoric in a Technological Age: Architectonic Productive Arts 1

2. Creativity and the Commonplace 25

3. Discourse, Demonstration, Verification, and Justification 37

4. The Methods of Rhetoric and Philosophy: Invention and Judgment 56

5. Symbols, Myths, and Arguments 66

6. Philosophy of Communications and the Arts 95

7. Rhetoric in the Middle Ages 121

8. Poetry and Philosophy in the Twelfth Century: The Renaissance of Rhetoric 167

9. A Philosopher Meditates on Discovery 194

Introduction: Richard McKeon and the Renaissance of Rhetoric

Rhetoric is enjoying renewed popularity in Western culture. Users of the term *rhetoric* frequently define its nature and purpose, and the variety of definitions points up the essential dynamism that has marked its complex history. To the composition teacher, rhetoric is an "art" of writing which focuses the student's attention on the strategic nature of communication. To the literary scholar, it is a critical "apparatus" that covers all the techniques by which a writer establishes rapport with the reader. To the philosopher of language, it is a "study" of misunderstanding and its remedies. To the self-described rhetorician, it is a "method" of argumentation which looks to an audience to discover the means of persuasion.

The dynamic nature of rhetoric fascinated Richard McKeon. During his long career at the University of Chicago he investigated the intricate relationship between rhetoric and the extraordinary number of arts and sciences it has penetrated. The essays in this volume result from that lifelong pursuit of rhetoric's fundamental qualities. Moreover, these essays constitute the critical core of McKeon's intellectual activities and frame his consideration of topics and problems that at first sight seem far removed from any concern with rhetoric as it is commonly understood. For McKeon's perception of rhetoric goes beyond the verbal art of persuasion with which the word is commonly associated. In these essays McKeon exposes a vibrant, vivifying rhetoric anchored in circumstances of application and understandable only in the context of ideas, assumptions, methods, and ends that condition its various uses throughout history.

Given the prodigious range of McKeon's intellectual curiosity, his longtime and pervasive interest in rhetoric suggests the unique place he assigns it in the scheme of humanistic arts. To limit rhetoric to an art of expression or to account for its continual rebirth in Western history by tracing the repeated appearances of its characteristic terms and concepts serves little purpose in his eyes. Rhetoric is not simply a verbal art; it is also a formative principle that both directs the systematic contemplation of any subject matter and contains the analytic tools necessary for the comprehension of diverse and often contradictory philosophic principles and systems. McKeon rejects the notion that rhetoric and philosophy are separate disciplines, each dedicated to different and even contradictory ends. Throughout history rhetoric has infused and ordered philosophy, and, more important, philosophy has often been an unknowing form of rhetoric. By bringing together McKeon's seminal texts on rhetoric and philosophy, this volume seeks to broaden the reader's appreciation of rhetoric as a central, critical method for the analysis of ideas.

McKeon produced few books, preferring instead the essay as the vehicle for his ideas. Among the approximately 140 essays he wrote between 1927 and 1985, one finds such a mixture of interests and directions that it is easy to see why commentators have had difficulty assimilating his work. Nevertheless, McKeon has profoundly influenced the method and content of our thinking about philosophy, rhetoric, education, culture, and the history of ideas. His long involvement with educators, philosophers, and academics from numerous countries and his leadership in international education circles exposed a large number of influential thinkers to his analyses and criticisms. Successive generations of his students have gone into the world as teachers, philosophers, and theorists, and their labors suggest the utility and scope of the rhetoric developed in these essays. McKeon's concern with the problems of communication in a culturally heterogeneous world contributed to the formation of UNESCO in the early years of the United Nations. In turn, his experience with international problems figured into his conception of rhetoric as a unifying, inventive method. These concerns inspired numerous conferences and seminars devoted to exploring the possibilities of world unity in an age of glaring political and ideological differences. Finally, his perception of the effects of technology on the grounding of knowledge have found expression in debates about the deleterious influence of rapid change on institutions of government, commerce, and education.

Richard Rorty's division of philosophy into two broad categories provides a framework for understanding McKeon's overall project. The first category, mainstream "systematic" philosophy, has been the preoccupation of most scholars and forms the subject matter of philosophy as a school subject. Centered in epistemology, it typically seeks one area, one set of practices that can serve as the paradigm of human activity. "In the mainstream of Western philosophical tradition, this paradigm has been *knowing*—possessing justified true beliefs, or, better yet, beliefs so intrinsically persuasive as to make justification unnecessary."[1] Against this Rorty sets the second type of philosophic activity, peripheral "edifying" philosophy, which is based in a suspicion about the pretensions of epistemology.

> On the periphery of the history of modern philosophy, one finds figures who, without forming a "tradition," resemble each other in their distrust of the notion that man's essence is to be a knower of essences. Goethe, Kierkegaard, Santayana, William James, Dewey, the later Wittgenstein, and the later Heidegger, are figures of this sort. . . . They have kept alive the historicist sense that this century's "superstition" was the last century's triumph of reason, as well as the relativist sense that the latest vocabulary, borrowed from the latest scientific achievement, may not express privileged representations of essences, but be just another of the potential infinity of vocabularies in which the world can be described.[2]

Richard McKeon clearly belongs among these edifiers. In his

1. Richard Rorty, *Philosophy and the Mirror of Nature* (Princeton: Princeton University Press, 1980), p. 366.
2. Rorty, *Philosophy and the Mirror of Nature*, p. 367.

hands rhetoric is turned to an analytic purpose that sets the contradictions and conflicts of philosophers and rhetoricians into a manageable scheme for comparison and evaluation. McKeon explores themes not theses and, in Rorty's terms, is more interested in "continuing a conversation rather than discovering a truth."[3]

> The purpose which I set myself, however, was not to present and develop a "thesis"—the thesis of Aristotle or of any other philosopher or even a thesis of my own—but to follow the evolution of "themes" in which theses influence and transform each other. The advantage of considering the themes within which [philosophic terms] acquire a variety of meanings is that interpretation is not limited to one aspect of discourse, and alternative uses of "argument" which do not fit one's thesis are not marked off automatically as erroneous or defective.[4]

According to McKeon, philosophic thinking is manifested in four ways: as personal statement, as social integration, as scientific formulation, and as insight into fundamental values.

> I had evolved a complete philosophy in the first sense, as personal expression, at the age of twenty. Indeed, I have never since been able to construct a scheme of solutions of problems, old and new, so nearly complete, certain, or systematic. . . . It could be applied to any field of philosophy or to any subject matter without the need of much effort to become familiar with intricacies of the subject matter or its problems.[5]

This complicated, ornate epistemology was badly damaged, however, by contact with philosophy

> . . . in its second sense, in which it serves as an instrument to treat problems in the specific forms which they assume in times, places, and circumstances, and . . . in its third sense, in which [philosophy] makes use of the methods and the accomplishments of science to adapt itself as a form of knowledge to its problems.[6]

3. Rorty, *Philosophy and the Mirror of Nature*, p. 373.
4. "Discourse, Demonstration, Verification, and Justification," *Démonstration, Vérification, Justification* (Louvain: Nauwelaerts, 1969), p. 67.
5. "A Philosopher Meditates on Discovery," p. 199.
6. "A Philosopher Meditates on Discovery," p. 199.

Inadequacies were further revealed, McKeon tells us, when he embarked on an inquiry into the problem of the "one and the many" at Columbia University under the direction of John Dewey and Frederick J. E. Woodbridge. These studies produced in him a clearer sense of philosophy as a penetration of the problems of human values.

> In the teachings of Woodbridge and Dewey the problem of the one and the many is restated in terms appropriate to the problems of our times—not as a problem of essence and existence, nor as a problem of reality and appearance, but as a problem of truth and modes of formulation. The richness and diversity required by the experience and the problems of our times . . . revealed the tenuousness and poverty of the philosophic principles with which I had been engaged.[7]

The increasingly important role rhetoric came to play in McKeon's philosophic investigations marks his private passage from a rational philosophy founded in universalizing vocabularies and derived from fixed principles of being to a rhetorical philosophy based in the circumstances of expression and conditioned by specific problems of action. His belief that the arbitrary separation of rhetoric from philosophy colors how we come to terms with change and transformation in the history of Western thought constitutes McKeon's most important contribution to contemporary philosophic analysis. The divorce of rhetoric from philosophy, of expression from content, prevents the intellectual synthesis essential to resolving the persistent problems of being, thinking, and acting. If we enforce this split, rhetoric and philosophy bear little importance to daily life. For McKeon, however, "philosophical issues are not merely intellectual puzzles . . . a philosophy is called upon to illuminate human problems of freedom and its absence, of life and death."[8] Rorty's edifying philosophy is for McKeon rhetoric in its highest form.

Although these essays share certain concerns and considerations, they differ in the subject matter they treat, the principles they de-

7. "A Philosopher Meditates on Discovery," p. 201.

8. Charles Hartshorne, *Creativity in American Philosophy* (Albany: SUNY Press, 1984), p. 209.

scribe, the sources they draw upon, and the intentions they fulfill. No single essay contains the overarching statement of McKeon's philosophy of rhetoric. Rather, each sketches a particular reification of rhetoric by examining the philosophic conditions and pragmatic applications that unite to produce concrete expressions of rhetorical theory and practice. This approach produces a history of rhetoric that emphasizes rhetoric's volatility throughout Western history.

One theme that McKeon explores is that the many renaissances of rhetoric have shaped and been shaped by new ideas and perceptions of nature, life, art, freedom, truth, history, knowledge, and science. McKeon's history of rhetoric complements but vastly differs from the standard history. This traditional, overt history, the "pedantic explorations of . . . an art of persuasion and belief," preoccupies scholars who treat modern rhetoric as the heir of traditional terminologies, functions, and forms. Since it fails to acknowledge the differing matters and often contradictory ends marking rhetoric's earlier uses, it takes little note of "the consequences of basic philosophic differences" that determine the place of rhetoric in the larger scheme of human knowledge. Shifts in the application of rhetorical concepts are usually regarded as arbitrary because underlying assumptions about the nature and function of rhetoric are lost in the analyses of similar terms. *Invention, disposition,* and *style,* for example, are examined as if they have fixed, unalterable meanings, while the new meaning given the original conception in the context of its novel application generally passes unnoticed. Modern rhetoric is treated as derivative rather than as original or inventive and is assessed and applied according to its theoretic affinity to ancient models. And though our rhetoricians often employ the same key terms in their definitions of a verbal art of rhetoric, they often do so to different ends. The ambiguity surrounding the vocabulary of rhetoric translates into confusing descriptions of its past, since "communication," "discourse," "intention," "audience," "argumentation," "persuasion," and "invention" also serve as the linguistic signposts for tracing rhetoric's historical development.

McKeon's history of rhetoric, in stark contrast to this traditional history, does not have as its subject an art confined by fixed form, content, or terminology. Rhetoric is an art that lacks a unique subject matter but can only be understood in the context of specific uses and ends. This conception liberates the historical analysis of rhetoric from classically determined functions and forms. According to McKeon, a modern history ought to make meaningful the often contradictory purposes assigned to rhetoric in the arbitrary scheme of the sciences and arts. Properly developed, "such a history . . . might give significance and lively interest to the altering definitions, the differentiation of various conceptions of rhetoric itself, and the spread of devices of rhetoric to subject matters far from those ordinarily ascribed to it."[9]

The traditional histories of a verbal rhetoric attempt to fix the past through microscopic inspection of rhetoric's role in the formation and spread of ancient cultures. Rhetoric, an archaic phenomenon, becomes clearer the nearer we approach its origins. McKeon's history is telescopic, projecting a role for rhetoric based on an understanding of the transformations and applications evident in past uses. The investigation of rhetoric along these lines reveals that we have not "moved away from the rhetorical world of classical antiquity"[10] but that the modern world is a product of rhetoric's pervasive and enduring influence.

McKeon's perception of rhetoric can be most vividly traced in the Middle Ages, when applications of rhetorical terms and concepts moved far afield of their classical subject matter. This no doubt will seem odd to the reader imbued with the traditional conception of rhetoric. How can an essentially argumentative art find room to grow during a period when universal truth conditions all aspects of life? Most modern historians beg the question by simply tracing the influences of the ancient rhetoricians and poets on medieval arts of letter writing, preaching, and poetry. Cicero's five divisions of rhetoric—invention, disposition, style, memory, and delivery—serve as focal points for the criticism of peculiar literary forms. The history of medieval rhetoric is marked, according to this approach, by a withering away of the exalted position the art enjoyed in Greece and Rome.

McKeon attempts to recover a history that reduces "the welter of

9. "Rhetoric in the Middle Ages," p. 124.

10. Walter J. Ong, *Rhetoric, Romance, and Technology: Studies in the Interaction of Expression and Culture* (Ithaca: Cornell University Press, 1971), p. vii.

changes in rhetoric to a significant historical sequence." His analysis of rhetoric in the Middle Ages elaborately investigates the reflexive relationship between rhetoric, poetry, philosophy, and the other arts. McKeon's analysis opposes traditional histories by seeing rhetoric as a dynamic method rather than a static art. All rhetorical theories, classical, medieval, or modern, are of interest for the light they shed on philosophic disputes and for the transformations they work in concrete application. When rhetoric acquires a theoretical basis, questions of philosophic significance penetrate and inform arts of expression. When philosophy acquires a pragmatic intention, questions of rhetorical significance modulate and guide systems of judgment. By demonstrating that rhetoric can be fruitfully examined as the complex interplay of theory and practice, McKeon challenges the notion that the history of rhetoric has as its goal the development of a unitary body of knowledge "by more or less adequate investigations of a constant subject matter."

Common opinion holds that in the Middle Ages rhetoric all but died as a vital art. Medieval scholars vary in their adherence to this judgment, but most subscribe in some degree to the complaint that the works that have come down to us are nothing more than a "misapplication and perversion . . . of terms traditional in ancient rhetoric."[11] Modern commentators seem to lament that there was "no medieval rhetorician who really advanced the study."[12] Consequently, they erect a tradition of rhetoric in the Middle Ages around disparate works on poetic and prosaic composition, preaching, and letter writing to promote the view that, busy as they were, medieval scholars never fully appreciated the ancient art with which they fiddled. One must await the Renaissance for the resumption of substantial work in rhetorical theory.

For McKeon, though, these analyses produce only "a brief and equivocal history of rhetoric in the Middle Ages." His purpose is to move the consideration of rhetoric beyond the well-worked ground of tracing Cicero's influence on medieval arts of composition and performance. To be sure, Cicero "fixed the influence and oriented the interpretation of ancient thought, Greek as well as Latin" during

11. C. S. Baldwin, *Medieval Rhetoric and Poetic to 1400* (New York: Macmillan, 1928), p. 152, pp. 191–193.

12. Baldwin, *Medieval Rhetoric and Poetic*, p. 62.

the Middle Ages. But rhetoric proceeds along another less obvious line of development in the tradition of philosophers and theologians "who found in Augustine a Platonism . . . formulated in terms refurbished and simplified from Cicero's rhetorical distinctions." Moreover, Cicero supplied a treatment of definitions and principles which informed a third line of development, the tradition of logic. Medieval thinkers in all the arts and sciences turned to rhetoric for methods, distinctions, and conceptions—not simply the ancient subject matters or vocabularies—to vivify their work.

> During the Middle Ages and the Renaissance many of the oppositions and agreements of theology and dialectic, no less than the problems internal to each, were stated in language borrowed from or influenced by rhetoric and reflected theories by which rhetoricians had in antiquity opposed philosophers and logicians; surprising parallels were disclosed in theology and dialectic as well as in other arts and sciences . . . expressed in language familiar to the rhetorician.[13]

Rhetoric was "the source of doctrines which have since become the property of other sciences . . . and of particular devices which have been applied to a variety of subject matters." The practical uses of rhetoric, in the Middle Ages and the present, have identified it with and opposed it to logic and dialectic, sophistic and science, civil philosophy and law, psychology and literature, and philosophy itself. McKeon believes that to confine rhetoric to a single subject matter denies it a vital history, in the Middle Ages or at any time: ". . . the innovations that are recorded during that period in the arts with which [rhetoric] is associated suggest that their histories might profitably be considered without unique attachment to the field in which their advances are celebrated."[14]

This principle directs McKeon's examination of poetry and philosophy in the Late Middle Ages, when philosophers often held conflicting opinions about the nature and purpose of poetic composition. Some felt that poetry "approximates closely the subjects and problems of philosophy," that the poet expresses the highest

13. "Rhetoric in the Middle Ages," p. 125.
14. "Rhetoric in the Middle Ages," p. 166.

ideas about man, his actions, and nature.[15] Others claimed that the constructions of poets are the chief sources of error and immorality, that philosophy alone explicates the truth. Still others held that poetry is completely lacking in doctrine and that philosophy requires a precision of proof uncharacteristic of poetic forms. In the face of these medieval disagreements, it is misleading to reduce the distinction between poetry and philosophy to differences in modes of expression, rigor in treatment, or usefulness. "Despite the temptation to claim the scientific method for literary criticism," poetry and philosophy cannot be classified as "purely natural phenomena or things," since they are artificial constructions that express ideas about art and life. Philosophy is often cloaked in poetic form, and both medieval poets and philosophers worked on themes and problems drawn from the conflict between reason and faith. Poetry and philosophy share similar subject matters and purposes in the Late Middle Ages, and the common method binding them together "is rhetoric, which assumes many forms and uses in the twelfth century." Because rhetoric provided the link between doctrine and aesthetic, the determination of its history along lines laid down by McKeon reveals the important connection between thought and expression. In this, medieval and modern times share a common disposition: ". . . for poetry is related to philosophy today in methods and matters as different as existentialism, Marxism, and pragmatism, and it has returned to themes . . . which recall that man is in a grave predicament, that words are ambiguous . . . and God is mysterious."[16]

Rhetoric informed methods for resolving conflicting assertions in canon law, theology, and philosophy. This facet of its medieval development is seen in the shift of rhetorical terms and concepts from questions of law to questions of faith. In the twelfth century rhetoric was directed to problems of sacred theology by Peter Abelard, whose *Sic et Non* adapted the traditional forms of canonic disputation to matters of mystic ambiguity. Abelard proposed that even the apparent doctrinal contradictions in the Fathers of the Church could be resolved through the judicious application of dia-

15. "Poetry and Philosophy in the Twelfth Century: The Renaissance of Rhetoric," p. 167.

16. "Poetry and Philosophy in the Twelfth Century," p. 193.

lectic and rhetoric. Abelard was condemned to silence for his innovation, but his method was picked up by numerous imitators and controlled the curriculum of the schools in one form or another for three centuries.

Rhetoric also guided the historical, allegorical, tropological, and anagogical modes of scriptural interpretation. Augustine's *On Christian Doctrine* introduced a rhetoric aptly suited to isolating and transmitting universal Christian truth through an unfolding, variable human history. His distinction between divine and human things and signs provided the matrix upon which medieval commentators worked out their inquiries into ethics, the nature of sin and redemption, the purpose and structure of sermons, the character of preachers, and the analysis of audiences. Clearly, rhetoric enjoyed a lively and fecund history during the Middle Ages.

McKeon examines rhetoric's pervasive role in medieval arts and sciences to reinforce the notion that our knowledge and use of rhetoric must be distilled from its obscured history. He plays upon the ambiguities that have come to surround rhetoric's traditional nomenclature in order to demonstrate that the history of rhetoric is at heart the story of new applications in changed circumstances for borrowed words, concepts, and distinctions. The exercise is dizzying, especially if McKeon is read in terms of the traditional history of rhetoric, where ancient definitions form the standard of comparison. He investigates the shared heritage of rhetoric and philosophy, for example, by examining varying notions of a variety of rhetorical terms and concepts, especially *commonplace*.

The idea of the commonplace originated with Aristotle, who was the first to distinguish between the general nature of rhetoric and dialectic and the special nature of science, or philosophy.

> Aristotle had differentiated rhetoric sharply from philosophy, and rhetorical persuasion from demonstrative proof, by means of the questions and the places proper to each. Rhetoric is a counterpart to dialectic. Rhetorical and dialectical syllogisms are concerned with places common to many sciences and subject matters. Proper places, on the other hand, are derived from propositions peculiar to each species and genus of things. . . . To the extent that proper places are used, a science is produced different from rhetoric and dialectic, and if first principles are

> encountered, the discussion has moved from rhetoric . . . to the science of which they are first principles.[17]

Subsequently, these conceptions were inverted. Rhetoric came to treat specific questions—this case, this cause, this effect—while philosophy and science came to treat general problems.

As devices of rhetoric, commonplaces have often served contradictory purposes. At times, they have referred to the seat of arguments and have been closely allied with the traditional rhetorical division of memory. At other times, they have referred to heuristic devices that suggest qualities, characteristics, and relations appropriate to all arguments. More recently, they have been identified with unvarying and repetitious formulae that offer an "easy substitute for the invention of a pertinent solution." Commonplace invention thus has alternately encompassed common categories, distinct relations, and universal truths. Moreover, commonplaces have been applied by philosophers and scientists to construct histories of their fields, by moralists to order fundamental values, and by politicians to define their communities.

The history of commonplaces is marked by degradations, narrowings, transformations, and novel applications. When applied to memory, the commonplaces threatened to become as numerous as the things remembered. Commonplaces moved from meaning an empty place, as an aid in the ordering of things, to meaning a special matter, or subject, to be discussed. As instruments of discovery, commonplaces have shifted back and forth, from devices used for discovering something unknown to formulae used for recalling stock quotations to be applied in a familiar manner. As a result, "commonplaces were memorized rather than used for invention, and they were recited when the occasion arose rather than used when the circumstances required."[18]

Invention and judgment have been joined at times within rhetoric and at other times within philosophy. They have also been separated to form distinct arts of knowing and telling. Invention has referred to things as well as words and has moved into all sciences and arts. Judgment is of characteristic qualities and virtues as well

17. "The Methods of Rhetoric and Philosophy: Invention and Judgment," p. 60.
18. "Creativity and the Commonplace," p. 28.

as of effective arguments. It directs the critical evaluation of behavior, experimentation, and first principles. For ". . . judgment adds to the demonstrative arts of deducing from assumptions, the deliberative arts of examining consequences, and the judicial arts of falsifying alternatives, while invention extends from the construction of formal arguments to all modes of enlarging experience by reason as manifested in awareness, emotion, interest, and appreciation."[19]

The movement of traditional terms of rhetoric from arts of eloquence, where they determine the shape of arguments, to arts of analysis, where they determine the proper scope of subjects and the methods of inquiry, indicates the presence of rhetoric as a dynamic tool shaping modes of thought. This history has been determined to a great extent by the ancient distinction between knowing and doing. The problematic separation of arts of knowing from arts of expression led Cicero to attempt to rejoin wisdom and eloquence in a "civic" philosophy controlled by the reformation of a rhetoric appropriate to Roman law. His effort has been repeated many times in circumstances far removed from classical legal culture. Rhetoric has expanded and contracted to fit the preferences of individual philosophers who have set out to construct intelligible systems of discovery and explanation. In the curriculum of the schools rhetoric has been assigned a much reduced role when the motive has been to establish discrete disciplines marked by unique subject matters and methods. Conversely, rhetoric has organized the entire course of study when the goal has been to bridge the gap between distinct subject matters. "When the philosophic arts are conceived of as arts of being or of thought, rhetoric is not treated as a philosophic art, although it is used extensively in the controversy and refutation which constitutes communication among philosophies. When the philosophic arts are arts of communication and construction, rhetoric is made into a universal and architectonic art."[20]

Inventions, discoveries, and judgments—of things, occurrences, phenomena, actions, accounts, systems, and statements—are expressed in language and genres of discourse. We determine our com-

19. "The Methods of Rhetoric and Philosophy," p. 59.
20. "Philosophy of Communications and the Arts," p. 108.

monplaces, whatever our purpose, through fictive narration, objective description, articulated argument, and sensible exposition. In these essays McKeon points the way to explorations of the connection of language to subject, not only in philosophy but also in politics, religion, art, and science. The history of Western thought turns on the successive rediscovery and novel application of commonplaces freed from the mindless repetition of things past, and rhetoric emerges as the crucial force in intellectual change. "The relevance of the methods of rhetoric to the problems of philosophy is due in part to the continuity of the influences, in which the methods of philosophy have influenced the methods of rhetoric and been influenced in turn by them, and in part to the orientation of contemporary problems to issues particularly suited to the methods of rhetoric."[21]

Clearly, rhetoric can be more than a verbal art, although expression has always been an important element. Most modern rhetoricians believe that words determine actions, that language is effective and affected. Rhetoric, for them, is essentially argumentative in structure and intent. As such, it has been widened to explain not only speech making and persuasive writing but also the argumentative aspects of film, fiction, and the entire range of artistic expression.

McKeon pursues another line of investigation. Invention refers not only to words but to facts, data, methods, and systems. Rhetoric is more than an expressive art; it is an organizational principle that provides the framework within which we can reveal and arrange the significant parts of any human undertaking. Ideas are expressed in structures developed to guide action—political communities, educational systems, business enterprises—as well as in the artifacts of literary or artistic creativity. Language is still an effective tool, but it *follows* from the creation of new ways of conceiving and acting upon change. That is, it trails the invention of new devices of science and new forms of cooperative action. The technological world literally "comes to terms" with the new after it has been uncovered by the application of scientific methods of discovery. Technological specialties shape our language, and thereby give rise

21. "The Methods of Rhetoric and Philosophy," p. 64.

to new ways of knowing, telling, doing, and being. Consequently, our commonplaces need to be innovative rather than repetitious because discovery "is not the simple fitting, or passive addition, of further items of information to a collection of data or to a structure of theory." Discovery leads to the creation of new forms, expressions, and ways of thinking rather than to doctrines grounded in the past.

McKeon believes that the expansion of rhetoric from an art of expression to a principle of organization makes possible the appreciation of diverse cultures, systems, and disciplines, since rhetoric seeks commonplaces that transcend the narrow confines of special perceptions. The power of rhetoric resides in its ability to discover, in the materials at hand, language and modes of interpretation suitable to immediate circumstances. "The new art of rhetoric is the art of discovery. It is not a heuristic method or radical interpretation but an art of topics or a selection of elements which opens the way to the recognition of new facts and to the perception of unnoticed structures or sequences."[22]

McKeon calls this rhetoric an architectonic productive art, a description he draws from Aristotle who "gave a technical meaning to the ordinary Greek expression *architecton*—'architectonic artist' or 'master craftsman'—and used it in his schema of the organization of the sciences."[23] McKeon's use of the term shares some features with modern usage, where "architectonic" carries a special meaning of structural design or skill in architecture. McKeon's sense of the word, however, is a residue of the more ancient definition. The rhetorician and the architect exist at two levels. As technicians, they are skilled with the tools of expression special to their trade—lines and planes for the architect, words and arguments for the rhetorician. As master craftsmen, though, rhetorician and architect transcend their specialties to take on greater responsibilities. They envision the formal design, coordinate the work of specialists, assess and assign the raw materials, and produce by their efforts the final product. An *architecton*—rhetorician or architect—employs an art different from that of the user, who knows only the form and func-

22. "Philosophy of Communications and the Arts," p. 110.
23. "The Uses of Rhetoric in a Technological Age: Architectonic Productive Arts," p. 2.

tion, because the master craftsman also knows the matter and makes the product. In Aristotelian terms, he commands the four causes: the formal, efficient, material, and final.

Rhetoric has always possessed an architectonic function, and it has grown or contracted according to the influence the art has assumed in relation to other methods and sciences. When rhetoric is a verbal art of persuasion, it is architectonic of attitudes and productive of arguments and words. Cicero divided the art of rhetoric into five parts and made disposition a major component. Once the key points have been discovered in the case at hand, they must be ordered to lead an audience to the desired conclusion. Ordering involves more than arguments, of course, since it also refers to the words and examples within the context of syllogistic structures. In terms of an audience the disposition of arguments produces the inclination to believe or disbelieve, accept or reject. When rhetoric moves beyond the realm of a verbal art, the concepts of disposition and ordering assume a more universal nature. They drop the specific subjects of argumentative communication and pick up the characteristic contents of whatever art or science they join. Cicero provides a ready example of this sense of disposition, for his "use of rhetoric as a productive architectonic art laid down the structure of a program of education and culture designed to reunite eloquence and wisdom in action."

Moreover, rhetoric is architectonic because, like Aristotle's *Politics*, it has its end in action, not knowledge. Since the "architectonic arts treat ends which order the ends of subordinate arts," rhetoric structures thinking about any subject matter. In this it is distinguished from all the other arts and sciences, including politics. "For Aristotle rhetoric is not a 'science,' because each science has a particular 'method' suited to its particular subject-matter and operative according to its proper principles."[24] McKeon develops this point in the brief histories that open most of these essays. Rhetoric lacks any special subject matter, although its transmission in Western culture has always been through its association with other arts and sciences. Rhetorical terms and concepts have influenced and been influenced by many disciplines and circumstances. Indeed, *circum-*

24. "The Uses of Rhetoric in a Technological Age," p. 4.

stance itself is a rhetorical concept that has enlivened philosophy, law, and science. Innovation, in any discipline, arises by means of rhetoric, when old terms and ideas are transformed by new problems and uses. Invention, first linked to the creation of arguments, now stands for creativity in every realm of human thought and action.

Rhetoric is productive because it leads to actions, systems, and structures. In Aristotle the productive sciences, like poetics, have particular content and result in things made or produced—plays, poems, artworks, and the like. Architectonic arts, in contrast, lack special products and focus on the means of production. Since Aristotle, however, "the sciences have become . . . sources of production, of new matters and new forms, in need of organizing methods and principles." The Aristotelian differentiation of the practical, productive, and theoretical arts and sciences breaks down in the technological age because technical innovation forces changes in areas remote from the sciences that first gave rise to new tools and devices. Invention in the technological age carries with it consequences in practice and product as well as in theory.

The explosion of new techniques has wreaked havoc upon static institutions of government, commerce, and learning because modern forms of special knowledge cannot be guided by the principles of any one science. Technology reinforces the disruptive separation of words and things by creating special places for action. Disagreements between experts have a way of becoming political and social controversies to be resolved by generalists. The age of technology militates against the orderly institutions of Plato's *Republic* and we cannot rely on a select group of guardians to make our decisions for us. McKeon's conception of rhetoric as an architectonic productive art provides an intellectual principle to organize considerations of change and its attendant dissonance in the modern world. Verbal rhetoric produces only words and arguments reinforcing differences.

McKeon's rhetoric collapses the distinction between words and things and seeks to remedy the division between wisdom and eloquence by inverting the traditional relationships of verbal rhetoric. Actions, situations, and organizations lead to the creation of new terminologies. Words do not determine actions; they bridge the gap between experience and the novel. Or, to put the matter another way, "The commonplace of commonplaces is the place in which the certainties of the familiar are brought into contact with the transformations of innovation."[25] McKeon's is a rhetoric of *invention* rather than *expression*, and familiar commonplaces are transformed into instruments for perception, creation, arrangement, discursive exploration, and inclusion.

> It is appropriate that commonplaces be transformed from collections of fixed and established, communicable clichés to neutral sources of new perceptions operative in new directions. Rhetoric again has assumed a dominant place in our thought and action. Whereas the rhetoric of the Romans took its commonplaces from the practical arts and jurisprudence and the rhetoric of the Humanists took its commonplaces from the fine arts and literature, our rhetoric finds its commonplaces in the technology of commercial advertising and of calculating machines.[26]

The exigencies of a technological age force us to deal with problems of communication that transcend and subsume the requirements of mere persuasion. Rhetoric is productive of actions as well as words, and it connects disparate things—cultures, disciplines, sciences, languages, ideologies—by extrapolating commonality from the uncommon. The conception of rhetoric as an instrument of cohesion breaks free of earlier formulations of rhetoric as a separate art: form is related to matter, presentation to content, agent to audience, and intention to reason through the inquiry into what is the case, rather than to semantic analysis of what somebody else has said.

Rhetoric emerges in the technological age in two distinct, related forms. As a verbal art of persuasion, it shrinks to a collection of commonplace techniques of argumentative communication. Writing, and communication in general, is seen as an action in itself. As an inventive, organizing principle, rhetoric grows to meet the demand for unity amid technological fragmentation. Communication in any form is a residue of action. The twofold history of rhetoric shows that at every stage in its development in Western culture, rhetoric operates simultaneously at the verbal and the architectonic

25. "Creativity and the Commonplace," p. 35.
26. "Creativity and the Commonplace," p. 34.

levels. In America, where culture is expressed in productive activity dominated by technological innovation, the new rhetoric grows out of and subsumes the traditional verbal art. Three realms of practical action—education, business, and politics—exhibit most clearly how rhetoric's twofold nature operates.

In education, the verbal art of rhetoric is the special discipline of the humanities and, as such, exacerbates the persistent division between words and things. Verbal rhetoric is an instrument of articulation and analysis which focuses on the products of human expression. It is used to teach writing, speaking, and literary criticism. In business, verbal rhetoric has found a place in corporate communications and advertising. The techniques of persuasion, culled from the long history of argumentative theory, are used to define audiences and sell the products of other arts and sciences. Verbal rhetoric is an instrument of differentiation and accommodation which seeks to match commercial appeals with special audiences. In politics, verbal rhetoric has found a place in legal reasoning, legislative debate, lobbying, and propaganda. It is an instrument of communication and negotiation which determines the realm of the possible in the allocation of limited resources among competing interests. The modes of commonplace invention focus on immediate judgments and decisions in order to convince dubious audiences of the similarity between present problems and past circumstances.

In each instance rhetoric is used to produce appropriate words and arguments. By searching for historical terms that can be made to fit existing conditions, rhetoric communicates established judgments or interprets what someone has said in light of what is known. It passively receives its content from precedent circumstances and uses. Most important, rhetoric proceeds here as a verbal principle, employing traditional language and concepts to configure new problems.

Architectonic rhetoric, however,

> . . . should become a universal art, an art of producing things and arts, and not merely one of producing words and arguments. . . . In an age of technology the diremption to be removed is the separation of theory and practice by the

> constitution of a technology which is theory applied, the *logos of techne*. We seek to produce it in concrete experience and existence by rejoining reason and sense, cognition and emotion, universal law and concrete occurrence.[27]

In education, architectonic rhetoric organizes the entire curriculum of study as well as courses in writing, reading, and speech. Rhetoric has always been associated with systematic education. Cicero's insistence that an orator be schooled in philosophy was intended to guarantee that the power to move men to act would derive from a knowledge of the nature and consequences of right action. The wise man who cannot speak is seldom helpful, he warned, and the eloquent man who lacks wisdom is always dangerous. Augustine sought to empower the Christian preacher to discern the truth among the flawed signs and ambiguous terminologies, analogies, parables, and examples of Holy Scripture by means of an interpretive rhetoric that organized learning and life in the Christian world. In the Renaissance Peter Ramus laid out several disciplines in his scheme for a rational system of education. Although he formally assigned style to rhetoric and placed invention under logic, the unifying framework for his division of the sciences is based on the five Ciceronian parts of rhetoric. Richard McKeon, Robert Hutchins, Ronald Crane, and others developed a pluralistic and practical course of study at the University of Chicago in the 1930s which sought to overcome the tendency of interdisciplinary studies to succumb to subordination to one well-established or popular discipline. As McKeon explained: "I inclined to argue for a broader conception of the liberal arts . . . one that would strive to combine universality of judgment with particularity of application of rules by joining considerations of the functions of liberal arts as ideas and actions to their functions as words and things."[28]

Architectonic rhetoric reorients the student to discover previously unnoticed connections between established disciplines. Current interest in "writing across the curriculum" is one expression of rhetoric's potential; it seeks to move responsibility for expression back

27. "The Uses of Rhetoric in a Technological Age," p. 13.

28. "Criticism and the Liberal Arts: The School of Chicago Criticism," *Profession 82* (Modern Language Association of America, 1982), p. 4.

into academic departments where a premium has been placed on "knowing well" at the expense of "telling well." Architectonic rhetoric rejoins knowledge and expression by incorporating the organizational aspects of rhetoric into the design and execution of all courses of study. It produces a pluralism of disciplines by establishing modes of discovery and discourse common to all sciences and arts.

In business, architectonic rhetoric organizes work among technologies isolated by their different languages, methods, and ends. By moving out of the marketing and sales division, where it is employed as a verbal art, rhetoric informs the conduct of commercial enterprise in all its phases. Modern business suffers from the fragmentation of internal processes and external audiences because the historic dialogue between special knowledge and common opinion in the technological age lacks an appropriate structure for its conduct. Communities of knowledge form around discrete and incommunicative special interests while control of rapid change, which spreads beyond the boundaries of its origin, is the product of chance, not art, in our time. The rise of "high tech" enterprise illustrates the point. Most successful undertakings are the work of a very few people who begin with a vision, however defined, and organize the instruments for its attainment according to ongoing adaptations to changing conditions. In other words, they conduct a dialogue between what is known and what can be done. This dialogue is shaped at every stage by "the calculation of uses that might be made of vastly increased available means." It aims to devise new ends and to avoid errors based on previous misunderstandings. In form and function the successful high technology company is an elaborate, eloquent conversation between the present and the past, special places and commonplaces.

Architectonic rhetoric provides the conceptual basis for understanding and managing change within fragmented technocracies. Communities are formed and reformed according to the vagaries of changing situations, recent discoveries, novel devices, and new concepts. Because the technological age is also the information age, the effects of novelty spread rapidly throughout the organizing structures of society. Our contemplation of the new and our attempts to control the processes by which it becomes real are thus locked up in a paradox. Novelty explained is no different from the familiar while discovery reduced to rules is indistinguishable from other actions guided by precept or habit.[29] Facts tend to overwhelm judgments. Collaboration in a climate of mass communication is made inefficient by institutionalized misperception and misunderstanding. Rhetoric is a managing skill that creates commonplaces for systematic action out of the data, facts, and consequences of actual cases. As an architectonic productive art, rhetoric produces a pluralism of technologies by establishing structures, forms, and procedures that transcend the unique languages of specialized sciences.

In politics, architectonic rhetoric creates communities of informed action out of diverse cultures, polities, interests, and ideologies. This is particularly crucial in an age dominated by technology, for politics and technological innovation are often joined in an unholy alliance to promote the centralization of authority and the obliteration of real differences—cultural, political, racial, spiritual—in the name of efficient government. When political forms are unable to adapt to rapid changes in techniques, the entire structure of social relationships is damaged. As one observer has noted,

> . . . social structures and political institutions are increasingly eroded by the impact of technological innovation which they cannot reject, regulate, or commit themselves to absorb. . . . The technological society is not threatened by the inescapable conflict of technology and politics, but rather by an avoidable conflation of technique and shallow rationality . . . Reason in the service of technique, employing only the categories and conceptions of conventional politics, is indeed inept.[30]

Architectonic rhetoric seeks to avoid the "conflation of technique and shallow rationality" by opening up the processes of dissent and divergence. More than an art of propaganda and conviction, rhetoric discovers commonplaces of unity and agreement rather than of opposition. It directs the inquiry into causes of political action in a manner sensitive to the influence of mass communication on a

29. "A Philosopher Meditates on Discovery," p. 195.

30. Raghavan Iyer, *Parapolitics: Toward the City of Man* (Oxford: Oxford University Press, 1979), pp. 144ff.

global scale. Rhetoric has always been concerned with the connection between stability and change, similarity and difference, and thus pays particular attention to the impact of technological innovation on the institutions of government and law. Architectonic rhetoric also looks to dissolve the traditional prejudices of past arguments about the means and ends of community by adjusting political structures and processes to changes in polity. Rhetoric alone among the humanistic arts can isolate and address problems peculiar to the circumstances of the present. The desire to come together, not the urge to persuade, is what makes politics rhetorical. Persuasion follows communication and the formation of communities since it is impossible to persuade "out of context." Isolation from the causes and consequences of belief—"true believing"—admits no capacity for change.

Further evidence for the transcendent nature of rhetoric is found in *On Christian Doctrine*, where Augustine uses rhetoric in both its verbal and architectonic aspects to distinguish his Christian conception from Cicero's classical art. As a verbal rhetoric *On Christian Doctrine* sets out precepts "for treating the Scriptures . . . so that they [students] may profit not only from reading the work of expositors but also in their own explanations of the sacred writings to others."[31] The principles and distinctions of classical rhetoric are transformed by Augustine to fit the particular requirements of persuasion in the setting of the universal truth of Christian doctrine. As an architectonic art, however, Augustine's rhetoric moves beyond the technical details of felicitous interpretation and suasive preaching. Through an evolutionary human history it encompasses the process of coming to terms with divine wisdom in the midst of confusing symbols of communication transmitted temporally. *On Christian Doctrine* develops a rhetorical method by which unchanging truth can be isolated and employed according to the needs of an ever changing and specifically determined Christian community. Augustine focuses the problem of developing a truly Christian history by dealing "explicitly with the ties that had bound educated

31. Saint Augustine, *On Christian Doctrine*, translated by D. W. Robertson, Jr. (Indianapolis: Bobbs-Merrill, 1958), p. 3.

Christians to the culture of their age."[32] These ties assumed two forms. Some were symbolic and were manifested in pagan literature and art. Others were structural and were embodied in Roman administrative institutions and educational curricula. Augustine invented an architectonic productive art of rhetoric to recast, in Christian form and content, the intellectual structure of human history, culture, and communication.

Augustine's task resembles our own in many ways. Rhetoric is a form of symbolic action, and its employment in the political realm predates its use in any other area of human activity. It treats "potentiality" as well as "actuality" and can serve to promote as well as inhibit the formation of articulate communities. Richard McKeon was keenly aware of this aspect of rhetoric, for he saw it work with limited success in the early days of UNESCO. Our confidence in the dynamics of international dialogue, signified by the numerous institutions we have created to promote the discussion of common problems of survival, underlies the role for a rhetoric that takes its commonplaces from beyond the immediate requirements of persuasion. While debate, discussion, and controlled confrontation contribute to mutual understanding and can lead to collaboration and cooperation, McKeon believed that international bodies founded on the architectonic principles of rhetoric provide the context for shaping philosophic ideas as well as for transmitting technical methods of government, industry, and education. In the context of international communication, of life in the "global village," rhetoric can help uncover a body of cultural symbols appropriate to a world marked by cultural diversity, rapid change, instantaneous communication, and the potential for mass destruction.

> Symbols, developed and used to make common values richer by the diversity of approaches to them and to make differences compatible by common courses of action that solve common problems even when the problems are differently conceived, provide the one practicable alternative to the imposition by force of a single set of symbols in the form of a single set of institutions interpreted by a single philosophy.[33]

32. Peter Brown, *Augustine of Hippo* (Berkeley: University of California Press, 1969), pp. 264 ff.

33. "Symbols, Myths, and Arguments," p. 94.

The works in this volume stand opposed to the new sophistries of the marketplace where unprincipled eclecticism is aided by computerized access to the world's storehouse of philosophic, religious, and ethical commonplaces. The technological revolution, with its demand for greater specialization, destroys the integrated perception modern life requires. The growth of modern technological sophistries directly reflects the isolation of education from the conduct of daily existence, and signals our acceptance of the division between words and things.

As an architectonic productive art, rhetoric operates largely unrecognized in human creativity, where ideas are expressed in the structure of knowledge, the organization of work, and the definition of community. In a world ordered by technical innovation and mass communication, the principles and practices of education, business, and politics flow through and inform each other. The practical actions of managers form the subject matter for scholars in schools of business administration. Public policy emerges from the debates of politicians, the commentaries of analysts, the claims of vested interests, and the arguments of concerned individuals. Its applications are detailed in case studies constituting the curricula in schools of public policy. In business and politics the organization of knowledge in the schools reflects and affects the organization of knowledgeable skills in the workplace. Work itself acquires new meaning in the liberation from menial tasks and the primacy of special knowledge. Life and labor are structured around the search for cohesion in an increasingly disrupted world where diverse, specialized arts and sciences make competing claims about the nature of the "truth."

> In the emerging community of the world the first problem of philosophy—the new metaphysics or at least the new prolegomenon to all future metaphysics—will expound the sense in which truth is one, despite the multiplicity of the forms of its expression, and the sense in which what is on some grounds or in some circumstances true is at other times false and dangerous.[34]

These essays address "the first problem of philosophy" by examining the relationship between thought and expression as it is

34. "A Philosopher Meditates on Discovery," p. 220.

played out in a variety of philosophic circumstances. They describe a concept of rhetoric rooted in practical application but mirrored everywhere in theoretical speculation. And they detail the history of rhetoric as a tool for creating disciplines, arts, systems, and methods. Above all, these essays anticipate a renaissance of rhetorical theory and practice which promises to discover new uses for rhetoric in contemporary problems of community, communication, and action.

—Mark Backman

RHETORIC
Essays in Invention
and Discovery

The Uses of Rhetoric in a Technological Age: Architectonic Productive Arts

I. Continuities and Revolutions in the Development of Rhetoric

Rhetoric has had a long and variegated history. It has been influential in the development of theory, practice, and art, and methods to produce and use the products of knowledge, action, and production. It has been influenced by truths of sciences, circumstances of times and communities, and analogies of arts; and it has been expounded in propositions of theory, in rules of practice, and in maxims of art. Its history has been a continuous one, because basic terms, distinctions, and schemata reappear and are put to new uses. It has been an ambiguous history, because continuing terms assume new meanings in their new applications, and the innovations are seldom guided by knowledge of how renewed terms were used in earlier traditions. Histories of rhetoric, which throw little light on the principles or purposes by which present methods and uses of rhetoric might be evaluated or changed, tend to be pedantic explorations of traditions of rhetoric as an art of persuasion and belief, of deception and proof, of image-making and communication, which follow through the consequences of pejorative or positive judgments posited as premises. Discussions of rhetoric in the past and in the present and projections of rhetoric in the future reflect estimations of its nature and operation. Apparently it has been practiced widely as an art of deception, public relations, alienation, and self-interest, and it has been one of the factors contributing to the degradation of knowledge, morality, and culture. Apparently it has also been practiced as an art of revolution and renaissance, and it has been one of the factors contributing to innovation and growth in theory, practice, and production.

Rhetoric is an instrument of continuity and of change, of tradition and of revolution. The history of rhetoric is the history of a continuing art undergoing revolutionary changes. It has played an important part at some points in the formation of culture in the West, notably during the Roman Republic and the Renaissance. In both periods it was enlarged in its operation, using an extended form of the rhetorical device of "amplification," to become a productive or poetic art, an art of making in all phases of human activity. It was systematized in its organization, using a comprehensive form of the rhetorical device of "schematization," to become an architectonic art, an art of structuring all principles and products of knowing, doing, and making. If rhetoric is to be used to contribute to the formation of the culture of the modern world, it should function productively in the resolution of new problems and architectonically in the formation of new inclusive communities. Rhetoric can be used to produce a new rhetoric constructed as a productive art and schematized as an architectonic art. At a second stage the new rhetoric can be used to reorganize the subject-matter and arts of education and life. What rhetoric should be and to what conditions it is adapted are not separate theoretic questions but the single practical question of producing schemata to guide the uses of the productive arts in transforming circumstances.

The nature and methods of an architectonic productive art and the technical languages in which arts and sciences are classified, like many of the processes of inquiry and analysis and much of the technical language of distinction and systematization in the West, can be clarified by going back to beginnings made in the distinctions and analyses of Aristotle. He gave a technical meaning to the ordinary Greek expression *architecton*—"architectonic artist" or "master craftsman"—and used it in his schema of the organization of the sciences. In that organization he gave a technical meaning to the Greek expression *poiesis*—"production" or "poetry" or "making"—and used it to name one of his three sciences "poetic science" or "productive science." Later thinkers, doers, and makers have revolted against Aristotle's metaphysics and poetics more frequently than they have used them. Nevertheless they have constructed like devices for making principles and relations, and the ambiguous history of architectonic productive arts affords some guidance in understanding and changing the uses of the productive arts in an age of technology.

Aristotle distinguished between the art of the user, who knows the form, and that of the master-craftsman, who knows the matter and makes the product, although the art of a user, such as a helmsman, has architectonic functions in determining the form in which the product, the helm, is to be made.[1] In the transition from things better known to us by sensation to things better known in nature by science the sequence runs from sensation to experience, to art, to architectonic art, to productive sciences, to theoretic sciences.[2] The architectonic arts are themselves principles and wisdom (or as it was later to be called, metaphysics) is the science of first causes or principles.[3] Metaphysics functions as an authoritative or architectonic art by organizing the sciences according to principles, subject-matters, and methods into the theoretic, practical, and productive sciences—the sciences of knowing, doing, and making.

An architectonic art is an art of doing. Architectonic arts treat ends which order the ends of subordinate arts.[4] The architectonic art is the most authoritative art. The practical science, politics, which has as its end action, not knowledge, is such an art, "for it ordains which of the sciences are to be pursued in a state, and what branches of knowledge each of the classes of citizens is to learn, and up to what point, and even the most esteemed capacities fall under it, such as strategy, domestic economy, and oratory."[5] The moral virtues are the sources of actions in accordance with the rule

1. *Physics* i. 2. $194^{b}1$–7.
2. *Metaphysics* i. 1. $981^{b}25$–35.
3. Ibid., v. 1. $1013^{a}1$–14.
4. *Nicomachean Ethics* i. 1. $1094^{a}1$–17.
5. Ibid., i. 2. $1094^{a}27$–$^{b}5$.

of right reason. The rule of right reason is put into effect by prudence, which is a calculative intellectual virtue, engaged in ordering and interpreting the variables of action, and it is in turn under the guidance of wisdom. Prudence and wisdom make use of architectonic arts to guide subordinate arts of doing.[6]

The second calculative intellectual virtue, art, likewise makes use of an architectonic art. Prudence is architectonic with respect to doing (and its sphere of doing includes sciences, actions, institutions, and arts). Art is architectonic with respect to making, and the architectonic art of making is rhetoric, in so far as rhetoric is an art of thought. Diction and thought are two of the six parts of tragedy which Aristotle distinguishes in the *Poetics*. Poetic diction is treated in the *Poetics*, and it is distinguished from elocution or the architectonic art of speech, which includes not only propositions, which are treated in logic, but statements in general, in aspects which do not bear directly on their truth or falsity—commands, prayers, threats, questions, answers, and other modes of simple and connected discourse. Thought is not treated in the *Poetics*; in the *Rhetoric* to which Aristotle refers in the *Poetics* for the treatment of thought, account is taken not only of cognitive processes of proof and disproof, but also of noncognitive devices of amplifying and restricting, that is, enlarging and diminishing, maximizing and minimizing.[7]

Later ages continued to use the vocabulary of these distinctions; and the overall characteristics and problems of ages may be stated by determining the architectonic productive arts by which theoretic, practical, and productive arts are organized and related to each other in production, and by which products of the arts and sciences are set up and justified in experience. Aristotle formulated rhetoric as a "universal art," limited to no one subject-matter but applicable to all. For Aristotle rhetoric is not a "science," because each science has a particular "method" suited to its particular subject-matter and operative according to its proper principles. One of the sciences, politics, is an architectonic art, for it is a science of doing, and it is architectonic of actions, individual and communal,

6. Ibid., book vi., esp. chapter 8. 1141^{b}22–28.

7. *Poetics* 19.1456^{a}32–^{b}19.

including actions which bear on the cultivation of sciences and arts. But the architectonic art of politics is to be distinguished from rhetoric. The vocabulary of the distinctions between architectonic and subordinate arts, and between practical and theoretical arts and sciences, continues to be used, but the distinctions are shuffled and the meanings and applications of the terms are altered: all the basic terms and relations undergo this transformation and transportation—art and method; theoretic, practical, and productive; being, thought, action, and statement.

Cicero enlarged rhetoric into a universal productive art, an *ars disserendi*, and applied it to resolve what he conceived to be the basic problem of Roman culture, the separation of wisdom and eloquence, of philosophy and rhetoric. The diremption between wisdom and eloquence had been a consequence of Socrates' great achievements in philosophy: earlier Greek philosophers and statesmen had practiced both arts, but after the development of the philosophical arts by Socrates, those who learned to analyze problems were unlearned in the arts of speech, while those who acquired eloquence were ignorant of what they talked about. Socrates had also been the first to bring philosophy down from the heavens to find its subject-matter in the homes and cities of men. Cicero therefore made use of Hellenistic readjustments of the earlier Greek philosophic distinctions and vocabulary to reformulate the practical subject-matter and methods of a philosophy rejoined to rhetoric. He based his method on questions or issues, the *constitutiones* of rhetoric operating as a productive art to construct or constitute the matter of problems or cases and of conclusions or judgments. The four constitutions are practical transformations of Aristotle's four scientific questions. Aristotle distinguished the methods of the sciences, which are applicable to particular fields, from the universal arts, which are applicable to all subject-matters. Both "methods" and "arts" are presented problematically, however, and in terms of the questions for which they provide means of inquiry. Aristotle enumerates four scientific questions—ways of discovering and establishing facts and causes in subject-matters—(1) is it? (2) what is it? (3) what properties does it have? and (4) why?[8] These are

8. *Posterior Analytics* ii. 1. 89^b21–31.

transformed from theoretic methodological questions into practical operational questions in Cicero's use of rhetoric as a productive architectonic science—(1) the conjectural constitution for the establishment of fact, (2) the definitive constitution for the definition of name, (3) the general or qualitative constitution for the justification of qualifications or evaluations, and (4) the translative constitution for the choice of proper or competent judges. Aristotle's questions provide principles for the methods of particular sciences which explore the structure of fact and cause within the subject-matters of those sciences. Cicero's questions construct issues for the arts of rhetoric which establish the facts and resolve the "causes" by relating facts, words, values, and judgments; they are not adapted to a pre-existent particular subject-matter but are used to constitute or produce a determined subject-matter.

Since differences of subject-matter are produced by discovering and justifying answers to questions, the arts and the sciences will not be organized according to differences in the subject-matter which they treat, but according to differences of question, action, statement, valuation, and judgment. Aristotle divided the sciences into theoretic, practical, and productive on the basis of differences of subject, method, and purpose or principle. He also divided rhetoric into three kinds on the basis of differences of audience, speaker, and subject, and he treated dialectic as a universal art and a counterpart of rhetoric. A productive architectonic art produces subject-matters and organizes them in relation to each other and to the problems to be solved. The changes in the names of the kinds of rhetoric are signs of the transformations they underwent when they became fields of action, production, or knowledge. Aristotle's "forensic" rhetoric, which is concerned with accusation and defense, with past actions, and with justice and injustice, became "judicial." His "political" rhetoric, which is concerned with exhortation and dehortation, with future actions, and with expediency and inexpediency, with utility and inutility, became "deliberative." His "epideictic" rhetoric, which is concerned with praise and blame, with present persons, their characters and actions, and with honor and dishonor, became "demonstrative." The difference between rhetoric and dialectic became the difference between eloquence and wisdom and is found in the difference between particular and universal questions.

Cicero's use of rhetoric as a productive architectonic art laid down the structure of a program of education and culture designed to reunite eloquence and wisdom in action. The great architectonic achievement of the Romans was the organization of Roman Law. But with the institution of the Roman Empire, political deliberative rhetoric ceased to play an important part in political deliberation and action, and the old dichotomy reappeared between eloquence and wisdom, between language and action, words and deeds. Justice, prudence, and wisdom were determined by the actions of the emperor, not by deliberation. Judicial and demonstrative rhetoric became verbal arts, the one an art of disputation, debate, and controversy in Roman Jurisprudence, the other an art of verbal construction and exhibition in the Second Sophistic. In the Empire two branches of rhetoric were cultivated, judicial or legal and demonstrative or sophistic. Judicial rhetoric exercised a productive architectonic function in the formation and organization of law by the jurisconsults, both the civil law of Rome and the *jus gentium* which universalized law to all peoples. It exercised a productive architectonic function in ordering the actions of men toward universal peace and justice in the *Pax Romana*. Sophistic rhetoric exercised a productive architectonic function in the formation of a literature of consolation, instruction, pleasure, and sublimity, of adroitly differentiated styles and intricately elaborated figures, of tales and histories, prose, poetry, and the merging of the two in *satura*, of drama, satire, philosophy, and the history of philosophy and of sophistry. With the spread of Christianity the dichotomy of eloquence and wisdom continued. Honor and dishonor, merit and sin, good and evil were determined by interpretation of revealed truths and by action of the church, not by *deliberative* rhetoric. The art of disputation developed in *judicial* rhetoric was used in canon law to establish the concordance of discordant canons and was adapted to education and to theology in the development of the scholastic method. Political or deliberative rhetoric was dichotomized in its productive architectonic function between the city of God and terrestrial cities, divine laws and human laws, and *demonstrative* or artistic rhetoric became one of the verbal arts of the trivium, and in the development the arts of words and the arts of things became technical, abstract, and empty of content and subject-matter.

Renaissance philosophers and rhetoricians sought to rejoin eloquence and wisdom and developed within the new rhetoric they constructed a new universal subject-matter. They sought to make rhetoric a productive architectonic art of all arts and of all products rather than a productive technical art of language and persuasion. To make that transformation they transformed the architectonic functions of rhetoric from the practical or legal organization of actions in virtues and institutions to the productive or poetic organization of constructions in art objects and cultures. They made use of Cicero in this rebirth and innovation, as Medieval rhetoricians and philosophers had used the schemata of Ciceronian rhetoric to build a unified religion and tradition. Indeed, Renaissance rhetoricians invented the "Middle Ages" first by revolting against "middle Latinity" to return to the Latin of Cicero, and they continued the task by discovering in that middle period, which separated them from ancient Latin and Greek wisdom further dichotomies of language and content to be removed by rejoininig rhetoric and wisdom. Instead of distinguishing divine and human letters, they edited and interpreted Greek and Latin authors and applied the philology and hermeneutics of the study of literature to interpret Moses and the prophets, Paul and the evangelists, as poets. Instead of distinguishing divine and human law, they constructed history and political theory from the study of the history of ancient institutions and of the problems of the new nation states and international relations. Instead of distinguishing knowledge of universal laws of nature from empirical experience of natural occurrences, they constructed heuristic devices of discovery in which they borrowed from the common and proper places of rhetorical invention. Nizolius, in *On the True Principles and True Method [Ratio] of Philosophizing against the Pseudophilosophers* (which was later edited by Leibniz under the title *The Philosophical Anti-barbarus*), placed among the five general principles of philosophizing, (a) knowledge of the science of precepts and documents developed by the grammarians and the rhetoricians, and (b) assiduous reading of approved Greek and Latin authors and understanding of language of authors and people. Francis Bacon made use of the Topics in the formulation of his New Organon for scientific discovery. Ramus exposed the errors of the rhetoric of Aristotle, Cicero, and Quintilian (Cicero adds to the errors of Aristotle, and Quintilian to the errors of both), and reformulated the disciplines of the liberal arts using materials from ancient literature, oratory, and history. A long line of commentators on Aristotle's *Poetics* make part of their interpretation the adjustment of Aristotle's *Poetics* to the rhetorical criteria employed in Horace's *Ars Poetica*.

The Renaissance use of rhetoric as a productive architectonic art laid down the structure of a program of education and culture designed to reunite eloquence and wisdom in art. The great architectonic achievement of the Renaissance was the discovery and organization of the beautiful arts and the beautiful letters, for which the names *beaux arts* and *belles lettres* had to be invented. But with the accelerating progress of science, poetic demonstrative rhetoric ceased to play an important part in poetic insight and construction, and the old dichotomy between eloquence and wisdom reappeared, not in its practical form as a distinction between words and actions, but in its poetic form as a distinction between art and nature. This was to develop into a distinction between values and facts, and then between the humanities and the sciences. Philosophers, philologists, and historians began to imitate the methods of the sciences in the seventeenth century. They found and used methods of proof, not methods of discovery, although seventeenth century scientists worked to develop a heuristic method. By the nineteenth century, scientific method was conceived as a method of proof, and even philosophers like Mill and Whewell who disputed concerning the processes of scientific discovery, agreed that there was no "method" of discovery. The architectonic processes initiated in the Renaissance to rejoin the poles of medieval dichotomies have been conceived as phases of a process of "secularization" in which arts and sciences have been turned from the contemplation of another heavenly world to the production of this secular world for secular men. The productive processes have produced new subject-matters—literature, history, philosophy, and science, each with its proper methods or arts, and the continuation of these processes have been conceived as phases of the "fragmentation" of knowledge, community, and communication. Rhetoric ceased to operate as the productive architectonic art initiating and guiding these processes. It was replaced by the numerous arts of making and disposing which prepared for and produced a technological age, and rhetoric itself became technical: it turned from applications in other subject-matters, even *belles lettres,* except as they could be treated as instances of the proper subject-matter of rhetoric conceived as the art of speech. The fragmentation of knowledge is diagnosed and treated by juxtaposing subject-matters in "interdisciplinary" inquiry and study, and the rival productive arts of the associated fields compete for the role of architectonic art in relating and organizing the parts.

At each stage of the evolution of the arts and sciences since the Renaissance, an architectonic art was sought and used. Seventeenth century philosophers sought to apply the methods of the physical sciences or the mathematical sciences to human thought and action and to construct a "universal mechanics" or a "universal mathesis." The revolt of Kant against theoretic or speculative or dogmatic metaphysics was a revolt against that architectonic art. His Copernican revolution consisted in turning from the search for an architectonic science in the principles of being to seek it in the analysis of the forms of pure reason. "Human reason," he says, "is by nature architectonic. That is to say, it regards all our knowledge as belonging to a possible system, and therefore allows only such principles as do not at any rate make it impossible for any knowledge that we may attain to combine into a system with other knowledge."[9] An architectonic is an art of constructing systems, and the final chapters of the "Transcendental Doctrine of Method," with which the *Critique of Pure Reason* closes, are a chapter on the "Architectonic of Pure Reason" and one on the "History of Pure Reason." The architectonic science against which Kant revolted was theoretic metaphysics or ontology; his critical epistemology was to provide an architectonic basis for treating the problems of Theology, Cosmology, and Psychology, the parts of the old metaphysics. It provided in fact a beginning to the controversies of the nineteenth century concerning theology and science (which have been conceived as phases of a warfare of science and religion), concerning

9. *Critique of Pure Reason,* I, Part II, Division II, chapter 2, section 3, p. B. 502.

the "methodologies" of the sciences (which have been conceived as phases of the developing opposition between materialism and idealism), and concerning the concepts and methods of sciences of facts and sciences of values, *Naturwissenschaft* as contrasted first to *Geisteswissenschaft* and then to *Kulturwissenschaft*, the natural sciences as contrasted to the human sciences or humanities and the social sciences (and the contrast has been conceived as an opposition and separation of two cultures based respectively on knowledge of universal, necessary laws and awareness of concrete, contingent facts). The twentieth century began with a series of revolts against metaphysics which were revolts against the methodologies of idealism and materialism rather than simple repetitions of Kant's revolt against the ontologies of empiricism and rationalism. Feuerbach placed the beginnings of modern philosophy in the "critique" of Hegel; G. E. Moore used critique of idealism and of utilitarianism as a propaedeutic to common sense.

As we enter into the final decades of this century, we boast of a vast increase of output in all arts, and we are puzzled by the absence of interdisciplinary connection and by the breakdown of interpersonal, intergroup, and intercultural communication. We need a new architectonic productive art. Rhetoric exercised such functions in the Roman republic and in the Renaissance. Rhetoric provides the devices by which to determine the characteristics and problems of our times and to form the art by which to guide actions for the solution of our problems and the improvement of our circumstances. The history of the development of culture in the West sketched in the preceding paragraphs is an application of the methods of rhetoric to the discovery of ourselves and our times. It is in opposition and refutation to many accepted or advocated interpretations, but more important than its use in adversary opposition, it opens up possible methods of directing and relating knowledge, action, and production, by instituting an architectonic productive art of improving and increasing both the production of utilities and goods (*utilia* and *honesta*) and the use and enjoyment (*uti* and *frui*) of the products. The guidelines for both tasks are found in the continuing use of basic distinctions made in the fundamental vocabulary of rhetoric, and the mark of the validity and relevance of those distinctions is found in the fact that the common vocabulary in which we discuss the problems of our times is already structured on those distinctions and that facts are as much determined by orientations as orientations are determined by facts.

The architectonic productive art in an age of "technology" is obviously technology itself given a rhetorical transformation. The architectonic productive art of the Romans was rhetoric with a practical orientation. In the Renaissance it was rhetoric with a poetic orientation. There is every reason to think that the art we seek is rhetoric with a theoretic orientation, and a rhetorical sign that this is the case is seen in the fact that, whereas the orientation of the seventeenth century, at the beginning of the modern period, found expression in "ontology," and that of the nineteenth century in "methodology," contemporary culture makes use of "technology," which combines a main stem meaning "art" with a suffix meaning "science," suggesting that it would be well to elaborate a "science of art." The subject-matter determined as the field of such problems and the methods to be instituted to treat them are foreshadowed in structure and direction, as they have been found in other innovations, by following the lead of rhetorical constitutions for questions and methods and the lead of rhetorical kinds for subject-matters and fields of activity.

II. The New Rhetoric, Its Methods and Its Problems

Determination of the problems of our times, and action to resolve them, stand in need of an architectonic productive art. The problem of constituting such an art and applying it once constituted is one of rejoining eloquence and wisdom, rhetoric and philosophy. The continuing vocabulary and schemata, of words and of things, afford guidance in the constitution of such an art. The initial exploratory applications of devices borrowed from older rhetorics is facilitated by the fact that the data of experience are labelled and classified in common language using the same vocabulary and schemata. The new architectonic productive art should become a universal art, an art of producing things and arts, and not merely one of producing words and arguments; but the first step in constituting and using an enlarged objective rhetoric should be the reformulation of the structure and program of verbal rhetoric and its subject-matter. Roman rhetoricians and philosophers made rhetoric an architectonic art which related all things by means of law and the actions of men. Renaissance rhetoricians and philosophers made rhetoric an architectonic art which related all things by means of art and the constructions of men. Rhetoricians and philosophers today might make rhetoric an architectonic art which relates all things by means of science and the experiences of men. Rhetoric in all its applications is focused on the particular, not the universal—particular questions or constitutions in law, particular works or compositions in art, or particular facts or data in experience and existence. In an age of technology the diremption to be removed is the separation of theory and practice by the constitution of a technology which is theory applied, the *logos* of *techne*. We seek to produce it in concrete experience and existence by rejoining reason and sense, cognition and emotion, universal law and concrete occurrence. A first step can be taken by sketching the methods and the fields of rhetoric on the analogy of revolutions in rhetoric in earlier periods.

A. The Methods and Principles of Rhetoric

Aristotle distinguished between productive *sciences*, like Poetics (which have particular *subject-matters*, kinds of things made or produced, genres of artificial objects or objects of art) and architectonic *arts*, like Rhetoric (which direct and organize thought concerning *any subject-matter*). The sciences have become, more and more, sources of production, of new matters and new forms, in need of organizing methods and principles. We have seen how Aristotle's four scientific questions concerning objective causes were transformed into four rhetorical questions concerning verbal issues. In the latter form, they have been enlarged from time to time to become universal in their scope and productive in their operation. The traces of such past distinctions and structures are present in our search today for inclusive methods, by which to understand our situation and problems, and operative principles, by which to reorient and open up actions. The echoes take on meaning when placed in their rhetorical contexts and suggest directions of inquiry and construction which might be followed to transform the methods of rhetoric and make them applicable to new problems.

(1) Creativity and Invention

Creativity has taken a conspicuous place in modern discussions of the objectives and methods of education, action, art, and inquiry. "Creativity" usually has no meaning and provides no guiding criterion for learning or doing other than those implicit in "innovation," in the sense of setting and following a course different from those pursued by others in the past or the present. There is no method or standard of creation, discovery, or innovation. "Invention" has always been an important part of rhetoric. During the nineteenth century, under the influence of the dichotomy of language and wisdom, it was questioned whether invention is essentially the same as, or fundamentally different from, discovery. This is one of the dichotomies which the new architectonic rhetoric must eradicate. Invention can be joined to discovery in an art which is productive of things and arts or skills rather than of words and arguments or beliefs. When a productive inventive art deals with content as well as form, it is an art of active modification—rather than of passive reception—of the data of existence.

The art by which the orator discovered or created arguments in the midst of debate and controversy was based on the topics, the places or seats of argument. From the beginning, on the testimony of Quintilian, commonplaces have commonly been degraded from instruments for discovery of new ideas or arguments to repertories for repetition of old devices or adages. Existence as well as documents is approached and illuminated by places which guide discovery, and experience is limited and obscured by commonplaces of existence which are often borrowed from commonplaces of literature and speech. We need a new art of invention and discovery in which places are used as means by which to light up modes and meanings of works of art and natural occurrences and to open up aspects and connections in existence and possibility. The data and qualifications of existence are made by attention and interest; and discoveries made in a book or a work of art should provide places by which to perceive creatively what might otherwise not be experienced in the existent world we constitute. It is a long time since topics have been used as an art of invention in rhetoric. Ancient and Renaissance treatises on invention can be used to rediscover the art of invention in the use of words, which can be applied to discovering invention in reading and to using the art of invention in one's own constructions from the elements of discourse and from the data of experience. A reconstituted verbal art of invention, adapted to our circumstances and arts, might be used to shadow forth the methods and principles of an architectonic productive art generalized from invention in language to discovery in existence.

(2) Fact and Judgment

Recent revolts against metaphysics have been motivated by distrust and distaste for *a priori* methods and universal principles. We seek to apply our methods to concrete facts, to what is happening in the world here and now, and we find our principles operative in concrete occurrences and processes. Older rhetorics had methods by which to determine what is the case, and these methods of judgment or definition by which facts were characterized in answer to the question, what is it? or what did he do? were distinguished from, and related to, the methods of invention by which data were discovered in answer to the question, is it? or did he do it? Cicero makes the difference between a conjectural issue and a definitional issue a difference between the determination of what the fact is and the determination of what word should be used to describe it. The dichotomy of words and things has been subject to question in our times, and the methods of rhetoric suggest that invention of words and symbols contributes to discovery of things and that things are delimited in the definition of words.

Judgment of the issue concerning what the fact is and how it is defined and named starts from hypotheses advanced for consideration and transforms one of the hypotheses entertained into a sentence or a true proposition. A sentence or a true proposition makes or states a truth or a fact. We need a new art of judgment to relate experience to existence, an art of recovery or recognition of facts to be used with the art of discovery or apperception of data to provide instrumentalities for our contemporary respect for concrete facts of experience and for our determination to adhere to them and use them in the formation of knowledge and attitudes, in the constitution of science, experience, and expression. A beginning can be made by reexamining rhetorical methods of interpretation in the perspectives of one's own age. A reconstituted verbal art of judgment, adapted to the recovery and reinterpretation of past circumstances and arts in their present significances and relevances, might be used as a step in the development of the methods and principles of an architectonic productive art generalized from judgment of motivations and acts in narratives and histories to judgment of hypotheses and facts in experience.

(3) Sequences and Consequences in Discourse and in Fact

Facts are questioned, and are defended when questioned, by argument. The adversary oppositions of court-room trials set the basic form of Roman rhetorical argumentation. Argument as debate continued in the concordance and systematization of medieval canon-law. In the scholastic method it was supplemented by methods of dialectical dialogue and of logical refutation and proof. Renaissance rhetoric took into account arguments of drama, tales, and histories, and in the eighteenth century rhetoric was applied systematically to the judgment and criticism of *belles lettres*, as in the *Lectures on Rhetoric and Belles Lettres* of Hugh Blair. This enlargement of the construction of sequences and consequences from pleading or persuasion to proof, question-answer, plot, action, motivation-action-reaction, cause-effect, experiment has never been brought together in schematic organization or by productive methods. They can be related to each other as answers to the third rhetorical question, the qualitative constitution: How is the fact or occurrence qualified or characterized? Approached in that perspective the arts of making connections can be related to the arts of invention and the arts of judgment. A universalized verbal art of making, and modifying, connections could be used to relate the separated fields of the arts and sciences and to trace themes as they move in variations from field to field; and a reconstituted verbal art of connections could prepare the way for moving from formulating the consequences of discourse to tracing the sequences of processes and actions and events in a generalized architectonic productive art of structures.

(4) Objectivity and Intersubjectivity in Communication and Knowledge

Metaphysicians and ontologists sought principles in the causes of things. Epistemologists and methodologists sought principles in the forms of thought and in the consensus of experts. We are suspicious of causes and concepts, and when the suspicion becomes doubt, we posit principles in postulates and theses. Yet the function of "principles" remains the same: they provide beginning points of verbal discourse and discursive thought which we can defend as beginning points of sequences of occurrences, facts, and objective relations. Theses are posited to account for positions, and positions are consequences derived from theses. We are suspicious of systems of being and of knowledge, but we organize and systematize information and raise questions and draw consequences from schematized data, facts, and relations. The arts of objective designation and intersubjective communication are practiced in new forms by machines and men in decision-making and mass-communication. A reexamination of the verbal arts of reference and systematization, of validification and justification, could be made a first step to the constitution of a generalized architectonic art of objectification and systematization in forming, and exploring the operations of, compositions of things, constitutions of communities, and constructs of communications.

B. The Fields and Problems of Rhetoric

Our concern with the "fragmentation" of knowledge and our "interdisciplinary" innovations to constitute new fields more relevant to the problems we encounter, and more viable to processes of inquiry and action, are indications that we do not find subject-matters ready made nor do we encounter problems distributed precisely in fields. We make subject-matters to fit the examination and resolution of problems, and the solution of problems brings to our attention further, consequent problems, which frequently require the setting up and examination of new fields. Rhetoric has replaced metaphysics as an architectonic art, in the past, when the organization and application of the arts and sciences was based, not on supposed natures of things or perceived forms of thought, but on recognition of the consequences of what men say and do. Cicero did not make use of Aristotle's classification of kinds of sciences according to subject-matter and method to provide subject-matter and data for the issues and decisions of rhetoric. He did make use of the Aristotelian differentiation of kinds of rhetoric and of dialectic according to speaker, audience, and subject, according to method, time, and objective, to constitute the fields and the subject-matters under discussion and adjudication. He did not adjust rhetoric to a subject-matter, but used the four kinds of issues or constitutions to develop the three kinds of oratory, that is, he used rhetorical methods to constitute relevant fields. We may well follow his example. Having examined the methods and principles of invention, judgment, disposition, and systematization, we can abandon the rigidities of accepted classifications of knowledge—institutionalized under headings like theoretical, practical, and productive; physics, logic, and ethics; science, poetry, and history; natural sciences, social sciences, and humanities—and return to rhetoric for hints concerning how to construct new interdisciplinary substantive fields by the use of the methods and principles formed for the resolution of problems for which new fields are needed. As in the case of our inquiry into methods and principles, we shall find signs of the relevance of the enterprise, and criteria by which to plan and judge steps to be taken in it, by the remnants of the terms of the art of rhetoric—"demonstrative," "judicial," "deliberative," and "dialectical"—which are found scattered in contemporary analyses and discussions of fields and problems.

(1) Demonstrative Rhetoric and the Data of Existence

"Demonstration" is a term which has wrapped up—in the meanings which we attach to it consciously as well as those which come to our attention unexpectedly, and in the applications which we make of it intentionally as well as those which extend the scope of "demonstration" unexpectedly—a rich variegated history of human thought, action, and production. Aristotle had two Greek words, *apodeiktikos* and *epideiktikos*, to apply to processes of presentation and manifestation: they are constructed from the same verb and, therefore, both mean "exhibit," "show forth," "make known," modified by prepositional prefixes which make "apodeictic" also mean "prove," that is, show forth "from" or "by," and "epideictic" also mean "display," that is, show forth "on" or "for." For Aristotle apodeictic proof was scientific proof, and epideictic oratory was display oratory. When "epideictic" became "demonstrative" oratory in the writings of Cicero, the certainties and necessities of proof were merged with the estimations and necessities of action. Aristotle distinguished three kinds of necessity, one absolute and two hypothetical, which are used in the apodeictic proofs of the three theoretical sciences. He argued that praise and honor are not reliable guides in the practical sciences, although praise and blame are the proper functions of epideictic oratory. For Cicero praise and blame are the functions of demonstrative discourse and action, in which he distinguished simple or absolute necessity from three necessities which govern actions taken to avoid or gain something: the necessity of the honorable (*honestas*), the necessity of security (*incolumitas*), and the necessity of convenience (*commoditas*).[10] Our most recent revolt against metaphysics has been a revolt against, or an adjustment of, the apodeictic certainties of nineteenth century idealism and materialism. Yet we seem to be surprised that "demonstrations" have become exhibitions, presentations, manifestations rather than inferences, inductions, proofs.

The architectonic productive arts are not adapted to pre-existent subject-matters for the solution of recognized problems. The transformation of demonstration from proof to manifestation is not an error to be corrected by returning from agitation to evidence: it is a phenomenon of our times to be recognized as a datum to be studied and an instrumentality to be reduced to art. We have had enough experience of demonstrations to recognize not only the problems they "presented" as demonstrations but also the problems they "presented" in the insufficiencies of our conceptions of subject-matters

10. *De Inventione* ii. 57. 170–58. 175.

and problems and the need for an architectonic productive art to change them. (1) Verbal demonstrative rhetoric is discourse for praise or blame. Recent demonstrations have not exhibited virtues and accomplishments for praise, but wrongs, injustices, and evils for blame. They have been effective as methods of discovery, of bringing to attention neglected data, but they have also made some use of the methods of judgment, disposition, and systematization. (2) Demonstrative rhetoric is designed to be productive of action as well as of words, that is, to arouse others to action and to accept a common opinion, to form groups that share that opinion, and to initiate participation in action based on that opinion. (3) The scope of demonstrative rhetoric is not limited to specific social, legal, and moral questions: it extends, even in application to those initial problems, to the whole field of human activity and knowledge, to all arts, sciences, and institutions. (4) Demonstration uncovers data, that is, "makes" them since data depend on the perspective in which they are "given." An assertion or demonstration by any one constitutes a datum, and affects the processes of judgment, disposition, and systematization. We need to constitute the field of demonstration in which such data can be treated without the distortions we feel justified in introducing by appeal to the assertions or demonstrations of experts. (5) The modality of demonstrative statements and actions is different from the necessities, contingencies, and possibilities of judicial, deliberative, and dialectical discourse. Epideictic oratory and modern demonstrations are about the present, and the statements they employ are assertoric. Judicial rhetoric is about the past, and judgments about the past can be necessary; deliberative rhetoric is about the future, and its proposals are contingent. (6) The field of demonstrative rhetoric is epideictic not apodeictic: it is not fenced off from, but fenced off for. In the nineteenth century when philosophers were seeking apodeictic certainties they explored the limits of concepts and of reason. The field of demonstrative rhetoric should provide the grounds for discovery and invention, going beyond the bounds of what is already known and the fields of that knowledge. The field of demonstrative rhetoric, set forth in assertions and explored by the art of invention or discovery, is a field of "topics" in the two senses which the term has acquired: subject-matters for consideration and places for invention.

(2) Judicial Rhetoric and the Facts of Experience

"Judgment" is a term which has been employed in action, art, and knowledge. Judgments are decisions or "sentences" in law-courts concerning past actions; they are appreciations or "criticisms" of works of art; they are conclusions or "propositions" which are true or false. After "forensic" rhetoric became "judicial" rhetoric in the vocabulary of Cicero, the interrelations among judgments as "sentences," "evaluations," and "propositions" have been uncovered at each turn of development. The methods of accusation and defense have been enlarged to become the methods of verification and falsification, and their field has been universalized from past actions to be judged to facts and values to be determined and to general truths and laws to be established. "Cause" shares the productive ambiguity of "judgment": "causes" are discovered in things, pleaded before judges, pushed against established powers, and won in the progressive solution of problems. Judgments are a central theme in Kant's three Critiques, and the *Critique of Judgment* forms a connecting link between theoretical and practical reason by analyzing aesthetic judgments and purposiveness. We have revolted against the separation of facts and values, and we have turned to actions and circumstances to rejoin them. This reformulation of our problems makes it necessary to constitute and explore the field of judgment in which the facts and values of experience are related to each other and to the data of existence uncovered in the newly constituted field of demonstration.

The growing interest in the new hermeneutics is further sign of the need to establish a working domain of judgments of knowledge and action. In that enlarged field the controversial opposition of verification and falsification is not resolved by victory or defeat of a protagonist but by the establishment or refutation of a hypothesis. Since the art of interpretation and judgment applies to known truths and values, the field of judgment includes all recorded literature, which is the subject of hermeneutics or semantics, but it includes the facts as well as the records of experience. It is in this field that hypotheses can become facts and the elements of invention and discovery can be joined in a statement or apperception of fact. One of the important tasks to be accomplished by the new architectonic productive art of rhetoric is to clarify the topology of the relation of the field of invention to the field of judgment. This will make it possible once more for the semantics of known facts and values to contribute to the discovery of new truths and the production of new accomplishments, and for places and elements to be used heuristically in the establishment of ideas and arguments, facts and values.

(3) Deliberative Rhetoric and the Structure of Connections

"Deliberation" and its companion terms "choice" and "decision" have already been universalized in our common language of diagnosis and action. They were terms in the practical science of ethics for Aristotle: they were limited to actions within our power; with respect to such actions we can deliberate and choose means, but not ends. The subject-matter of political rhetoric was future actions. When "political" oratory became "deliberative" oratory after Cicero, the terms of art, of ethics, politics, and rhetoric merged, and deliberation could be applied not only to ends as well as means, but to theoretic and productive as well as practical problems. We deliberate not only about the expedient and the inexpedient, but also about the good and the bad, the true and the false, the pleasurable and the distasteful. Decision-making and methods-analysis require a universal field, and our universal methods could be used more effectively if that field could be subjected to positive definition rather than only the negative limitations provided by lack of limits, infinity, or indefiniteness. When the verbal rhetoric was universalized, it included all discursive sequences—inference, narrative, plot, lyric, history, aphorism, paradox—with related forms and methods. We have become accustomed to statements of the relations among their arts—that poetry presents truths, that mathematics expresses beauties, that history sets forth universal laws—but we have not constructed the subject-matter which provides the content for the operation and interrelation of these arts. As we proceeded with its constitution we would give substantive meaning to the "structures" which appear so frequently in our discussion of problems of education and action and which need grounding if the formal precision derived from mathematics is to be translated into concrete processes of operation determined by context and subject-matter. A beginning can be made by using the fields of invention and of judgment for data and facts to be related in structured sequences and intelligible consequences. This is the field of "arts" and "methods," in which themes are continued and undergo variations which reflect changing arts and constitute changing regions of the structure of connections which constitute the field of deliberation.

(4) Dialectic and the Principles of Objectivity and Communication

Aristotle treated dialectic as a counterpart of rhetoric. The differences between them were in part consequences of the difference between the particular audiences of rhetoric and the universal audiences of dialectic. Arguments can be adapted to the predilections of groups or communities of men. They can also be framed by art so that anyone who uses art or intelligence can follow them and appreciate them. The differences between dialectic and rhetoric became for Cicero a difference between universal questions of philosophy and science and particular questions concerning particular actions of particular men at particular times and places. The growth of science and communication, the increase of knowledge and the formation of world community, have begun to lay out the field of systematic organization both as a system of communication for a universal audience, mankind, and as a system of operation of an ongoing development and inquiry, technology. It is a field which provides grounding for the intersubjectivity of communications of persons and groups and for the objectivity of conclusions of inquiry and action. It is within this field that the possible worlds, which are discussed in plans and policy, are constructed, and theses which are posited are stabilized into principles. Theses and principles have a history which carries back in tradition to principles that were called eternal and universal but were also derived from theses which posit being in the context of an agent, his environment, and his subject. It is the field of reflexivity and responsibility, which must be explored in rational action concerning rights and justice, laws and conventions, sanctions and obligations, utilities and values, and opinions and truths. The field of the new dialectical rhetoric, of debate and dialogue, is being travelled and cultivated by chance and by art. An architectonic-productive survey of the field of these activities could make its beginning by orienting rhetoric from the oppositions of the past to the understanding and projection of the new processes and needs of the present.

Verbal rhetoric is productive of arguments and architectonic of attitudes. It provides the principle, in both the sense of beginning-point and of guide-line, for the construction of an architectonic productive art of rhetoric and philosophy which can be used to create a method productive of the arts and a subject-matter substantive to the problems of an age of technology. It should be a rhetoric which relates form to matter, instrumentality to product, presentation to content, agent to audience, intention to reason. It should not make technology the operation of a machine, in which the message is a massage; it should not take its form from its medium and it should not be adapted to use to communicate established judgments (which are jostled commonplaces) or revolutionary convictions (which are repeated dogmas) on the supposition and intimation that they might be related to traditional ends or novel objectives and that they are somehow means to those ends. It should be adapted to inquiry into what is the case rather than to semantic analysis of what somebody else has said. It should be positive in the creation, not passive in the reception, of data, facts, consequences, and objective organization. It should be an art in which what any one says to be the case, judges to be good or evil, connects in relations, and establishes with some show of system and principles, is relevant as subject-matter, content, and product. In a technological age all men should have an art of creativity, of judgment, of disposition, and of organization. This should be adapted to their individual development and to their contribution to forming a common field in which the subject of inquiry is not how to devise means to achieve accepted ends arranged in hierarchies but the calculation of uses and applications that might be made of the vastly increased available means in order to devise new ends and to eliminate oppositions and segregations based on past competitions for scarce means.

Creativity and the Commonplace

That creativity takes its beginning in the commonplace may be taken as a familiar and accepted commonplace. Invention, discovery, and insight are creative modes of departure from accustomed circumstances of the commonplace to transform the customary or the unnoticed into novelties. Widely known and authoritatively established novelties in turn become commonplaces and provide circumstances and subjects for new innovations. Such "commonplaces" of common opinion and ordinary language, however, are examples of the changes and alterations which the "commonplace" undergoes. Both "creativity" and "commonplace" are ambiguous words. Places, topics, loci, commonplaces and proper places have had long paradoxical histories since they entered into the languages of the West. They were as ambiguous in ordinary Greek as they are in ordinary English, and the nature of "place" and "space" was a subject of dispute in the beginnings of Greek physical science. They became terms of art in Greek rhetoric, acquired fixed meanings in Roman rhetoric, and spread, with the widespread use of rhetoric in the development of the arts of practical philosophy, jurisprudence, history, and literature, to commonplace meanings which are frequently at variance with their uses as terms of art. Creativity, invention, discovery, recovery, and innovation were ambiguous in their ordinary uses and in their philosophic uses, to such an extent that Plato sought to rectify the errors of poetic invention by truths discovered in the recollection of ideas. In the subsequent history of philosophical speculation on creativity, memory is the basis of invention, invention provides the materials for memory, and commonplaces are the devices of both invention and memory.

Cicero defined places as seats (*sedes*) or sources of arguments. Since rhetoric is composed of five parts—invention, disposition, elocution, memory, and pronunciation—he used places as fundamental devices in two parts, in invention and in memory. For the places of memory he went back to the poet Simonides; for the places of invention he built on the topics of Aristotle. Cicero attributes the invention of the art of memory to Simonides of Ceos. Simonides had been commissioned to present a poem in honor of his host at a banquet. In the course of his poem he also praised Castor and Pollux, and his patron, when the poem had been read, argued that the praise had been divided and proposed to pay only half of the fee that had been set for the panegyric. At that point Simonides was notified that two young men wished to see him outside. In his absence the roof of the banqueting hall collapsed, crushing the diners so badly that it was difficult to identify the corpses. Simonides used his memory of the places at which the guests had been seated to identify the persons, and he argued that the faculty of memory may be trained by selecting places, forming mental images of the things to be remembered, and placing them in the places distinguished, so that the order of the places would preserve the order of the things, likening the places to a wax tablet and the images to the letters written on it.[1] The wax tablet and the letters or images were to continue in the figurative philosophic language used in the history of the discussion of memory and thought—of impressions, likenesses, and images—together with the signet ring and its impression on the wax of a seal, and the footprint (*vestigium*) and its mark in soft earth.

At the beginning of his *Topica* Cicero recalls to his friend Trebatius that when he had picked up a copy of Aristotle's *Topics* in Cicero's library and had asked what it was about, Cicero had explained that it "contained a discipline invented by Aristotle for inventing arguments so that we might come upon them by a structure and a path (*ratione et via*) without any error."[2] He had prom-

1. Cicero, *De Oratore* ii. lxxxvi. 351–4.
2. *Topica* i. 2.

ised to explain this discipline more fully, and the *Topica* was his fulfillment of that promise written from memory on a voyage to Greece, when he had no books with him.[3] The absence of books has provided scholars with a rich field of investigation to relate the discipline expounded by Cicero to the topics and their uses set forth in either Aristotle's *Topics* or his *Rhetoric*. Every ordered structure of discourse (*omnis ratio diligens disserendi*), Cicero argued, has two parts concerned respectively with inventing and with judging. Aristotle established both, whereas the Stoics limited themselves to the ways of judgment, which they called dialectic, and neglected the art of invention which is called topics, in spite of the fact that it is more useful and certainly prior in nature.[4] Cicero divides the topics into technical and atechnical, that is, places from which arguments are derived by art and places from which arguments are derived without art. Aristotle makes a like distinction in the *Rhetoric*, but Cicero's treatment of the two kinds of topics differs from his. For Cicero the atechnical places have to do with testimony. He enumerates four technical places—"definition," "enumeration," "etymology," and "circumstances"—and divides "circumstances" into thirteen kinds—"conjugates," "genera," "species," "similarities," "differences," "contraries," "adjuncts," "antecedents," "consequents," "contradictions," "causes," "effects," and "comparisons" with things "greater," "equal," or "less." They are not Aristotle's topics, and they combine topics, with the predicables which Aristotle uses with the commonplaces in his *Topics*, with the kinds of opposites which he distinguishes in his *Categories*, and with the "circumstances" of action which he examines in the *Nicomachean Ethics*. But some of them also call to mind topics that have recurred in later inquiries into inductive logic and logic of discovery, and others give color to objections brought, again and again, against "traditional logic" and "verbal rhetoric" and against formalisms and subjectivisms of art and authority unrelated to the concrete things of existence and experience.

Commonplaces underwent degradations and criticism. Topics of memory threatened to become as numerous as things to be remem-

3. Ibid., 4–5.
4. Ibid. ii. 6–7.

bered, and therefore to provide no aid in retaining or ordering them: the word "topic" changed periodically from meaning an empty place by which to order things to be remembered to meaning a subject matter or a placed subject, as "the topic" on which to speak, to think, or to act. The commonplaces of invention changed periodically from meaning devices for discovering something previously unknown to meaning familiar quotations in which something well known and widely esteemed is stated. Quintilian complained that many orators made collections of sayings and arguments concerning subjects likely to recur in the practice of their art instead of fortifying themselves with places by which to discover new arguments that had never occurred to them before. Commonplaces were memorized rather than used for invention, and they were recited when the occasion arose rather than used when the circumstances required. Commonplaces ceased from time to time to be ways to the new and unknown, and commonplace-books became collections of aphorisms and verses rather than arts of invention. From time to time commonplaces reappeared and were schematized as devices and in the Renaissance they were organized in numerous arts of invention or arts of discovery and arts of memory, or mnemonic arts or arts of artificial, or technical, or topical memory, and the listed commonplaces or topics underwent changes in successive versions of the arts. Seneca the Elder reports prodigies of memory and subtleties of invention in the Roman schools of rhetoric. The Second Sophistic carried the practices of adepts and the informed appreciation of audiences to new extensions and embellishments. Aristotle did not enslave men's minds during the Middle Ages in logic, science, philosophy, or even topics. Boethius did not translate Aristotle's *Topics*, but he wrote a vast work in four books, *De Differentiis Topicis*, in which he combined the topics of Cicero with those of Themistius and gave the version of Aristotle's logic which was to be studied in the Middle Ages, a Platonized form, by basing knowledge on the opinions used in dialectical syllogisms of the *Topics* rather than on the scientific principles used in demonstrative syllogisms of the *Posterior Analytics*. Commonplaces gave shape to the method of canon law and to the scholastic method which was developed from it in the twelfth century.

The commonplaces contributed, in their alternations from invention to repetition, to the aridity and obtuseness of the medieval liberal arts against which the Renaissance revolted. The Humanist revolt inspired a return to Cicero, who had also been the source and inspiration of the medieval liberal arts, and invention and the commonplaces were again prominent in the revolt. Aristotle had distinguished between commonplaces and proper places. Cicero had distinguished between particular questions about concrete events and persons and general questions about philosophical problems; and he used the "paths" or "ways" of places in both kinds of questions as part of his program to rejoin wisdom and eloquence, rhetoric and philosophy. During the Renaissance, letters were revived by proper places used in a new form of the discipline of philology, and commonplaces came into their own in new versions of logic, dialectic, and rhetoric developed in numerous treatises on method. "Method" (*methodos*) was used by Aristotle to signify a "path to" the investigation of a scientific subject matter or the solution of a scientific problem and he distinguished "methods" from "paths" or "ways" (*hodos*) constructed in universal arts for the statement of arguments or descriptions or accounts applicable to any problem or subject matter. The Ciceronian and medieval treatises were "paths" or "ways" (*via*), and "methodus" did not become a Latin word until the translation of Aristotle's *Topics* in the twelfth century. Lully devised a Combinatory Art which had an inventive part. Rudolph Agricola wrote a *De Inventione Dialectica* which influenced Ramus in his revision of the liberal arts—and for all his criticisms of Aristotle, Ramus was at pains to point out the superiority of Cicero's treatment of the topics to Quintilian's, and the superiority of Aristotle's approach to both. Nizolius wrote a treatise *On the True Principles and True Reason of Philosophizing against the Pseudophilosophers* basing metaphysics on principles derived from literature and rhetoric. The art of memory was also developed in a large number of diversified systems of mnemonic art.

The beginnings of modern philosophy were in these innovations in philology, philosophy, history, and science, and many of the heralds of the new advancement, philosophers like Francis Bacon, Leibniz, and Vico, were aware of the work of their predecessors with commonplaces and proper places. Bacon was critical of the methods of Lully and Ramus. He sought proper places for the discovery of things and of arts rather than commonplaces for the invention of words and arguments. Leibniz continued the tradition of the combinatory art and the universal characteristic, and he edited and commented on Nizolius' rhetorical metaphysics. He found place for topics in both the demonstrations of combinatory logic and the probabilities of moral science, jurisprudence, and history. The subtitle of his *Dissertation on the Combinatory Art* promises that it will sow "new seeds of the art of meditating or logic of invention." He divided logic into two parts, an inventive logic or topics and a logic of judgment or analytics. The practical sciences are based on probability logic, that is, on Topics or Dialectic, used, in the absence of analytic, as an art of estimating degrees of probation. The art of invention, however, was poorly developed, and only a few samples of it could be found. Vico attacked Descartes' method as a method craftily feigned to exalt mathematics and Descartes' own philosophy and to degrade all other studies and philosophies. Vico proposed instead a program which would exercise memory, imagination, and perception (*ingegno* from *ingenium,* a faculty of the mind comparable to what Aristotle called "quick wit," the immediate perception of middle terms, the faculty of genius or immediate perception on all levels, sensitive and intellectual, of end terms to be related). One of the pernicious practices which afflicts the study of philosophy today, he said, is to introduce philosophy by the study of the Port-Royal Logic, "full of rigorous judgments concerning recondite matters of the higher sciences, remote from vulgar common sense." In the program he proposed, youthful mental gifts would be regulated and developed each by a separate art—memory by the study of languages, imagination by the reading of poets, historians, and orators, and perception (*ingegno*) by plane geometry, which is in a sense a graphic art which invigorates memory by the great number of its elements, refines imagination with its delicate figures as with so many drawings described in the finest lines, and quickens perception (*ingegno*) by surveying all these figures and collecting among them all those which are needed to demonstrate the magnitude which is required. Such a regime will bear fruit, at the time of mature judgment, in an eloquent, lively, and acute wisdom. If, on the contrary, students are led by logics prematurely into criticism

(that is to say, are led to judge before properly apprehending,

> against the natural course of ideas—for they should first apprehend, then judge, and finally reason), they become arid and dry in expression, and without ever doing anything set themselves up in judgment over all things. On the other hand if in the age of perception [*ingegno*], which is youth, they would devote themselves to Topics, the art of discovery that is the special privilege of the perceptive (as Vico [in the *Autobiography* Vico refers to himself in the third person], taking his cue from Cicero, did in his youth), they would then be furnished with matter in order later to form a sound opinion on it. For one cannot form a sound judgment of a thing without having complete knowledge of it; and topics is the art of finding in anything all that is in it. Thus nature itself would aid the young to become philosophers and good speakers.[5]

Vico had returned to Cicero's ideal of joining wisdom and eloquence, and he used commonplaces to form programs of study and to open up insights in research which were to guide and inspire later inquiries into literature, history, and jurisprudence.

Bacon, Leibniz, and Vico extracted, and developed from Renaissance speculations on methods of discovery and on topics, the diversity of topical uses that were implicit in Cicero's use of them to rectify the predicament of philosophy and rhetoric both of which had become "technical" disciplines in his day, producing on the one hand experts who had knowledge but were unable to express themselves, and on the other hand experts who had mastered the arts of language and communications but had nothing to say. Cicero had used them as devices by which to achieve his ideal of uniting eloquence and wisdom. But he had used them on only two of the five parts of rhetoric, while Bacon, Leibniz, and Vico had extended them to all five parts and had made them ways of advancing science, reforming philosophy, conceiving and studying culture, and framing universal history. They saw that Cicero's places of "invention" were more than sources of argument for orators and philosophers pressed or cornered in debate and controversy, and transformed them into places for the perception, discovery, and explanation of the unknown. The places of "memory" were transformed from the storage

5. *The Autobiography of Giambattista Vico*, trans. M. H. Fisch and T. G. Bergin (Cornell University Press, 1944), pp. 123–24.

places of known facts assorted for easy reference into an organization of what has been discovered and what is known into interacting schematisms of arts and sciences. "Disposition," or the arrangement of what has been discovered, involves judgment; and the connections of discourse are found in the places of judgment and argument, in the figures of syllogisms and of proofs, and in the figures of speech and of thought: "tropes" have been connected closely with "topes" in the history of devices of placing and of turning. "Elocution" is language adapted to the arguments, narratives, and myths of presentation and proof; and the places of statement and judgment are the sources and determinants of lines of inferences and flows of styles. "Pronunciation" or delivery includes the motions of the body as well as those of the voice; it is action, and the places of doing govern all arts of action, not only the dramatic and oratorical actions of the stage and the podium, but also the practical arts, the liberal arts, and the fine arts, that is, the arts of prudence, the arts of wisdom, and the arts of imagination. The places of the warranted, of the asserted, and of the done have developed out of the places of the known and of the unknown; and the newly invented places are places both of memory and of invention.

The mnemotechnics and the heuristics of the Renaissance have fallen out of fashion, or have been altered beyond recognition; and we have wearied of, or forgotten, the voluminous investigations and schematizations of methodologies of the nineteenth century, which developed methods for natural sciences, cultural sciences, social sciences, human sciences or humanities, for history, bibliography, and criticism. We are more apt to remember the paradoxes, which came to life again in the controversies among proponents of those methods, concerning whether an art or method of invention and discovery can be constructed, or whether they must be regarded as products of genius and quick wit, which cannot be learned or acquired. John Stuart Mill and William Whewell agreed that there can be no "method" of discovery, while disputing for years, through several editions of Mill's *System of Logic* and through several books of Whewell on inductive logic and the philosophy of discovery, concerning the nature of discovery and its place in philosophy and logic. Yet in the twentieth century we have had books and articles on the logic of discovery as well as on the logic of chance and of the artificial. The new interest in creativity has made "creativity" a commonplace with many meanings and with many places in art and science, in practice and theory, in logic and method. "Creativity" is frequently used as a commonplace, meaning to do something differently than is customary. Used in that meaning it seldom gives rise to problems that require appeal to an art, or a method, or a logic of discovery: spontaneity, chance, obstinacy, or animosity is sufficient to account for change; and if questions of value are raised, they are reduced to commonplace disputes concerning the relative worth of the new and the conventional, or the relative attractiveness of revolution and tradition, or the relative effectiveness of innovation and revival. Considering such formulations of the questions, and using such arguments for resolving the debates, the decision may as easily go against as for novelty, and any step of progress or innovation may as easily be shown to be due to rebirth as to revolution. The battle of the books, of the ancients and the moderns, was such a commonplace battle for creativity. Commonplaces begin to emerge in the course of such set disputes of value, however, and they begin to function once more as arts of invention and as arts of memory—beginning with the commonplace of the relation of fact to value, followed by a cluster of related commonplaces of the relation of imagination to memory, of invention to judgment, of myth to logos, of history to theory, and of sequence to structure.

The places of invention and of memory are places of things, thoughts, actions, and words. They are explored as sources of invented novelty and of established fact by faculties of symbolic imagination, factual memory, discursive reason, and intuitive understanding. In communications, in sciences, and in arts, there are no things or thoughts, only known things and significant thoughts, expressed things and thoughts, ordered by actions of art which produce and make them as objects, understandings, consequences, and expressions. The inventions and discoveries, the recollections and recoveries of things and occurrences, of thoughts and imaginations, of arts and actions, and of statements and accounts, are expressed in inventions of language and in genres of discourse—fictive narration, concrete description, sequential argument, and intelligible exposition; and they are constructed by arts or actions of innovation and fixation—invention, recovery, discovery, creation. By the use of such discourses and arts, we are able to make confidently our commonplace, concrete distinctions of things, thoughts, actions, and statements. If there is a philosophy of discovery and creativity, it cannot be a philosophy established by consensus concerning the nature of things, the powers or faculties of thought, the devices of arts, or the meanings or warrants of statements. It must be a pluralistic philosophy which establishes a creative interplay of philosophies inventing their facts, their data, their methods, their universes. It must be a rediscovery of the commonplaces of invention and memory for innovation rather than the establishment of a doctrine for proselytizing and conversion among marked-off heresies and dogmas.

It is appropriate that commonplaces be transformed from collections of fixed and established, communicable clichés to neutral sources of new perceptions operative in new directions in the thought and culture and philosophy of the twentieth century. Rhetoric again has assumed a dominant place in our thought and action. Whereas the rhetoric of the Romans took its commonplaces from the practical arts and jurisprudence and the rhetoric of the Humanists took its commonplaces from the fine arts and literature, our rhetoric finds its commonplaces in the technology of commercial advertising and of calculating machines. As in past rhetorics, the art of memory has developed more elaborately and more rapidly than the art of invention, and retrieval often passes for innovation and motivation for ratiocination. The great problem of creativity is "creativity" itself. It is a commonplace, a meaningless word which assumes clear and fixed meanings in well-known commonplaces that express what everybody knows about it, or which preserves a productive systematic ambiguity from which new insights may be derived and new consequences constructed. But the products of creativity—acquired insights, made things, planned actions, composed statements—become the commonplaces of our familiar world, while the commonplaces which innovate and transform, invent and discover, may be detected in their effective use but can never be stated univocally, clearly, or distinctly. The present exposition of "creativity and the commonplace" is not designed to uncover and state truths about creativity but to explore the commonplaces which determine the varieties of meanings it assumes in statements about it and the variety of ways in which it functions in exploring the old and constructing the new. If it had been designed to be a history of commonplaces or a theory of the commonplace, it would have had the radical defect that it never defines a commonplace or enumerates commonplaces: Cicero's commonplaces are not Aristotle's, Boethius departs beyond both, Lully and Ramus innovate, and Bacon, Leibniz, and Vico refashion their innovations. The only list that is given, with unconcealed reluctance, is Cicero's list, and it was chosen obviously because it is short and its terminology is traditional and has been fashioned into the language of new and later traditions—that is, the listed commonplaces have ceased to be commonplaces of invention and have become commonplaces of repetition. If the adepts of commonplaces have used different commonplaces, what is the commonplace of commonplaces, and how are commonplaces used to depart from the commonplace?

The commonplace of commonplaces is the place in which the certainties of the familiar are brought into contact with the transformations of innovation. A commonplace term, like "creativity," is meaningless in isolation. When it is combined with another term in a statement, the statement may be true or false, and the term is ambiguous. When reasons are brought to warrant a meaning, the meaning of the term becomes a variable adjusted to the variations of other terms in the formulation of the argument. When principles are sought to ground the argument, the meaning of the term becomes a function of the system, and the doctrine of creativity becomes a comfortable commonplace in an established universe. This is the genesis of doctrines of creativity from the commonplace word "creativity"; like accounts of that genesis might be given from the commonplace thing, thought, or action "creativity." The commonplaces of creativity differ from the doctrines of creativity in all four stages of this progress: a term may be meaningless in the sense of being undefined or in the sense of being stripped methodically of vestiges of meaning; ambiguity has productive uses as well as equivocal dangers; variability appears in accounts which are variations of an argument or theme as well as in stages of arguments or occurrences; functionality is a relation among things and statements, thoughts, and arts as well as a relation among the constituent parts of what is the case. The present exposition is an account of the commonplaces of creativity: "creativity" was used as a commonplace; it was expanded to the commonplace "known-unknown" and used to distinguish and merge the arts of invention and memory, which were explored in the commonplace "term-statement-argument-system," and systematized in the creation of commonplace "things-thoughts-actions-words." Many doctrines of creation have been moved along the first path; they have all used the structures of the commonplaces sketched along the second path. The commonplace "known and unknown" has some advantages over the customary commonplaces of philosophic discussion, like "subjective and objective," "mind and matter," "real and ideal," because it retains an easy reversibility by which the known becomes unknown as well as the unknown known, and by which its inventive openness as a commonplace is preserved and the commonplaces derived from it provide structures for all philosophies in a pluralism of philosophies of invention and of varieties of creativity.

The commonplaces of creativity operate in the interpretation of texts as well as in the writing of texts, in the interpretation of experience as well as of statements, in the interpretation and formation of character, thought, actions, and things. In the interpretation of the text of a philosopher, past or present, commonplaces of invention may open up the perception of new meanings and applications even in a familiar text, which in turn uncovers previously unperceived lines of arguments to unnoticed conclusions which were not there until they were made facts by discovery. The newly perceived facts of interpreting a text may in turn lead to the discovery of new powers of perception and their use in the discovery of new existential data and new experiential facts, set in relation by new arts and methods, to discover new universes of discourse, thought, consequential occurrence, and systematic organization. The use of the commonplaces of creativity erects and fills the commonplace as a storehouse of the familiar to provide materials for commonplaces as instruments for the perception, creation, arrangement, and establishment of the new in existence, experience, discursive exploration, and inclusive organization.

Discourse, Demonstration, Verification, and Justification

The history of things and events, the history of ideas and theories, the history of statements, presentations, and communications run separate courses which are ambiguously intermingled in occurrences, meditations, and narrations. They are histories of what has been the case, leading up to, and in the light of, what is now the case; of what men have thought, preparing for, and judged according to, what is now known; and of what men have said and expressed, reconstructed relative to, and interpreted under the influence of, what is now perceived and valued. They are all histories of facts, of concrete existences and occurrences; yet no facts enter the sequences of our histories except known facts and stated facts, and we still recognize, with Parmenides, that what can be said and thought must be. Thoughts and statements are adapted to facts; and facts are discovered, invented, and created in and by thought and statement. Discourse presents sequences in occurrences, in thoughts, and in expressions. It is *discursus*, a running around or a running to and fro; and since it is impossible to separate actual discourses from known discourses or stated discourses, the structures of discourse are sometimes found in things, sometimes in thoughts, sometimes in words, sometimes in actions. Science, poetry, and history are modes of discourse whose structures are similar, as Aristotle observed: poetry is more philosophic (or scientific) and serious than history, for poetry narrates particularized universals rather than historical individuals and singulars. Discourse presents things, thoughts, and symbols, the abstract and the concrete, and relates them in the omni-existent; it presents past, present, and future, the timeless and the timed, and relates them in the omnipresent.

From the beginning of speculation on human action and the environing world, the arts of what men know and do have been conceived as arts of discourse. From the first, the arts of discourse have united saying and doing with what is said and done; and from the beginning, the arts of discourse have been distinguished into arts of words and arts of things, and the verbal and substantive arts have been given meaning in pragmatic interpretations. During the Middle Ages the arts of the Trivium—grammar, rhetoric, and logic or dialectic—were often treated as the arts of words; and the arts of the Quadrivium—arithmetic, geometry, astronomy, and music—as the arts of things. Yet analysis of words or of the *logos* has produced grammars of science, of politics, and of assent, as well as grammars of languages and of Language; and inquiry into things or into the *cosmos* has produced the symbolism of mathematics and has generalized music from the harmonies of sounds to the spheres and to all proportions; astronomy from the motion of the heavens to the planetary orbits of stars and atoms; geometry from two- and three-dimensional figures to mechanics and dynamics of motion; and arithmetic, even in antiquity, included logistic, the art of calculation. The history of poetry and the arts lays the foundation for the history of politics, religion, and science; and in the sequences of each, ideas and connections are borrowed from the other histories. The arts of words and of things—grammar, rhetoric, logic, dialectic, and mathematics—are not set apart by definite dividing lines but borrow methods and subject matters from each other. Any one of them may be, and each of them has been, shown to contain the basic statement of the principles of all knowledge; and the relations among them, on analysis, contain all the problems of philosophy and science.

The problems of philosophy and their resolution, the relations among philosophic positions and the evolution of philosophic interests and perspectives, when they are not determined by chance and fortune, are produced and discovered by philosophic arts. The arts applied in philosophic inquiry are employed in the resolution of problems and the establishment of unambiguous, coherent, and fruitful truths. The same arts applied in philosophic semantics are employed in the interpretation of statements of problems and resolutions which are ambiguous in their common statement in two or more philosophies and often contradictory in their proper significances. The philosophic arts applied in the continuities of the history of philosophy and of the debates to the present, trace or guide the common themes of philosophic discussion through concrete precisions and ordered consistencies, productive ambiguities and suggestive inconsistencies, from the topics or commonplaces of discussion to philosophic innovations and discoveries. The problems of demonstration, verification, and justification are problems for the philosophic arts. In philosophic inquiry they assume fixed meanings and functions. Examination of other philosophies reveals their ambiguities in the different methods by which the different ends of different philosophies are achieved. Yet they have a character as arts which provides the common problems of philosophic inquiry and the connecting links for philosophic discussion; and they isolate topics which start new turns of themes, initiate new perspectives and new ambiguities for discussion, and set new problems for inquiry.

The ambiguities of "demonstration," "verification," and "justification" are apparent in the philosophic semantics of ordinary and technical usage. Demonstration is a process of proof from immediate or axiomatic premises in logic, mathematics, or science; it is a manifestation of feelings and convictions by an individual or a group; it is an exhibition, portrayal, or presentation of what is the case and what are the noteworthy characteristics of a situation, occurrence, or object; it is verification or justification by verbalization or activization. Verification is the communication to another of the reasons for crediting conclusions from experience or knowledge; it is an investigation of grounds in fact, probability, or scientific law for descriptions or explanations; it is an analysis of the relations of consistency, relevance, and appropriateness of statements in exposition, narration, or inference; it is demonstration or justification by establishment of applications in things and convictions in minds. Justification is a defence or condonation of oneself, one's attitudes, or opinions; it is a proof of theses, hypotheses, or positions questioned or rejected or a refutation of arguments against them; it is an adjustment or arrangement of things or parts of things in coherent, well-proportioned wholes; it is demonstration or justification by presentation or performance. There are arts of demonstration, verification, and justification in each of these senses as well as in the many senses which emerge from merging two or more of them and from further differentiating among them.

The ambiguities of philosophic semantics provide the materials of controversy in philosophic inquiry. From the standpoint of the meanings given to demonstration, verification, and justification in any one philosophic position, the processes followed and the results alleged in other philosophies use badly organized and unreliable methods to arrive at meaningless results in resolution of misconceived problems. The ambiguities and the controversies are the materials which are woven into themes by the philosophic arts, and the adjustments and borrowings of the philosophic arts therefore provide insights essential to an understanding of demonstration, verification, and justification. Any account of the origin and development of the philosophic arts, even brief accounts prefixed to new inquiries into science, logic, phenomena, experience, existence, or language, attest to their versatility as methods and their heterogeneous adaptability as devices.

The beginnings of the philosophic arts in the West are encased in a massive ambiguity. We have learned their names, their basic distinctions, and their methods from Aristotle. Moreover, Aristotle claims or implies immodestly that he originated all or most of them and that he worked at best on the lisping anticipations of his predecessors: he first distinguished the causes systematically and completely and, since we know when we have discovered the cause, it follows that he originated scientific method; he first analysed and formulated the parts, the structures, and the objectives of logic; he concentrated attention on the essential part of rhetoric, arguments or persuasions, which were omitted by his predecessors. He was convinced that each science has its own peculiar subject-matter, method, and principles. In many of his scientific treatises he therefore first examines previous theories dialectically; then he makes a new beginning and methodically investigates the problems of the science and verifies his conclusions; finally, he makes use of causes to adjust what has been shown to be the case and the properties and functions of things to the broader context of the problems of adjacent sciences and of the cosmos. This conception of the philosophic arts contains the reasons for Aristotle's criticism of his predecessors: the dialectical definitions of Plato reduced all things to thoughts or ideas; the physical definitions of Democritus reduced all processes, including thinking, to things and motions of things; the eristic of the Sophists reduced all thoughts and things to connections and interpretations of words. Once the results of inquiry have been established by the methods of the sciences—theoretic, practical, or productive—they can be reformulated, organized, and tested by the universal analytics of logic. Aristotle also distinguished and laid down the procedures of two other universal arts, which did not apply to the particular subject matters or problems of the sciences: dialectic or the method of treating the opinions of men to establish one opinion and to refute opposed opinions; and rhetoric or the method of treating the convictions, interests, and feelings of men to move and persuade particular audiences.

Despite its clarity and its crucial position in the history of thought in the West, Aristotle's conception of demonstration, verification, and justification does not throw much direct light on the history of the development of these arts employed to achieve them in their various senses, because the influence of his distinctions was slight, and his arguments and arts were adjusted and interpreted to support the methods and conclusions he opposed. Historians of philosophy from the first have been amused or offended by his *hubris:* they found the beginnings of science in the Presocratics, Pythagoras, Plato, or Democritus; they found the distinctions and devices of logic in the Eleatics, the Pythagoreans, the Sophists, and the Socratics; they adjusted Aristotle's rhetoric to that of Isocrates with little attention to argument or persuasion. His commentators practiced the universal arts, not the particular methods of the Aristotelian sciences: from the time of the Greek commentators, who were Neoplatonists, to the time of Brandis, Jaeger, Burnet, Taylor, Ross, and Cherniss, who saw Aristotle as a Platonist, they have been dialecticians; during the Renaissance when Medievalism was invented and discovered, and when philosophy and culture were refurbished, the task was done by rhetoricians who gave rhetorical force to their interpretation by the thesis that Aristotle had enslaved men's minds for two thousand years; with the coming of modern science and the impact of scientific method on philosophers, Aristotle's critics have been physical scientists or philosophers of science who continue the dialogues of Galileo against the restated errors of Aristotelian science.

Since the theme of the development of the philosophic arts has evolved in the reinterpreted terms and the rediscussed distinctions of Aristotle, the influence of Aristotle on the meaning and methods of demonstration, verification, and justification can be seen more clearly from beginnings in his treatment of methods in the universal arts than in methods of the sciences. One of the paradoxes in the evolution of the themes of philosophic discussion is that the universal arts which were distinguished by their differences from the scientific methods, have repeatedly been transformed into methods of scientific discovery and proof; and scientific questions have taken on new meanings relative to new subject matters by transforming moral ends in action into scientific objectives in inquiry and proof or into esthetic insights in statement and communication. The ambiguities of methods in interpretation are a source of fruitfulness in their adaptations as well as of stagnation in their repetitious uses. Since the methods of rhetoric were not adapted to characteristics of subject-matter treated, Aristotle distinguished them according to the audiences addressed. Political rhetoric is addressed to assemblies or individuals faced with problems of policy or mode of life; it employs devices of exhortation and dissuasion to determine the expedient or useful and the harmful in future behavior. Forensic rhetoric is addressed to judges and juries in accusation and defense to determine the just or right and the unjust in past actions. Epideictic rhetoric is addressed to a general public in praise or blame to mark the honorable or good and the disgraceful in present records of accomplishments and of recognized values. By the time that Cicero reformulated these distinctions, they had acquired three names—deliberative, judicial, and demonstrative—which became fixed as three universal methods in the developing art or science of discourse, the *ratio disserendi*. The commonplaces of the themes of these methods grow out of consideration of deliberation (or decision-making), judgment (or criticism), and demonstration (or exhibiting) as methods of applying reason to the problems of science, art, and action.

Deliberation takes its meanings in a context of choice and decision. It treats of means, not of ends which are determined by wishes, with the possible influence of prudence and wisdom. Its subject matter is utilities—moral, political, and social—in matters whose issue is indeterminate or uncertain. When deliberation becomes a universal method, it is not restricted to the subject matter of practical action but determines all subject matters. All questions are matters for deliberation and decision, and all matters are uncertain and indeterminate. Probability takes the place of necessity and certainty. Deliberation extends to ends as well as means and to the issues of science as well as those of policy. Deliberation is a kind of weighing; it is disputation, which is a kind of calculating. When subject matters are determined by communication and discourse, ends are found in the opinions and feelings of those who enter the disputation, and the method of deliberation is to discover means to realize those ends. Deliberation is involved in the future of planned actions or predicted outcomes. The better course of action or the truth is set forth as some one's conception or conviction, and the scientist establishes his truth as the moralist or statesman establishes his policy or morality, by exhortation and dissuasion consisting of statements of what is the case and predictions of what will be the outcome if events are left to themselves and if other sources and influences are brought into play. Deliberation has become a universal method of science, art, and action.

Judgment takes its meanings in a context of definition and opposition. It is an estimation of persons in the light of their actions and accomplishments and of things in the light of their qualities and effects, with the possible influence of sensibility and taste. The judge or the critic pronounces on things done and things made in matters which affect the interests and pleasures of others. When judgment becomes a universal method, it is not restricted to subject-matters under the jurisdiction of courts of law or under the scrutiny of aesthetic criticism but determines all subject matters. Judgment becomes the synonym of proposition, and any statement about any subject is a judgment. A thing or event is what it is judged to be until the judgment is invalidated. The judgment of common opinion and of experts extends to manners and morals, to persons and values, to facts and truths. Judgment is a kind of pronouncement or sentence for or against, and the methods of securing judgment are methods of attack and defense. Oppositions of judgment are oppositions of controversy, a kind of turning against, which are resolved by securing agreement on one of the opposed judgments. When subject matters are determined by communication and discourse, what is just and right extends its meaning from the determinations and judgments of law, to custom and accepted determinations of what is and what should be. The laws of nature are likewise judgments, and the history of science is a series of controversies resolved by successive judgments of scientists. Judgment is involved in the past of actually formulated views and hypotheses of facts judged relevant. The method of the philosopher, the scientist, the politician, the critic, and the molder of common opinion or received doctrine is to invalidate opposed judgments and to test his own judgment by considering all attacks by which it might conceivably be falsified. Judgment by the tests of falsifiability has become a universal method of science, art, and action.

Demonstration takes its meanings in a context of inquiry and presentation, of principles and consequences. It seeks to set up principles which are unquestionable and to derive inferences that follow necessarily from them. The proofs of mathematics and physics have long provided the models of demonstration. The subject-matter of demonstration is knowledge well enough established to be set down in formal proof. *Mathemata* meant whatever is learned, in Greek educational theory, before the mathematical sciences were separated from other learning to provide the model structure of learning. When demonstration becomes a universal method, it is not restricted to the subject-matter of quantity or of mathematics but extends to and establishes all subject matters. Learning begins in experience as well as in postulates and axioms, and all structures, including those of mathematics, can be exhibited by ordering as well as be constructed by deduction. Demonstration is a kind of discussion, a breaking asunder or distinguishing by analysis and synthesis. When subject matters are determined by communication and discourse, structures and sets are found in any organized wholes encountered in statement. Demonstration is involved in the present formulations of what is and has been and will be, and in present formulations of values brought to bear in ordering these structures.

It is the method of forming lawlike statements and of applying them to actual states of occurrence and circumstance; it is the establishment of what is thought to be the case, relative to what is conceived to be value. Demonstration by exhibition of facts and values has become a universal method of science, art, and action.

Discourse takes its being and its meanings in a context of deliberation, judgment, and demonstration. When they are universalized as methods of science, art, and action, discourse is their embodiment. It constitutes or constructs their media of communication and expression; it discovers or creates their subject matter; it sets or expresses their objectives; and it establishes or applies the criteria of their success. The intelligible structure of the universe and the objective structure of thought have been transformed into the consequential structure of discourse. The sequences and consequences of things, thoughts, actions, and statements are inseparable, and they establish connections between fact and theory, fact and value, fact and fiction, fact and non-existent, which in turn make the connections of sequences in discourse possible and intelligible. There is no pre-established priority of being, cause, or rule among things, thoughts, actions, and statements; each in turn may be made fundamental in deliberation or judgment or demonstration. Speculation concerning discourse must avoid the fixities of categories, doctrines, methods, and assumptions which discourse assumes in any one form of philosophy or inquiry, if it is to include all the forms which discourse takes in philosophy and in inquiry, action, and production. This is possible because the variety of categories or elements is approached in discourse by way of common topics or "commonplaces"; the variety of facts or statements of what is the case by way of common hypotheses; the variety of arts or methods of treating problems by way of common themes; and the variety of assumptions or principles by way of common theses. In what follows, the nature of demonstration, verification, and justification will be sought, first, by examining some of the commonplaces or structures of meaning which underlie and connect the particular positions taken with respect to common ambiguous problems, and which make discussion and continuity of discussion possible; and, second, by tracing the perspectives in which common questions take on particular forms in the lines of discourse when theses are accepted and are employed as principles with consequences in thought, action, and statement and therefore in occurrence.

One of the functions of commonplaces is to determine what discourse is about, what the subject matter of inquiry, discussion, and controversy is. When Aristotle tried to fix the subject matter of the theoretic sciences by listing four scientific questions, the distinctions he made were broadened to provide commonplaces for all subjects, processes, and functions. Whether a thing or occurrence is? what it is? how it is characterized? and what its cause is? became the basic questions about the nature of things in medieval metaphysics and science, and the basic issues of decision and debate in Roman rhetoric and law. Their remnants are in modern speech: we still use "quiddity" in answer to the question, what? and "quality" (a linguistic innovation of Cicero) to answer the question, of what sort?; and one medieval philosophy invented "anity" to name the answer to the question, is it? and "curity" to name the answer to the question, why is it? In legal rhetoric the questions become the stages of establishing a case or a "cause" rather than the steps in discovering an essence or in grounding a scientific demonstration in a "cause." The "conjectural" issue is a question of fact, did the occurrence take place and was the accused present?; it is followed by the "definitive" issue, what is its name?, the "general" or "qualitative" issue, what is its genus or characterizing quality?, and "translative" issue, under what law or before what court shall it be judged? that is, who is competent to determine the case. The structure of things and the structure of thought are assimilated to the structure of discourse and of presentation, and the four questions are transformed in their continuous but ambiguous history from questions adapted to subject-matters to questions for the resolution of any problem or for the accomplishment of any purpose, including the total and integrative relation of all problems and all experience. The transformation may even seem to be a substantive philosophic innovation for the questions are no longer questions of essence and cause but questions of process and structure in which essence and cause survive as anachronisms or figures of speech. Discourse is not about actual, potential, or imaginary things, nor about being or becoming, nor about necessary, probable, chance, or impossible occurrences: the subject of discourse is the possible, and the realm of universal discourse is the omni-possible.

Since discourse is not differentiated into kinds by its subject-matters, the second function of commonplaces is to distinguish the purposes which discourse serves and the means by which it achieves the values to which it is addressed. When Aristotle separated the methods of the universal art of rhetoric from the characteristics of particular subject-matters and related them to audiences, the distinction of three ends of persuasion which he made was broadened in later discussion and speculation to provide commonplaces for all values and for all activities in pursuit of values. The end of political rhetoric was the expedient or the useful and the inexpedient; the end of forensic rhetoric was the just or right and the unjust; the end of epideictic rhetoric was the honorable or the good and the disgraceful. When rhetoric is distinguished from ethics and politics, as it was by Aristotle, questions concerning what is desired as useful, what is accepted as just, and what is praised as honorable can be distinguished from what is desirable, what is just by nature, and what is good in itself. But when the method of rhetoric becomes the universal art of discourse, one deliberates not only about means but also about ends; one judges not only according to what is accepted but also according to what is acceptable because it is a source of pleasure; and one demonstrates or exhibits not only what is praised but also what is praiseworthy and good in itself. The "useful" (*utilia*) and the "good" (*honesta*) not only provided the matrix for Kant's treatment of moral imperatives, and the commonplaces for the opposition between utilitarianism and the morals of synthetic *a priori* categorical imperatives, but also, with the "right" and "pleasure" of judicial rhetoric, a structure of commonplaces for the whole of moral and political philosophy and for the relations of theoretic and practical philosophy. We still treat questions of the good and the right, of the good and the useful, of disinterested and interested pleasures, of values and existence; and questions of the useful and pleasure, the right and good are transformed in their continuous history from limited or arbitrary ends to the ruling purpose of any process and of all experience. The transformation again seems substantive, for the question of fact is separated from the question of value, and the question, what is it? is balanced, not by the question, why is it? but by the questions, what should be and why should it be? The ends of discourse are not superimposed *a priori*, or by tradition, or authoritative revelation: the inclusive objective of discourse is the desirable, and the realm of the ends of discourse is the omni-desirable.

The determination of subject-matter and the ends of discourse, of the what and the why, raise questions of fact and existence, of the what sort and the whether. The third and the fourth function of commonplaces is to find general qualifications of facts when facts are universalized and all-inclusive, and to formulate the marks and tests of existence among all existences. Beginning from Aristotle's rhetoric, rather than from his metaphysics, deliberation is concerned with what is useful in policy for the future, and deliberative proof is not distinct from exhortation and dissuasion; judgment is concerned with what is just in punishment and reward for past actions, and judicial proof is not distinct from rectification and differentiation; demonstration is concerned with what is honorable for praise and criticism of present agents and personalities, and demonstrative proof is not distinct from securing agreement and esteem. When deliberation becomes a universal method, planning and prediction as a method of determining what should be is transformed into definition and prediction as a method of determining the nature of existent things and processes. When judgment becomes a universal method, refutation and defence as a method of determining how past actions should be rewarded or punished is transformed into falsification and defense as a method of determining whether formulated statements should be credited or discredited. When demonstration becomes a universal method, devaluation and estimation as a method of establishing what is honorable or dishonorable in the accomplishments and character of present agents is transformed into alienation and estimation as a method of achieving more goods for more people. The facts of the future, past, and present are known in example and prediction, in argumentation and falsification, and in maximization and estimation. We still differentiate past determinancies and future contingents, but we make them both relevant to present processes. The change seems substantive, for the perspective of the present enters not only into the determination of simultaneity, priority, and posteriority of observed past, present, and future facts, that is, into when they are, but also into the determination of what they are, how they are qualified, and why. The facts of inclusive discourse are seen and presented as present facts, and the realm in which they evolve and take form is the omnipresent.

A fourth function of commonplaces is essential, once discourse has supplanted metaphysics and epistemology as architectonic methods, for when facts of existence take the place of principles of being and indubitable truths, they take on the characteristics of being and truth, and become at once inclusive and the basis of discrimination. Marks and tests of existence are needed to move and think and communicate within the totality of all existences. No questions arise unless there is an answer to the question, is it? Whether it is or is not, the methods of examining "it" are not unlike the methods of metaphysics and epistemology, for they continue the same commonplaces. The transcendentals of the Middle Ages were predicated convertibly of each other: whatever is is a thing, a something, a unity, a true, and a good. So too, to run through the commonplaces of discourse which we have examined, whatever is alleged to be fact may be analyzed to determine what it is, how it is qualified, and why the results of these analyses may be presented as warranted. Whatever is is desirable, if only because whatever is came to be and continues within structures judged to be right, and what is provides the beginning point and grounds for modifications and innovations in the structure of what is and of what is right. Whatever is is a connecting link between what was and what will be. Discourse as an inclusive whole provides the system within which facts and values are stated and determined. An initial immediate experience is a confused whole from which selections and simplifications are made in perspectives determined by attention and interest. They are stated in particular propositions and generalized in universal propositions. They fit into a compendent whole or are isolated into irrelevancies; they are ordered in inferential sequences or are opposed in contrarieties or contradictions. Neither existence nor experience is *ab initio* an ordered whole of constituted facts or of spaced or sequential events. Occurrences, observations, errors, illusions, and fictions are all facts; and errors are sometimes as illuminative of experience as controlled, well-grounded experimental observations. A coherent system of relations may cease to apply to relevant facts, and an incoherent, opaque system of variables may be reinterpreted to become relevant and fruitful. The change seems substantive since we have abandoned the revealed verities of theology and the self-evident truths of metaphysics and have sought models in the new authoritative paradoxes of mathematics and of relativity physics and quantum mechanics; but we have learned to be comfortable with the paradoxes of facts and the coincidence of contradictories in experience without building the inclusive structures of facts which explain and justify the contradictions. The facts of inclusive discourse are existential facts, and the realm in which are ordered in lines and hierarchies of influence and reaction, dependency and rule is the omni-existent.

The commonplaces provide the linkages of communication and the sources of innovation. Discussion and inquiry are possible only when questions are ambiguous, for no problem (except problems of fact) is posed by questions which have a single interpretation and simple univocal answers. An ambiguous question may be interpreted in different ways to constitute different questions about the same concrete but general experience; and those different unambiguous questions are relevant to different aspects of the experience, constitute different facts, and provide different data to be explored and used by different arts and methods. The lines of discourse are continuities of a sequence and consequence bound by coherency and directed to novelty. Since the questions of communication and discovery are ambiguous, the arts of discourse and inquiry, which disclose and organize facts, explore orders and connections in which they return one on another, and the themes which they develop borrow matter and method from different disciplines and find their continuity in common ambiguous questions faced in thought, action, and art. The arts, thus, are formative and creative; they have natural bases and ordered natural contents; they embody and express values and achieve purposes; they raise problems and have consequences. Again, the emotions presented and produced by poetry are in turn subject of inquiry and use in psychology, ethics, and rhetoric, and each of these arts has borrowed nomenclature, description, and analysis from the others. Philosophy is a systematic ordering of lines of discourse into perspectives.

Philosophic analysis of discourse may take its perspective from discourse itself. The intelligible structure of discourse is at once a structure of symbols related and transposed, of actions performed or projected, and of things signified and ordered. The frameworks of things, thoughts, actions, and symbols are assimilated in the common framework of discourse. When dialectic was the method of metaphysics or epistemology, the assimilation was to being or ideas, but the dialectic of discourse is an assimilation to concrete facts and contextual statements structured in processes rather than in essences or concepts. Facts have their meaning and existence in structured wholes of which they are interpreted parts. Statements have their references and consequences in structured discourses of which they are constituent parts. Facts reflect or approximate the ordering principles which give them form; they are orderings in a manifold, and they are adjusted to the environing circumstances and conditions in which they develop and evolve. They are formulated in lawlike statements and described in narrative statements. Statements of fact reflect the interests and information of the agent or formulator and the values and opinions of his culture; and scientific, historical, and mythical statements of fact supplement and reinforce each other. Discourse is a structure of systematization, argumentation, proof, and discovery, and each of the four structures takes many forms because the arts by which they are developed are commonplaces. To examine the interrelations and interplays of the modes of discourses is to assimilate them into discourse and to treat discourse in the perspective of systematization.

Philosophic analysis of discourse may take its perspective from the known and from conditioning circumstances. Facts are known facts; and since known facts present problems which vary with circumstances, they orient inquiry to the unknown. The scope and significance of problems expands as problems are solved and as the body of stated and known things increases and is ordered. The perspective of discourse is determined by the structure of emerging problems and hypotheses for their resolution. When logic was a method of definition and demonstration, of terms and rules by which to relate them, the resolution of problems was an ordering of variable and constant terms, but the logic of discourse is a resolution of problems of communication in which the definition and structure of symbols, the nature and functions of things, the character and intentions of agents, and the available knowledge of facts and relations are all structures of fact and statement, and in which consequences are established in historical narration, creative imagination, and purposive action as well as in symbolic implication. Facts are encountered and stated; and the adequacy of their statement is tested by comparing the consequences anticipated in statement with the consequences observed in occurrence. The method of deliberation is generalized from planning policies of action to predicting continuities of process and function. It includes the anticipations prepared in literature, music, and the arts, the expectations established in experimentation and theory, and the inferences and porisms grounded in logic and mathematics as well as the outcomes forecast or projected in practical action. Discourse is a sequence of assumptions and consequences, of observations and expectations. To treat discourse in the perspective of known facts and conditioning circumstances is to treat it by the method of deliberation and verification.

Philosophic analysis of discourse may take its perspective from the knowable and the underlying nature of things. Facts are the data of experience and the evidence for the structure of elements, which in turn provide the grounds and explanations of facts and their relations. Proof is a synthesis of elements of discourse, and it is a synthesis of elements on the subject-matter of discourse. The verification of proof depends on the double movement by which conclusions are related to the elements or principles on which they depend, and elements are related to the facts of experience from which they are derived. The Greeks used a single word, *stoicheion*, for the letters of the alphabet, the elements of physical nature, and the fundamental principles of mathematics and proof. When grammar was a linguistic method of constructing and analyzing statements and discourses, the constructions of things, of attitudes, and of proofs were ordered and examined by different grammars analogically related to the grammar of the discourse in which they were expressed; but the grammar of discourse is a vocabulary and syntax in which the construction of character and thought, of occurrences and sequences, of responses and style are inseparable from the construction of periods and the literature of communication. The method of judgment is generalized from the debates of law and the interpretations of criticism to include all analytic judgments of appropriate elements and all synthetic judgments of plausible consequences. Judgments of science, art, and action are based on analyses of facts and syntheses of elements, judged basic to the facts, into conclusions judged consequential on the elements. The element of debate which is prominent in judgments in law continues in the expansion of judgment to all discourse, for the test of a judgment is by placing it in the context of alternative judgments and by trying all means of refuting and falsifying both the opposed judgment and one's own. Discourse is an organized series of judgments set forth to secure credit concerning what is judged and consensus in the judgment expressed. It is justification of purposes and attitudes, of appreciations and interpretations, of facts and conditions as well as of statements of fact and of regularities of occurrence. To treat discourse in the perspective of the knowable and of nature and human nature is to treat it by the method of judgment and justification.

Philosophic analysis of discourse may take its perspective from the agent or knower or speaker. Facts are discoveries or inventions or innovations to be demonstrated or shown to others. The intelligible structure of the universe or of discourse, the known and the objects of inquiry, the unknown and the objects of experience are all facts discovered and made, or to be discovered and to be made. When rhetoric was a method of speaking to arouse passions and create attitudes, the art of invention was an art of forming arguments, but the commonplaces and topics of rhetoric have been extended in the rhetoric of discourse to the discovery of things and of arts as well as of words and ideas. Commonplaces have provided patterns, structures, and matrices subject to heuristic interpretation and application. The method of demonstration is generalized from the deductions of scientific proof and the manifestations of display oratory to include the exhibition of any structure particularized to any constants—the exhibitions of poetry and propaganda, of power and protest, of skepticism and proof. Demonstration as establishment of conclusions and certification of facts, demonstration as manifestation of convictions and advocacy of actions, and demonstration as stimulation of pleasure and inducement to adherence have modified and supplemented each other in the demonstrations of discourse since structures, things, and objectives are all projections and inventions in the perspective of the agent. The demonstrations of discourse are discussions which supervene in and transform the disputations of deliberation and the controversies of judgment. Discourse orders all experience into a series of manifestations which are the facts and meanings and values of communication. It is demonstration as designation, definition, and proof; as acquaintance, appreciation, and criticism; as reaction, connection, and integration. To treat discourse in the perspective of the agent or knower is to treat it by the method of demonstration.

There are sequences and consequences in things, thoughts, language, and action. At times in the history of the West they have been treated, in the dominant interests and in the philosophy of the times, as structures of communication. In Rome the structure of legal rhetoric provided commonplaces and methods which were extended to all problems. In the Renaissance the structure of a rhetoric of criticism of art and culture provided methods of innovation and demonstration that moved from the fine arts to the problems of science, society and religion. Today the structure of the rhetoric of communication and decision-making is in process of constructing universal arts of life and knowledge. Law and the fine arts become universal arts of discourse and communication, and we have recognized that universalizing tendency by seeking our art not in the practical or the poetic but in the scientific, by making a science of art, a *logos* of *techne*, and naming it ambiguously "technology." When discourse is a universal art, it is a matrix from which an indefinite number of patterns may be derived, and those patterns may be viewed from the point of view of the audience, the subject matter, or the agent of communication. Each perspective isolates a form of discourse, which is distinct from the others in methods and history, and which none the less may dominate and transform the others and assume their functions. The use of discourse as an inclusive structure, therefore, introduces flexibility while retaining methodological precision; it opens up dangers, repetitions, rigidities and wandering ambiguities. Deliberation is verification, not only in the sense of establishing propositions as true of what is the case and of what will happen, but also of planning action and policy, of communicating reasons for conclusions and evaluations, and of establishing satisfactions and enjoyments. Judgment is justification, not only in the sense of establishing the right or wrong of an action, but also of defending a position and belief, of extending and applying an interpretation, or of adjusting a thing to a context. Demonstration, finally, as manifestation, exhibition, or portrayal, has become an architectonic art, an art of arts. We verify and justify by demonstrating, and in so doing we exhibit the structures and unity of discourse. We move commonplaces from one mode of discourse or discipline to another, and we trace the lines of discourse according to the perspective selected; but the assimilation and discrimination are both achieved by demonstration, for they are achieved from the perspective of the agent who makes them.

The Methods of Rhetoric and Philosophy: Invention and Judgment

Periodical revolutions occur in the history of philosophy which change the perspectives of philosophical inquiry and transform the meanings of philosophic words and the natures of things meant. Kant called the insurrection in which he participated a Copernican revolution. Revolutions are to be distinguished from inversions and refutations by opponents and subversions and modulations by disciples, for revolutions abandon or dismiss positions rather than reconsider them. Revolutions prepare ways for different questions and occupations. The revolutions in the first decades of the twentieth century which set directions in modern philosophy abandoned methods of criticism and the construction of systems, and turned to methods of rhetoric and the grounding of statements. They revolted by seeking meaningful questions in the concrete and the real; by cultivating experience and phenomena, existence and nature; by appealing to science and history, common sense and language. They refuted no metaphysical or epistemological proposition, but they exhibited the absurdity of metaphysical statements which purport to be about all things, and idealistic statements which confuse thinking with being. Since it is absurd to seek to base meanings on alleged characteristics of being or on supposed forms of thought, inquiry into what men say and what they do may be used to provide clarification and test of what they say they think and of what they think is the case. Things and thoughts are in the significances and applications of language and in the consequences and circumstances of action.

The vast and difficult task undertaken in these revolutions lacked instrumentalities needed to carry it out successfully, because no art of rhetoric had been formed adequate to the possibilities of communication or to the contents or ends to which communication might be adapted. The techniques of public relations, propaganda, politics, and advertisement might afford data for the formation of such an art, but the interpretation of those data lacks a philosophical basis today. The nature of the problem is linguistically apparent in the solecisms, like "logical empiricism," "cognitive and emotive uses of language," "transcendental phenomenology," in which the analysis of language and experience finds adjectives for its linguistic and experiential nouns in epistemology, metaphysics, or popular psychology. The arts of rhetoric by which similar transitions from philosophy to rhetoric were effected in the past afford fuller indications of the methods that might save us from the amphibologies constructed to explore the implications of such solecisms and leave us time for inquiry into the philosophic problems of statement and action.

The nature of the transition is not as apparent as it should be because we tend to repeat the histories of philosophy—of wisdom and eloquence—set forth in the terms of the several traditional philosophies. The history of learning, culture, and interpretation is recounted differently by rhetoricians, and the revolutions become intelligible for deliberation and speculation in the lines of development those accounts follow. According to Cicero, the Greeks included under "wisdom" both the method of thought and its expression and the faculty of speaking. The two wisdoms or arts, of action and speech, were inseparable in the careers of ancient statesmen and philosophers, and there were also professional teachers of the double wisdom, like Gorgias, Thrasymachus, and Isocrates, who did not themselves engage in politics or oratory. Socrates, who was versed in knowledge and expression, put such emphasis on content that his teaching had the effect of limiting "philosophy" to knowledge of subject matters and of making a false separation of the art of thinking from the art of speaking.[1] Quintilian traces, in a like historical account, the origin, parts, and methods of the art of rhet-

1. *De oratore* iii.15.56–16.61.

oric. Rhetoric took its start from the work of a philosopher, Empedocles, and from the textbooks (*artes*) written in Sicily (responding to problems raised in the newly established democratic city-states) by Corax and Tisias. Gorgias was a Sicilian and a pupil of Empedocles. Protagoras and Gorgias were the first to treat commonplaces; Prodicus, Hippias, Protagoras, and Thrasymachus were the first to treat emotions (*adfectus*). Isocrates, the most famous pupil of Gorgias, and his opponent Aristotle both wrote textbooks of rhetoric. Thereafter, the philosophers, especially the Stoics and the Peripatetics, outstripped the rhetoricians in the cultivation of the field.[2]

In histories of ancient philosophy the Sophists are usually the villains of the piece, and accounts differ primarily in the kinds and degrees and qualifications of villainy ascribed to them. In this version of the history of learning and policy, the Sophists are the originators and movers; and, although only occasional philosophers deserve mention, the basic problem is a reconciliation of philosophy and eloquence, of knowledge and the ability to set forth what is known effectively and persuasively. In this version, moreover, the emerging problems are set forth in terms of the methods by which they have been, and may be, treated; and a fashionable modern note is anticipated when the problems of method of inference are brought to a point in the oppositions of Stoic and Aristotelian logical and linguistic analyses of creativity and credibility in discursive consequences and *rationes disserendi*. The invention of "commonplaces" was the provision of instrumentalities for *invention*. The investigation of "emotions" (when Descartes produced what he proclaimed to be the first scientific treatment of the emotions in the seventeenth century, he makes large use of rhetorical distinctions and analyses) was to uncover the causes and structures of *judgment*.

Invention and judgment had been parts of philosophic method, both as subjects of analysis and instruments of use, but the emphasis which was put on the methods of invention in rhetoric transformed philosophic methods even in application to problems far removed from those of language and speech. Cicero argued that every systematic treatment of discourse (*omnis ratio diligens disserendi*) has

2. Quintilian, *Institutio oratoria* iii.1.8–15.

two parts, one concerned with invention, the other with judgment. Aristotle treated both, and the Stoics developed the art of judgment but neglected the art of invention, which Cicero finds more useful and certainly prior in nature.[3] Invention is the art of discovering new arguments and uncovering new things by argument, while judgment is the art of testing arguments, proving conclusions, and verifying statements. In the context of inquiry and invention, judgment adds to the demonstrative arts of deducing from assumptions, the deliberative arts of examining consequences, and the judicial arts of falsifying alternatives, while invention extends from the construction of formal arguments to all modes of enlarging experience by reason as manifested in awareness, emotion, interest, and appreciation.

The achievements of rhetoric in invention and judgment, like all advancements of arts, suffer attritions in use and simplifications in misuse. The characteristic degradations of devices of invention and judgment are marked by the shifts of meanings attached to their terms of art. A commonplace is a place or seat of arguments; it is not itself an argument but a heuristic device by which issues that have never been considered before suggest distinctions and relations to be examined in search for solutions. Some problems recur frequently, however, and a "commonplace" has come to mean the irreflective repetition of identical formulae as an easy substitute for the invention of a pertinent solution.[4] Judgment is the art of considering the appropriateness of a formulation to the invention it expresses, to the problem it treats, and to the content it formulates. It is not formal, but rational, emotional, habitual, conative, and deliberative. The richness of the varieties of judgment appears in the ways in which Kant uses judgment in his three Critiques. Judgment occurs in the consideration of method in simplified meanings: in idealistic logics it has been a synonym for "proposition," and in revolts against idealisms it reappears in "decision-making."

Method is needed in invention to define the question and to order the data pertinent to it. The distinction between the questions of philosophy and those of rhetoric may then be stated as an antithesis

3. Cicero, *Topica* ii.6.
4. *Cf.* Quintilian, ii.4.27.

or as an assimilation of the two kinds of questions when rhetoric is transmuted into philosophy. Kinds of questions must be distinguished without predetermining the properties which will be found in the subject matter as a result of later discovery, and places must be formulated appropriate to the kinds of issues without anticipating the answers which will be discovered and explored by use of them. Aristotle had differentiated rhetoric sharply from philosophy, and rhetorical persuasion from demonstrative proof, by means of the questions and the places proper to each. Rhetoric is a counterpart of dialectic. Rhetorical and dialectical syllogisms are concerned with places common to many sciences and subject matters. Proper places, on the other hand, are derived from propositions peculiar to each species and genus of things, and propositions proper to physics furnish no arguments about ethics and the arguments of ethics are inapplicable to the subject matter of physics. To the extent that proper places are used, a science is produced different from rhetoric and dialectic, and if first principles are encountered, the discussion has moved from rhetoric and dialectic to the science of which they are first principles.[5] This distinction became the basis for the differentiation of indefinite questions (*quaestiones infinitae* or *universales* are also called *theses*, or simply *quaestiones*) from definite questions (*quaestiones finitae* or *speciales* are also called *hypotheses* or *causae*) which was the subject of controversy in the development of rhetoric. Cicero reports that Hermagoras mistakenly divides the matter of rhetoric into causes and questions, whereas he should recognize that questions are the subject matter of philosophy and that only causes (which are specific to individuals and circumstances) are the subject matter of rhetoric.[6] Quintilian reports the progress of the discussion and resolves it by arguing that the basic issues or *status* of both questions and causes are the same, citing in support of this conclusion the authority of Cicero in his later works, the *Orator*, the *De oratore*, and the *Topica*.[7]

A question—in the broad sense of either a thesis or a hypothesis—is rendered precise by determining the issue (sometimes called *status*, sometimes *constitutio*, sometimes *quaestio*). The complex and

5. Aristotle, *Rhetoric* i.2.1358a10–26.
6. Cicero, *De inventione* i.6.8.
7. Quintilian, iii.5.5–16.

changing relations between philosophy and rhetoric, and the effects of the transmutation of philosophy into rhetoric, are shadowed forth in the history of the schematisms and distinctions used to differentiate issues or questions. In Quintilian's account, the devices used to determine what is at issue in a question range from lists of categories to formulations of the basic questions of science—the issue is determined by conflict or antithesis, by the way in which the subject thing (*subiecta res*) is understood, by categories (beginning with Aristotle's), and by the reduction of all questions to one, two, three, or more. The solution which Quintilian reports many writers favor is the three questions of Cicero, who had argued that everything which enters into controversy or contention is contained in the three questions—whether it is, what it is, and of what sort it is (*Sitne? Quid sit? Quale sit?*).[8]

Aristotle's "categories" can be interpreted as issues or questions, but the three issues of rhetoric have a more apparent relation to Aristotle's four "scientific questions." What is involved in the transition from philosophy to rhetoric can be clarified by examining the changes in basic philosophic method which result from using his four "questions" of inquiry and proof as "issues" of controversy and contention. Aristotle finds as many questions in inquiry as there are things known—whether it is, what it is, of what sort it is, and also why it is.[9] In this list, the questions whether it is and of what sort it is are questions of fact, while the questions what it is and why it is seek the reasons or causes for facts.[10] The sciences make use of special places and principles determined by the facts, and rhetoric makes use of general places common to the subject matters of several sciences or regions of experience. As means of inquiry the questions are as numerous as the things known; but as means of discovery the questions are as numerous as the judgments made. The answer to the question "why" is found not in a cause which connects the terms in a proposition but in a judge who determines the issues in a question.

There is consequently an inversion of Aristotle's distribution of kinds of questions—rhetoric, not philosophy or science, treats of

8. Ibid., 11–44.
9. Aristotle, *Posterior Analytics* ii.1.89b23–35.
10. Ibid., 2.90a31–34.

specific questions, and science treats of general questions, if indeed they too do not fall as Hermagoras thought within the purview of rhetoric. But this inversion is due in part to the fact that the marks of general and specific questions, of common and proper places, have changed in the transition. In the orientation to facts a place is proper to the subject matter of one science or common to a broader field of data. In the orientation to judgment, a definite question or a proper place derives its specificity from reference to individual persons and determinate times, places, and circumstances, while an indefinite question or a commonplace derives its universality from reference to kinds. The earlier philosophy and the later rhetoric is each "objective" or "concrete" in its respective way, and the transition from philosophy to rhetoric is recorded in the language of the rhetoricians who call the "definite question" a "hypothesis" or a "cause" and the "indefinite question" a "thesis" or a "question." The issues (or constitutions) are the same in definite questions or hypotheses, and the names acquired by hypotheses are again marks indicating the significance of the transition. The question "whether it is" is a *conjectural* issue or an issue of fact; the question "what it is" is a *definitive* issue or an issue of name; the question "of what sort it is" is a *general* issue or an issue of genus or kind. Moreover, Aristotle's fourth question, "why it is," had not disappeared in the transition from indefinite questions or theses to definite questions or hypotheses. Cicero had distinguished four issues. In addition to the three reported by Quintilian he considered the *translative* issue or the issue of who should bring the action, against whom, how, or before what court, and the problem of the *cause* of a process is transformed into the problem of the cause considered and resolved by consensus of the proper body of experts.[11]

Questions of judgment are found in the products of invention as well as in the process of invention. They include the statement and proof of what is discovered, and they apply to problems of expressing, establishing, and falsifying conclusions as well as to problems of raising questions, determining issues, and framing hypotheses. In the classification of the parts of rhetoric, judgment was sometimes listed as one of the parts; Cicero placed it under invention; Quin-

11. Cicero, *De inventione* i.8.10 and 11.16.

tilian held that judgment is involved in three of the five parts, in invention, arrangement (*dispositio*), and expression (*elocutio*).[12] The emphasis on judgment does not depend on the unique qualifications or authority of specific judges or experts, for the argument would, if that were the case, be circular: judges are good because their judgments are true, and judgments are true if they have the authority of good judges. Judgment does not depend uniquely on facts or on words, or ideas, or emotions. Its function is not to adapt statements to known ideas and emotions of audiences, but to form ideas and arouse impulses. Rhetorical judgment retains the marks of its transformation from dialectical proposition as described by Aristotle: a dialectical proposition is a question which accords with the opinion of all men or most men or the wise—either all the wise, or most of them, or the most famous; but dialectical propositions also include views similar to received opinions and views contrary to them.[13] A thesis is a conception contrary to general opinion but propounded by someone famous as a philosopher.[14]

Aristotle differentiates the sciences, according to principles, methods, and propositions appropriate to different subject matters, into theoretic, practical, and productive. He differentiates dialectical questions, according to commonplaces rather than particular propositions, into three kinds—ethical, physical, and logical.[15] One of the marks of the influence of the transition of philosophy into dialectic and rhetoric is found in the long history of subsequent divisions of philosophy into ethics, physics, and logic. The more specific influence of rhetoric is found in the kinds of judgments differentiated according to the three kinds of oratory, and once again the transformation of their names is a summary indication of the pertinence and importance of the change. What Aristotle called epideictic oratory became "demonstrative"; political oratory became "deliberative"; forensic oratory became "judicial." There is a pun in each of the terms "demonstration," "deliberation," and "judgment" which permits them in turn to take over the whole field of inquiry, while the differences raised in their oppositions provide

12. Quintilian, iii.3.5–6.
13. Aristotle, *Topics* i.10.104a8–37.
14. Ibid., 11.104b18–28.
15. Ibid., 14.105b19–21.

the basic problems of philosophy. Quintilian was convinced that *demonstration* had been unduly neglected, yet by considerations of praise and blame it focuses on the good, *honesta*, and gives objectivity to all modes of argumentation and judgment. *Deliberation*, on the other hand, by considerations of expediency and inexpediency focuses on utility, *utilia*, and there is more than an intimation of the philosophical convictions of Kant, G. E. Moore, and Pritchard, in Quintilian's objection that inclination is an insufficient base for precepts for action, since they should be based on *honesta* rather than on *utilia*. *Judgment*, finally, seeks objectivity by considerations of accusation and defense, not in the good or the useful, but in the necessary; and the true emerges from the trial of opposed alternatives as warranted or as not falsified. The foundations of judgment are in the structures employed in demonstration and system-building, in the consequences examined in deliberation and calculation, or in the necessities encountered in judgment and decision-making.

The relevance of the methods of rhetoric to the problems of philosophy is due in part to the continuity of the influences, in which the methods of philosophy have influenced the methods of rhetoric and been influenced in turn by them, and in part to the orientation of contemporary problems to issues particularly suited to the methods of rhetoric. This orientation is manifest in philosophy in the importance assumed by facts and data, experience and existence, the circumstantial and the concrete. Yet despite this orientation of contemporary problems the discussion of those problems is betrayed into verbal, abstract, and fantastic formulations. The methods of a new rhetoric, transformed to philosophic uses, is needed to bring invention to bear on innovation of insights rather than on repetition of verbal forms and to bring judgment to bear on issues of causes rather than on adjustments to formed habits, characters, and prejudices. A new schematism of commonplaces is needed to make the exploration of the new a proper method of philosophy; and a new examination of demonstration, deliberation, and decision is needed to lift judgment from formalisms and mechanisms and to make the treatment of what is the case or what may be made to be the case a proper method of philosophy. The new problems encountered in the world today as a result of increase in things known must be considered in commonplaces of invention rather than in commonplaces of past problems. The interplays of peoples and of subject matters suggest new issues which must be explored by stating new questions rather than by facilely reducing them to old theses.

Symbols, Myths, and Arguments

The development of language and the arts of its use are accorded an important place in several phases of human and social history, and the chronicles that recount the effects of language in each phase deal with happenings which have obvious relations to each other in each account. Yet the several accounts depend on uses of languages which are mutually independent, and each comprehends the others in its scope. As early as the first speculations of Greek poets, historians, and philosophers, language was considered an indispensable instrument for the establishment of human association and society, an unexcelled matter for the creation of poetic forms and statements, and a clear and testable structure for the discovery and statement of scientific proofs. Poetry and science develop within societies and are treated properly as part of social communication since they contribute to, and in turn are influenced by, human ties and associations. The relations of men—the destinies of kings and the sufferings of commoners, the campaigns of generals and the wanderings of peoples, the loves of men and women, the education of youths and their coming to maturity, the mysteries beyond life and the fear of death—have furnished the subject matter of poetry; and poets have expressed, in the opinion at least of some poets and philosophers, truths beyond the range of science. Society and art, finally, like all other phenomena, afford a subject matter and present problems which are, or should be, susceptible of analysis and treatment according to the scientific method; and science, in turn, is an art and the republic of scientists and scholars a community.

To talk about these interrelations is to commit oneself to one of these or similar frames of reference. The characteristic frames in which language is discussed today tend to set its social and moral, its esthetic, and its scientific problems and uses in antitheses and oppositions, which are frequently stated as some form of an opposition between the "scientific" and the "non-scientific" or "anti-scientific." The resulting problems of semantic systems have so little relation to the interpenetration of the problems of actual languages and the means they actually employ that it is difficult to know whether the methods of semantics are newly devised to meet characteristic problems of our times or the problems discussed in semantics are consequences of characteristic methods in vogue. Two problems come to the center of discussion when these relations of problems and languages are in question. One is the question of the relation of the language of poetry to the language of science or, in the objective form in which it is sometimes thrown, the effects of science and technology on poetry. The second is the question of the relation of the language of communication and persuasion, of discussion, negotiation, and agreement to the language of science or, in its objective form, the effect of science and technology on society. The distinctions examined in this paper are set up and elaborated to isolate the social use of symbols and to distinguish the problems of symbols in that use from the linguistic and semantic problems of art and science.

Once questions concerning the relations of languages are stated, in any form, it is easy to recognize the facts to which they are relevant, and the temptation is strong to construct the history by which man has passed from earlier or "primitive" uses of symbols to later or "scientific" uses which destroy not only the supposed efficacy of magic, incantation, and ritual but also the positive operation of social and religious symbols, moral precepts, and poetic constructs. The possibility of such a history and its scope and truth depend, however, on distinctions, ultimately philosophic in character, concerning the nature of language and the modes of its use. There is no dearth of such linguistic and semantic theories; indeed, if one were to catalogue the characteristics of our age, the widespread tendency to treat all fundamental questions in terms of the language in which they are stated and to describe such linguistic treatment as factual and empirical should occupy a prominent place in the list. These theories, however, despite their number and diversity, all reinforce rather than correct the simple view of our present situation, together with the simple account of the stages of its evolution, which we expound in our accounts of the effects of the achievements of the "scientific method" and the history of their ramification. The basic distinctions of most semantic theories are not derived from linguistic phenomena or from scientifically ascertained facts, nor are they justified by the structure of scientific proof or the history of scientific development. They are built on fragments of metaphysical or physical principles, epistemological or psychological doctrine, and social or cultural theories. These vestiges are not expressed fully or examined carefully, and they are borrowed for the most part from the doctrines of a bygone age to construct the novel doctrines by which we are to break away from those earlier commitments. Since they are simple distinctions they can be made to reinforce each other and thereby lend an air of factual substantiation from many sources to any of the variety of semantics.

We assume without much discussion, as a cryptometaphysical basis for language, that words are denotative or connotative, that they are or should be defined by things they designate, preferably particular things experienced in sensation and situated in time and space, and that all other aspects of the operation of language are or should be explained by the interrelations set up in linguistic combinations and structures which correspond to like combinations and structures in the experience of men, their passions and presumptions, and the association of their ideas. This assumption provides ready means for cataloguing and describing the numerous uses of language which do not designate things perceived by the senses without crediting the apparent designation of many things dreamed of by philosophers and scientists, expounded by poets, and negotiated for by diplomatists and politicians; but no very enlightening or practical means of treating the problems in which those things are involved results from this catalogue. We assume in similar fashion, as a crypto-epistemological basis for language, that the scientific use of language is cognitive, and that poetic and practical uses are non-cognitive inasmuch as they are emotive or persuasive. This is a reasonable enough distinction, but its theoretic scope and practical utility are limited, since the arbitrary restriction that it places on the "cognitive" translates all rational and causal uses of language in practical action and esthetic construction into problems of emotion and power accessible to cognition only at the removal from which science views them; and it translates the numerous aspects of language employed in the development of scientific knowledge, proof, and expression into problems of proof and verification. We assume, finally, as a cryptosociological basis for language, that the vocabulary and syntax no less than the semantics of a language reflect the character of the culture in which it is developed, and that languages acquire intercultural generality by borrowings from other languages and from the common language of science and technology. Yet this distinction limits our treatment of both culture and science in ways that we recognize more easily in rival forms of the theory than in our own, as, for example, in the Marxist reduction of the language of science to the objective devices of dialectical materialism and the language of ethics, art, law, politics, and even "bourgeois" science to "ideologies" explained by the circumstances of the classes that use the language rather than by the nature of the things they treat.

These three sets of basic distinctions—between denotation and connotation, between cognitive and non-cognitive, between common and cultural—all come to much the same consequences when they are applied in the discussion of symbols and language. Whether the distinctions are true or false and, further, whether they provide an adequate basis for a philosophy of language, would be nice questions and important ones. They are not, however, the question that I wish to consider. I have raised the question of the adequacy of these basic principles of contemporary theories of signs, symbols, and language to provide practical means by which to analyze or to treat practical problems—not to focus on theories of "symbols" in general but to provide, in the inadequacies that have been sketched, a background against which to restate the practical problem of "symbols" in particular, as they operate as bonds of association and motives of action. In current debate the practical problem of symbols is discussed as a problem of the "decay" of symbols or as a problem of propaganda analysis. The distinctions on which the discussion is based lead to hypotheses which explain the present impotence of symbols and the decline or perversion of the arts of influencing the actions of men in communication and association as consequences of differences between our more advanced civilizations and the more primitive cultures in which symbols were effective; or as consequences of the development of science, which has made us insensitive to symbols and has faced us with the dilemma of either constructing symbols in which we do not believe, to influence people on whom they might be effective, or relying on the effectiveness of a propaganda of truth and of facts, which people do not always believe; or, finally, as consequences of confusion of facts and emotional preferences. Like the theories on which they are based, these three attitudes toward practical symbols are not different in their basic distinctions or practical consequences. They are, however, taken together or separately, implausible or at least impoverished as theory, and they reduce us, in practical programs based on their use, to dilemmas in which the balance of incompatible courses of action forestalls any action, while it multiplies knowledge that is not employed in the actions that are taken.

If symbols operate in practice simply as instruments of power to be manipulated, the problems of symbols in application reduce to the two for which linguistic theory provides a terminology: a problem of knowledge, which can be solved either by employing knowledge in the more effective use of symbols, even when they are not demonstrably true, or of the construction of true symbols on the assumption that they are more effective than symbols in some sense false; and a problem of emotions, which can be solved either by constructing symbols to appeal to the emotions that groups are known to have or by manipulating symbols calculated to arouse in them emotions that they should have. In the face of antinomies such as these, one is tempted to simplify a precept of Kant and say that theoretically neither solution is correct, but practically both are. In practice we follow Kant's precept by excusing the course of action we continue to follow, but when we are engaged in the theoretic consideration of the grounds of what we do, it is worth considering the possibility that our basic distinctions are among the causes of our confusion.

The use of symbols occurs in contexts: the context of a subject matter, particular and universal, to which the discourse is related; the context of speaker and audience related in expression, communication, and reaction; and, finally, the context of conditions and circumstances which influence the discourse, the view of the subject matter assumed in it, and the attitudes reflected in the statement and in its reception. The marks and effects of these influences and these environing or conditioning forces might supply principles for the discussion of symbols, but if the influences are taken themselves as principles, what is said about symbols may afford information about things or thoughts, emotions or cultures, but it yields only elliptical knowledge of the nature of symbols and indirect paradoxical guidance in their use. The distinction between denotation and connotation tends thus to slip off into questions about the character of the things designated by symbols and about the character of the psychological connections on which the association of symbols is based; on the other hand, if those questions are translated into questions concerning the means by which symbols attain particularity and make use of devices of connection and universality, the problems that are encountered and the distinctions by which they can be stated and treated are relevant to the discourse itself rather than to the influences that condition it. Much the same is true both of the problems involved in the ideas which discourse conveys and the emotions which it excites and of the problems of the common and particular values it reflects and embodies. Moreover, the linguistic devices can be examined in the language of science, of poetry, and of action, whereas the external distinctions locate these languages *a priori* in separate categories, since cognition, emotion, and power are obviously distinct; and, what is more important when the problem is one of the practical use of symbols, linguistic devices are related directly to the character of the symbols and their uses, whereas the external distinctions lead to "sciences" of language which have no immediate or obvious practical consequences.

Symbols attain particularity, usually by means of devices that depend on their generality or universality, in a variety of ways. Two such means may be distinguished, using terminology long traditional, as argument and myth. "Argument" in its most general sense, as the primary meaning of the Greek word *logos* suggests, includes all kinds of calculation. It is a mistake to suppose that we encounter individual things as given elements in immediate experience. Whatever the experience of organisms which do not employ symbols may be, a long preliminary process is prerequisite to applying a sign to what it is to signify in the experience of men and even in the more limited use of signs that can be detected among other animals. Arguments—whether they are scientific, dialectical, or rhetorical—employ these devices in a calculation which focuses the generalities employed in analysis and discourse, however rudimentary and non-verbal, on conclusions which can be identified in a particular instance. "Myth," as the primary meaning of the Greek word *mythos* suggests, puts emphasis on what it said rather than on what is presented for calculation, and it attains particularity by narration. It is a mistake to suppose that "myths" or the accounts of happenings deal with particulars in a peculiar sense distinct from the generality of "arguments," that is, of discursive inferences from premises. Rather, the two employ different means of achieving particularity by means of different modes of generality. The construction of an argument concerning particulars depends on the establishment of premises from causally related particular instances; the construction of a likely story depends on the use and suggestion of causes to relate the incidents or the parts of the narrative plausibly. "History" played an important part in both processes in earlier discussions of their operation: "natural history" assembled the instances and observations which the biologist employed in formulating scientific laws, and "history" provided accounts of what actually happened from which the epic or tragic poet constructed the probabilities and the necessities of his poem. Moreover, the question of truth is not the peculiar province of either process, but depends on the interrelations of both in argument and myth, for the use of argument itself makes clear that the verification of a scientific truth is not a question simply of reference to particulars, and Aristotle has indicated the sense in which poetry is truer and more philosophical than history.

The complexity of the effective interrelations of particularity and generality in discourse begins to appear once these distinctions, or others similarly based on discourse itself, are made. For although argument is a calculation and not a story, the plot or the "myth" of a tragedy is its "argument." Dialecticians, from their first appearance in history to their current activities in developing forms of Marxism and Hegelianism, have found an equivalence between the devices by which universal truth and concrete particularity are achieved in the processes of change and the devices by which they are treated by reason: Croce would reduce philosophy to historiography, and some evolutionists as well as some Marxists find the pattern of sciences in the developmental processes, while other biologists and metaphysicians undertake to expose the basic principles and assumptions on which the arguments that justify evolutionary processes depend. Plato, more than most philosophers, was subtly aware of the interpenetration of argument and myth. The dialectical method which he employed, not only to derive consequences from presuppositions, but also to test and refute premises, to establish the principles that underlie hypotheses, to explore the indeterminacies of the infinite, and to demonstrate the existence of the highest things—of the Ideas, the Good, and the gods—is supplemented throughout the dialogues by myths which put in concrete narrative form particulars whose simplicities defy expression according to the distinctions of analytic and discursive proof. Such particulars include the principles of proof (such as the contact of the soul with Ideas), the sources of action (such as the commitment of an individual man or state to a character and a way of life), or the application of a conclusion to a set of facts (such as the variety of reasons leading to error and vice and the variety of objects in the hierarchies of loves). To accomplish these purposes of demonstration, verification, and application Plato invented or refurbished some of the great myths which poets and historians have continued to repeat—the myths of prenatal choice and posthumous reward, the golden age, cycles of growth and catastrophe, the gift of Prometheus, the age of Cronos, the destruction of Atlantis. Moreover, he recognized that, without confusion of myth and argument, myth is in some perspectives an argument and argument a myth: the *Republic* is a complete and masterly dialectical construction set in a context of related inquiries; yet the argued account of the perfect city becomes a "myth" which must be transported into the realm of truth by an account of what has actually happened, that is, true "history" and true "argument";[1] the true history related to accom-

1. Plato, *Timaeus*, 26C–E.

plish this purpose is the account of the ancient city of Atlantis, which editors, notwithstanding Plato's elaborate argument to the contrary, treat as a myth, and part of the grounds alleged for crediting the history is that it was told by Solon who was not only the wisest of men but the noblest of poets;[2] myth and history are then supplemented by an inquiry into cosmology and physics which is, likewise, not a demonstration, but a "likely story" or "myth."[3]

The differences and interrelations among the devices by means of which argument and myth employ generality to achieve particularity, may be used in contrast and counterpoise to indicate the devices by which "symbols" serve as bonds of community and stimuli to action. The fact that symbols are prominent in our discussion of human relations and yet difficult to enumerate—except for the flag and the cross—and the quaint conundrums to which problems of the use of symbols are reduced, are both consequences of the tendency to confuse them either with arguments or with myths. These are inevitable confusions when symbols are analyzed in the terms available in most modern schemes of semantics. Thus, symbols in their social uses would seem to be neither cognitive nor designative in any strict sense, and the distinction between myth and argument suggests, at most, that symbols are mythical but might be made true and reliable, if not argumentative. Even in theory, the cost of applying the simple dichotomy between cognitive and non-cognitive is tremendous, for it would mean that the difficulty of separating them in philosophies like Plato's throws doubt on such philosophies and makes plausible the expectation of better results from a purer and more cognitive language. The labor of theory, however, is long, and the expectation should be given its test; but the consequences of the distinction in practical application are disastrous, since the only directions that are left intelligible and practicable by the distinction are to try to remove the mythical element in symbols (or to employ it deliberately) and to ground symbols more firmly in truths established by arguments (or to conceal the argument whose truth might destroy the efficacy of the symbol).

2. Ibid., 21A–C.
3. Ibid., 29B–D.

Symbols differ from myths and arguments in respect both to the universality on which they are based and the particularity which they achieve—as well as in many other ways which would have to be examined if our purposes were to develop a theory of symbols rather than simply to indicate their characteristics and to suggest distinctions to guide their use. Arguments are calculations which proceed from universal grounds and may be used to identify particulars—things, relations, events—and to justify the properties and operations attributed to them. Myths are narratives which construct particulars in discourse—persons, institutions, events—by means of sequences and structures which may have the universality of recognized necessity or probability. If causes are sought, they are found in the premises of arguments (for even the postulates of mathematics and the principle of indeterminacy, which is the reason for denying causes in quantum mechanics, are formal causes) and in the sequences of events and interdependence of parts in myths and histories. "Symbols," as the primary meaning of the Greek word, *symbolon,* suggests, are tallies. They were the two halves or corresponding pieces of the bone or other object which two strangers, or any other two contracting parties, broke between them in order to have proof of the identity of the presenter of the other part. In its more general use, "symbol" includes any token which serves as proof of identity and any like guarantee in the relations and affairs of man. The particularity and the universality of the symbol are inseparably conjoined; it is the mark, immediately and unmistakably recognizable, of a relation which requires, without question or argument, actions of a particular kind. So far as particularity is concerned, the symbol is more concrete and evocative than myth or argument, and although what it accomplishes can be accounted for by history and justified by proof, restatement of a symbol in either form is less precise and less pertinent than the original symbol. So far as generality is concerned, the symbol is richer and more relevant than myth or argument, and although it is an inexhaustible source of interpretation in narrative and in proof, it provides a ground of action and cooperation at once more reliable and more direct than the continuities of history or the consequences of demonstration, for it can move men who are ignorant of history and insensitive to argument.

These characteristics of symbols are not mysterious nor have they been passed unnoticed by philosophers or by men who have influenced action, in spite of the tendency of recent linguistic theories to make them disappear into poetry and science, passion and power, ambiguity and attitude. Jean Jacques Rousseau, who sought to base his philosophy and his theory of education on deeds rather than words, on facts rather than language, was particularly sensitive to the operation of symbols, and presented both aspects of their use—the vividness of their particularity exceeding that of myth and argument and the cohesive force of their generality justifying and exceeding multiple interpretation by myth and argument—although he was unconcerned with their characteristics or uses. The context in which he treats the particularity of symbols is in his discussion of the modern error of appealing to the ear and the reason rather than to the eye and the heart of men:

> One of the errors of our age is to use reason in too naked a form, as if men were all mind. By neglecting the language of signs, we have lost the most energetic language. The impression of words is always weak, and we speak to the heart much better by way of the eyes than the ears. In the effort to reduce everything to reasoning, we have reduced our precepts to words; we have embodied nothing in deeds. Reason alone is not active; she occasionally restrains, she rarely excites, and she never has done anything great. To reason always is the mania of small minds. Strong souls have an entirely different language; it is by this language that men are persuaded and led to act. I observe that, in modern centuries, men only get a hold over others by force and interest, whereas the ancients acted much more by persuasion, by the affections of the soul, because they did not neglect the language of signs. . . . What the ancient accomplished with eloquence is prodigious; but this eloquence did not consist only in beautiful discourses well arranged; and it was never more effective than when the orator said least. What they said most vividly was not expressed by words but by signs; it was not said, it was shown. The object which is exposed to the eyes shocks the imagination, excites the curiosity, and keeps the mind on the alert for what we are about to say. Thrasybulus and Tarquin cutting off the heads of poppies, Alexander placing his seal on the mouth of his favorite, Diogenes walking in front

> of Zeno, do they not speak better than if they made long speeches? What circumlocution of words would have expressed the same ideas as well? Darius, engaged in Scythia with his army, received from the king of the Scythians a bird, a frog, a mouse, and five arrows. The ambassador deposited the gift and retired without a word. In our days this man would have been taken for a madman. This terrible harangue was understood, and Darius withdrew to his own country with as great speed as he could. Substitute a letter for these signs, and the more threatening it was the less it would terrify; it would have been merely a piece of blustering at which Darius would only have laughed.[4]

Rousseau, concentrating on the distinction between the heart and the mind, simplified somewhat the operation of symbols. They lead to action, not because their meaning is unambiguously clear, but precisely because it is not; and their effectiveness depends, not on an appeal to emotion in the absence of reason, but rather on an intermingling of emotions and reasons. As Herodotus tells the story, the meaning of the Scythian's gift was not immediately clear to the Persians; rather it suggested two interpretations: Darius argued that the Scythians were surrendering themselves, their earth, and their water to him, while his captain, Gobyras, reasoned that their gift meant, "Unless you become birds and fly up into the sky, or mice and hide in the earth, or frogs and leap into the lakes, you will be shot by these arrows and never return home."[5] Diogenes, walking while Zeno demonstrated the impossibility of motion, established either the absurdity of Zeno's position—and the persistence with which philosophers have continued to discuss Zeno's paradoxes is evidence against the success of his effort—or the enigmatic character of philosophy.

The particularity of the symbol resists statement in myth or argument. The effectiveness of symbols depends on that particularity and is diminished by exposition and interpretation; they are immediately pertinent to attitudes and directly effective on actions. The generality of symbols is found in the community or unity of

4. Jean Jacques Rousseau, *Émile, ou de l'Education, IV, Oeuvres Complètes de J. J. Rousseau,* edited by V. D. Musset-Pathay, P. Dupont, Paris, 1823, III, pp. 134–137.

5. Herodotus, iv. 132.

men which has access to them and which is divided into factions and heresies by histories and arguments. Symbols are immediate bonds by which men are conscious of being joined to each other. Rousseau also presents vividly this aspect of generality not in terms of the use of symbols, but again by opposing natural feelings to acquired ideas, our hearts to our manners and customs. Conviction based on natural feelings is part of the profession of faith of the Savoyard vicar, and beliefs are, in general, so closely bound to symbols that the traditional term to designate a basic creed is "symbol."[6] Rousseau's statement of the opposition between basic and superposed symbols is as concrete as his illustration of operation of symbols in communication.

> Cast your eyes over all the nations of the world, run through all the histories; in the midst of all these inhuman and bizarre cults, in the midst of this amazing diversity of manners and characters, you will find everywhere the same ideas of justice and integrity, everywhere the same principles of morality, everywhere the same notions of good and evil. Ancient paganism gave birth to abominable gods who would have been punished as criminals here below, and who offered as models of supreme happiness only crimes to be committed and passions to be gratified. But vice, armed with sacred authority, descended in vain from the eternal abode; the moral instinct drove it back from the heart of men. While the debaucheries of Jupiter were celebrated the continence of Xenocrates was admired; the chaste Lucretia adored the shameless Venus; the bold Roman sacrificed to Fear; he invoked the god who mutilated his father, and died without murmur at the hand of his own father. The most contemptible divinities were worshipped by the most noble men. The sacred voice of nature, stronger than that of the gods, made itself respected upon earth, and seemed to relegate crime together with the criminal to heaven.[7]

This unanimity of mankind in the judgment of actions, which Rous-

6. Cf. H. Denzinger, *Enchiridion Symbolorum*, Freiburg, 23rd edition, Herder, 1937, in which seven forms of the *Symbolum Apostolicum* are presented, pp. 1–16, as well as the Athanasian creed or *Symbolum "Quicunque,"* pp. 17–18, the *Symbolum Nicaenum*, pp. 29–30, the *Symbolum Nicaeno-Constantinopolitanum*, pp. 41–42, 278, the *Symbolum Tridentina*, pp. 346–349.

7. Rousseau, op. cit., III, pp. 62–63.

seau finds innate in the souls of men, is overlaid by differences which take explicitly symbolic form in the religions that divide two-thirds of mankind into Jews, who follow the revelation of one book, Christians, who follow the revelation of two, and Mohammedans, who acknowledge three, and which derive from those books different traditions, meanings, customs, and prejudices.

I have gone to Rousseau to illustrate the meaning and operation of symbols, not because symbols concerned him especially in his philosophy, for the contrary was the case, but because he was sensitive to the operation of symbols in action, and his vivid presentation, by removing symbols from the vague mysteries which our symbolic philosophies have cast about them, makes them easy to identify in their operation today without recourse to myth or argument. Once they are identified and recognized, it is clear that we face two fundamental problems in the use of symbols in our times.

Symbols have always had two distinct but related uses. Myths and arguments are poor substitutes for symbols in both uses; yet, in both, the development and operation of symbols is attended and furthered by related myths and arguments. Symbols are used, in the first place, as a means of external communication to express the intention, attitude, desire, or expectation of one person or group to others. The Scythian's gift to Darius was a symbol of this sort. Darius's advisers might have gone to the history of the Scythians and their culture for an interpretation of the symbol or they might have presented arguments in support of opposed theories; but as Rousseau suggested, neither the myth nor the argument would have conveyed the message or achieved the effect of the symbol. Symbols are used, in the second place, as a means of internal cohesion in a group and, consequently, as a cause of joint action. Our actions relative to others are governed by a sense of rightness (whether or not Rousseau was correct in thinking it innate and in calling it "conscience") which can seldom be justified by histories constructed to account for the origin of the group or by arguments constructed to justify its existence; and even when such justification can be found, an appeal to history or to argument would be an impractical substitute for the immediate response elicited by the symbol. When I begin to justify what I must do for my family or for my country by myths about my relatives and my countrymen, or by arguments about the institution, the symbol is no longer operative and my inventions are a sign that the relation it symbolizes is weakened. The institution itself—my family, my church, or my country—may be considered a symbol, or the term, symbol, in its primary sense, may be reserved for those concrete symbols which are attached directly to the institutions—the hearth, the threshold, the Lares and Penates, the star of David, the Cross, and the Crescent, the fasces, the flag, and the sceptre. The significance of that symbol is expressed in other secondary symbols: the epic or origins of the institution, the creed or principles that animate it, the gospel or purposes it fulfils. The two kinds of symbols are distinct in their uses—communication and unification—and they present distinct problems, but they are interrelated since the symbols that unite a group determine the significance of the symbols that set forth its intended actions.

In the light of these distinctions it is easy to enumerate symbols other than the flag and the cross and to identify their operation in negotiation and action today. But it is extremely difficult to hold them in view for theoretic examination, or to determine what should be done about them in practical programs, by examining them to determine whether, once identified, they are "discursive" or "expressional," whether they are "fact pointers" or "value eliciters" or "emotion inciters." They may be any or all of these, but the problem of using them as symbols is not primarily a problem of arousing an emotion, or presenting a fact, or establishing a truth. The empirical problem they present is not one of differentiating fact and discourse—people confuse words and things only in the philosophies of their opponents or the diagnoses of their therapists—but rather one of identifying symbols. The practical problem is not one of demonstrating that symbols are often false and dangerous—when I am a member of a group whose beliefs are opposed and whose power and existence are threatened, the argument that my beliefs are not true and are contrary to a larger common interest is only a symbolic restatement of the fact that the group, the sect, the class, or the nation is opposed and menaced—but the practical problem is rather one of the operation of symbols.

Symbols in their use as *external means of communication* are numerous and easily identified in the practical affairs and communications of nations today. The atom bomb is a symbol, but so also are the numerous reports of committees that have tried abortively to work out an agreement concerning the development of atomic power and atomic weapons; the Saar valley, NATO, UN, the intervention in Korea, the independence of Indonesia, forced labor camps, satellite countries, imperialism, the plight of the Negroes and Hindus in the Union of South Africa, and the status of minority groups in the United States are all used as symbols in negotiations similar to those Darius engaged in long ago with the Scythians. Symbols are concrete representations of objective situations; they are constructed in diplomatic negotiations; they emerge in the view taken by one group or nation of the institutions and actions of others.

In all forms of external communication symbols indicate or threaten actions which are not explicitly delineated. Neither the fondness for symbols nor the skill in constructing them, illustrated in the Scythian's gift to Darius, has been lost. But we have tended to neglect in our use of symbols for this purpose a problem with which the ancients were familiar and for which they had devised techniques of interpretation less to our taste than the enigmatic signs on which they were employed. In all negotiations, one side can profit by ambiguity while the other side must, unless it finds an alternative symbol practicable in the situation, remove ambiguity by action—the Scythian ambassador could depart without a word, but Darius had to decide whether to remain in Scythia or to withdraw his army. It is not the case that wisdom, honesty, or effectiveness in the use of symbols requires precision in their use and avoidance of ambiguity. There is a region of necessary and fruitful ambiguity in all communications designed to lead to action, precisely because symbolic communication is necessary only when both parties are in agreement on the problem that calls for action but not on principles and purposes. Some clarity would be introduced into modern forms of this ancient problem of symbols by distinguishing the circumstances in which, from the point of view of each of the parties to the negotiation, ambiguity is tolerable and desirable from those in which precision and definition by action is indispensable. Thus, to use an obvious illustration, the Soviet Union is opposed to Western plans of atomic control and it abstained from voting to approve the Universal Declaration of Human Rights, not because of a professed opposition to the control of arms or to human rights, but because of the means by which definition and control would be attained in both cases—by external inspection and common adjudication—which seemed, or which Soviet diplomatists could argue were, devices by which to attain other objectives. Conversely, the Western democracies have all but permitted the Communists to appropriate "peace" as a symbol, not because of opposition to peace, but because of suspicion concerning the devices by which "peace" is to be defined and because of lack of ingenuity in constructing an equally effective contrary symbol; and powerful groups in the United States oppose the genocide convention, threaten the success of the proposed convention on human rights, and criticize the United Nations in general because of dangers they see, or profess to see, to our "sovereignty."

A second problem in the use of symbols in practical communication is new in our times. The symbols which the ancients used, and the arts which they developed for their interpretation, were instruments of opposition—threats of action or claims for performance addressed by members of one nation, religion, or class to another—and even questions of peace, alliance, or federation were negotiated by symbols of power and recorded in treaties constructed to secure performance by like guarantees. Cooperation among groups today is still negotiated by symbols of power, yet symbols of opposition are enmeshed in symbols of concord, which have emerged in the relations of the groups, but which have found no adequate corresponding symbols in statement and negotiation. Thus, the relations of people today are profoundly affected by the new symbolic importance of man's ancient aspiration to own a plot of land of his own. The Department of State of the United States has given wide publicity to its policy of land reform in its Mutual Security Program, but not only is the policy extremely difficult to elaborate in practical form and to set in operation once elaborated, but it is also surrounded by symbols that reduce or destroy its effectiveness—"capitalism," and "imperialism," by which all American policy is tagged, borrow plausibility from the fact that materials and goods are involved and that agreements are negotiated with existing governments and governing classes; "freedom" and "rights," including property rights, have little meaning or appeal since they correspond to no experience or desire of men who seek primarily means of subsistence or symbols of such means—and it is opposed, often successfully, by implausible symbols, such as the Communist program of breaking up of landed estates as a preliminary step to the establishment of communal farms. The oppositions among the symbols of concord that are being constructed are again oppositions determined by universality and particularity, by ambiguity and action; and the difficulties and advantages encountered in the formation of symbols of American policy therefore arise from precisely the same circumstances: American recognition of the legitimacy of claims for action requires the presence of American funds, goods, and personnel in foreign countries and these may be made either the symbols of disinterested concern that belies allegations of isolationism or the symbols of aggressive interference that belies professed goodwill.

The effectiveness of symbols in communication concerning action depends on their concreteness, which makes myths and arguments, factual statements of what did occur or reasoned statements of the truth, poor substitutes for symbols, even when they remove the ambiguities implicit in the use of symbols. The effectiveness of symbols as means of providing and preserving the homogeneity and adhesive unity of the group in action in a variety of circumstances, on the contrary, depends not on their concreteness but on the adaptability which makes them a fertile and coherent source of actions, and for which the predictions and extrapolations of history and the deductions of arguments are poor substitutes. Rousseau was led by his enthusiasm for primary symbols of unity, the sense of justice and right innate in all men, to undervalue the importance of secondary symbols by which primary symbols find expression in different manners, customs, and cultures. Yet the development of human conscience and sensitivity to values is precisely the history of the operation of symbols which in their fullest statement in art, philosophy, and religion are subject to repeated and divergent interpretations. It would be difficult to exaggerate the importance of the Homeric epics in bringing a sense of unity into the motley collection of racial and tribal strains and the heterogeneous city-states that comprised what we call the "Greeks." The Romans felt the need for a like document even before the *Aeneid* was composed and put to like employment. The Jews, the Christians, and the Mohammedans had their Books, and put them to uses which Rousseau failed to appreciate because he was distracted by the myths and arguments which obscure and disguise the symbols. The Bible and Cicero were of crucial symbolic importance in the development of British liberalism and constitutionalism, and it would be difficult to determine how far Shakespeare wrote with insight into the British character and how far the British character was developed by later statesmen repeating the lines and adapting the actions of Shakespearean characters. Finally, failure to consider the symbolic uses to which the writings of Marx have been put has led us into the error of supposing that their effectiveness in the development of Communism and in the promotion of the ideological conflict can be countered by proving that they expound false history and state unsound philosophy.

The use of such highly developed symbols—and *a fortiori* the use of the less elaborate but more directly cohesive symbols of which they are a refinement—has been formalized in arts which have fallen out of our more recent practice and out of the scope of our more fashionable philosophies. The lessons of the development of both Christian and Communist society are therefore difficult to read, and they have little effect in the formation of a new symbolism. St. Augustine, who gave system to the doctrine which was to have continuing influence in the development of Christian thought and Christian society, has left the record of his discovery of his method. When he read the Old Testament literally he found it full of the absurdities which he had learned to detect following the arguments of the Manichaeans; those absurdities were removed, not by counter-arguments, but by the spiritual interpretation he learned from Ambrose.[8] Augustine says that he was won over to the Catholic doctrine by the conviction that the injunction to believe what has not been demonstrated was sounder than the Manichaean promise of knowledge on which to base belief. He reinforced this conviction by enumerating the beliefs on which one acts without prior knowledge, and the absurdities he had previously found in the narrative

8. Augustine, *Confessions*, v. 14.

and the argument of Scripture became a further sign of the authority of the book.

> For I now referred the absurdity, which was wont to offend me in those Scriptures, when I had heard many instances of it expounded probably, to the depth of the mystery; indeed, that authority appeared to me the more venerable and the more worthy of sacrosanct faith, the more it was ready at hand for all to read and the more it preserved the dignity of its secret in a more profound meaning, offering itself to all in the most apparent words and in the most humble mode of speech and influencing the intention of those who are not light of heart, in order that it might receive all into its common bosom and move on through narrow apertures some few, yet more than if it neither rose to such eminence of authority nor attracted crowds to the breast of holy humility.[9]

The method which worked this profound change in Augustine was the allegorical method of interpretation which Ambrose had learned from Philo and the Eastern Fathers.[10] It was the method which the Greeks had earlier practiced in the interpretation of Homer; it was the method which theologians and practical men employed to develop Christian doctrine and to establish Christian Community and which Christian poets employed in writing and interpreting their poems.

I put this emphasis on the importance of the allegorical method, not to advocate a return to a method which we think to be out of the spirit of our times, but to make concrete the way in which we react to symbols when we are not trying to check them against facts or reduce them to arguments as well as the way in which symbols operate in the creation and continuation of a community as distinguished from the histories and arguments by which we trace the development and analyze the forms of the community. To begin

9. Ibid., vi. 5.

10. Cf., for an example of the details of the method, Philo's interpretation of the building of the tabernacle, which becomes in the interpretation a comprehensive symbol. The interpretation proceeds in Platonic fashion from immaterial prototype to material construction and in Platonic context by demonstrating that Moses was not only philosopher and king but also lawgiver, priest, and prophet. *De Vita Mosis*, ii, 15, 71 ff.

with, many of the narratives that have influenced men profoundly have no literal interpretation, and many of the arguments have no verifiable premises or unambiguous conclusions; yet they are no less intelligible, and rather more effective on action, becauase of their departure from the literal and the concrete. The Bible is full of such narrative and argument. The conversation between Jesus and the Samaritan woman, thus, begins with a simple request made at a well for water, wanders through countersenses concerning the water that quenches thirst and the water of eternal life, and ends with a dialogue that has no literal plausibility and no literal connections.

> The woman saith unto him, Sir, give me this water, that I thirst not, neither come all the way hither to draw. Jesus saith unto her, Go, call thy husband, and come hither. The woman answered and said unto him, I have no husband. Jesus saith unto her, Thous saidst well, I have no husband: for thou hast five husbands; and he whom thou now hast is not thy husband: this hast thou said truly. The woman saith unto him, Sir, I perceive that thou art a prophet. Our fathers worshipped in this mountain; and ye say, that in Jerusalem is the place where men ought to worship. . . .[11]

In this conversation the interlocutors answer statements that have not been made to work out the solution that has not been stated in literal propositions.

In addition to a vast body of such narratives, there is a similarly vast wisdom literature extending from the sayings of the pagan sages to the precepts of prophets, kings, and evangelists which cannot be reduced to syllogisms but which have been examined for insight into nature and used for guidance in practical action.

> There are four things which are little upon the earth,
> But they are exceeding wise:
> The ants are a people not strong,
> Yet they provide their food in the summer;
> The conies are but a feeble folk,
> Yet make they their houses in the rocks;
> The locusts have no king,
> Yet they go forth all of them by bands;

11. John, 4:15–20.

The lizard taketh hold with her hands,
Yet she is in kings' palaces.[12]

Primitive people recounted myths and formed arguments such as these, and although modern men profess to be uncomfortable in the use of parable and analogy, they have acquired, even from the study of history and the principle of policy, no substitute symbols for action.

Allegorical narratives and analogical arguments have no literal interpretation, and the allegorical interpretation which draws meaning and guidance from them is suited to find like mysteries at the center of more literal histories and more formal arguments. The higher criticism demonstrated, during the nineteenth century, and in the same philosophic context that saw the beginnings of Marxism, that the narratives of the Scriptures are dubious history and the precepts of the Old and New Testament are an insubstantial and inconsistent basis for a philosophy and a life; the new ethics demonstrated that the effective morality of men's action has never conformed to the Christian precepts. Yet Augustine employed most of the basic contradictions of literal meanings that are exploited in the higher criticism as part of his discovery of the mystery of symbols, and his distinction between the City of God and the terrestrial city is a more drastic and consistent prototype of the Open and Closed Societies of recent moral speculation. Bacon, who shared the modern tendency to separate history, poetry, and science by sharp boundaries and to remove mysteries from scientific discovery and proof, was nonetheless aware of this dimension of enigma. For he made "parabolical" poetry one of the varieties in his classification of poetry, and he reserved to the interpretation of Scripture an extensive though well guarded function.[13] The mystery which symbols

12. Proverbs, 30:24–28.

13. Francis Bacon, *Of the Proficience and Advancement of Learning Divine and Humane*, Book II, *The Works of Francis Bacon*, edited by J. Spedding, R. L. Ellis, and D. D. Heath, Longmans, London, 1857, III, p. 344: "But there remaineth yet another use of Poesy Parabolical, opposite to that which we last mentioned: for that tendeth to demonstrate and illustrate that which is taught or delivered, and this other to retire and obscure it: that is when the secrets and mysteries of religion, policy, or philosophy are involved in fables or parables. Of this in divine poesy we see the use is authorized. In heathen poesy we see the exposition of fables doth fall out sometimes with great felicity. . . ." Cf. also ibid., pp. 484–485: "As to the interpretation

open up and the authority which they exercise permit their diversified application in different situations: the influence of Scripture on the relations and associations of men is not a deduction in which actions follow from principles nor is it affected by arguments which show that Christianity has never been tried; its influence is a living adaptation of symbols in the cohesive life of the community which has taken many forms in Christian communities and Christian governments. Its test as symbol is not the abstract justification of the designation, "Christian," but the effectiveness of its impulse to a common life and to common actions.

The operation of symbols in communication is not wholly an enigma to contemporary modes of thought in the West, for although their effectiveness is blunted by reduction to myths and arguments, they are still recognizable in forms that resemble the stories told and the inferences drawn in commercial advertisements. The operation of symbols in producing cohesion and unity in a group, on the other hand, has become an almost total enigma, since the symbol is a source of actions and of arguments which often seem absurd and unpredictable when restated in arguments uninfluenced by the symbol. The basic problems of symbols in this use are two. In the present conflict of the communities of the world, the Communist countries have a symbol of unity in the Marxist-Leninist philosophy; for the most part we wholly misconstrue the power and significance of that symbol, and the analogies we see between it and religious symbols lead to doubtful conclusions because of the simplifications we introduce into the interpretation of the operation of symbols in religion. Communities caught between the two extremes in the conflict are likewise often bound by symbols which we misconstrue as badly as we do the symbols of Communism. Conversely,

---

of the Scriptures solute and at large, there have been divers kinds introduced and devised; some of them rather curious and unsafe, than sober and warranted. Notwithstanding this must be confessed, that the Scriptures, being given by inspiration and not by human reason, do differ from all other books in the author; which by consequence doth draw on some difference to be used by the expositor. For the inditer of them did know four things which no man attains to know; which are, the mysteries of the kingdom of glory; the perfection of the laws of nature; the secrets of the heart of man; and the future succession of all ages." In the *De Augmentis*, Bacon lists as one of the desiderata Philosophy according to the Ancient Parables and subjoins three examples of the interpretation of parables. (*Works*, IV, pp. 317 ff.)

the Western democracies in general and the United States in particular do not make intelligent use of the symbols available to guide them in their common purposes and common actions. The first problem of symbols is the problem of understanding the operation of the symbols we oppose; the second problem is the problem of reconstructing and using opposed symbols to give coherence to what we think, say, and do.

It is a mistake to treat the Marxist-Leninist-Stalinist philosophy simply as a body of doctrines that can be weakened by demonstrating that it entails a theory of history which is not borne out by the facts, a conception of science which runs counter to the practices of science, and a science of the history of society that is poorly calculated to achieve even the ends to which it is oriented and much less the fuller rich potentialities of human life. The primary fact in the operation of that philosophy as a symbol is that it provides a body of statements, facts, arguments, and principles widely disseminated, not only among the members of the Communist Party, but also among the vast numbers of people who fall under their control and influence. It is difficult to judge how wide its influence has been as a common body of data and a common method of argument which unite those who share it and provide them with a means of common understanding and unambiguous communication, but the common facility with which even minor representatives of Communist countries at international conferences employ the dialectical method is a significant mark of the influence. No other nation or group of nations has a similarly well defined body of accepted data or a similarly well organized method of proceeding to conclusions from any problem. The doctrines are not fixed and the party line changes, but there is no reason in the dialectical method that would lead to commitment to an abstract view of consistency. Indeed, the virtue of the philosophy is found precisely in its adaptability, according to the official history of the Communist Party: "The power of the Marxist-Leninist theory lies in the fact that it enables the Party to find the right orientation in any situation."[14] To be sure the party line is established and maintained by a ruthless

14. *History of the Communist Party in the Soviet Union*, International Publishers, New York, 1939, p. 355.

use of force, but it is based, nonetheless, however tenuously and however differently from the previous interpretation, on the doctrines of that philosophy, and the processes of citation and denunciation of deviation are not mere ritual. From other points of view than that of the Marxist philosophy, its interpretation of history and of facts, past and present, is fantastic and demonstrably false, but one who practices the method of dialectical materialism would be no more surprised by the need to rewrite history than St. Augustine was by the need he saw, and urged on Orosius, to rewrite the history of the Roman Empire as part of the defense of Christianity set forth in the *City of God*.

Symbols are not refuted by arguments or by facts; indeed, the threat of refutation reinforces the cohesiveness of the group joined in attachment to the symbol. Acceptance of the symbol may take either the form of continuing to adhere to a doctrine in spite of the weight of evidence against it or of shifting from one doctrine to another in spite of apparent absence of connection, or even contradiction, between them. If arguments and myths are powerless against symbols, however, symbols as they serve as bonds of unity are sources at once of myths and arguments and of credibility attached to both. The study of the operation of symbols in the development of Communism should be undertaken, consequently, in two distinct stages. The first should be concerned with the operation of Communism itself as symbol, not only in attaching different men—farmers, workers, artists, scientists—to Communism by different appeals, but also in providing motivation for common action strong enough to run counter to the claims of all other symbols.[15] The second should be concerned with the use of a philosophy or a body of doctrine as a symbol and with its effect on action and on response

15. Symbols, in this sense, have come to occupy an important place in psychiatry, and psychiatric studies have shown the force and complexity of their influence on action. The political operation of Communism as a symbol and the complexities of its relations to the use of power are brought out excellently in studies like the Report of Subcommittee 5 of Committee on Foreign Policy of the House of Representatives, *The Strategy and Tactics of World Communism* (House document 619, Washington, 1948) and its various documentary supplements. But psychiatric and political analyses are for the most part used as a substitute for the examination of symbols rather than as a means of indicating the problems with which the study of symbols should be concerned.

to facts and arguments. It is easy to caricature such arguments, but we shall not have disposed of them as effective instruments of action by labeling them fallacious or extra-logical: the eventual emergence of the classless society is inevitable, whatever occurs is a step toward it, and the dictatorship of the proletariat, which is the dictatorship of the Communist Party, is at once preparation for it and scarcely distinguishable from that eventual society; war and violence result from internal conflict, and since there is no internal conflict in a Socialist state, Socialist states are never guilty of aggression; Socialism frees men from the bonds resulting from economic shortages, restrictions, and alienations, and although it must be advanced by force, it is nonetheless the source of all freedoms—political, civil, and cultural, as well as economic and social; the Russians were held back by their imperial rulers and their accomplishments were discouraged or were sold to foreigners, consequently history must be rewritten to vindicate the contributions of Russians to science, technology, and the arts.

The operation of symbols seems irrational and erratic in the action of groups, parties, and peoples whose symbols one does not share. It is tempting, therefore, to think that opposition to such action, to be rationally motivated and consistent, should be based on knowledge, or science, and on facts, as indeed the symbols opposed claim to be based. Such a supposition, however, arises from a misconception of symbols and from an arbitrary limitation put on the forms reason takes in rational action. The second problem of symbols in their use as bonds of unity and sources of action centers on our own symbols and their operation in the context of antagonistic symbols. Even the most highly rational man does not operate always at the highest pitch of rationality, and few men, even among the well educated and scientifically trained, make much consistent use of reason in their actions. Action in groups is rationalized by symbols, and symbols provide an immediate and coherent response to practical problems, which are usually encountered in circumstances that do not permit long inquiry and proof and are little conducive to dispassionate reflection. The symbols that we in the United States have, and the symbols that we should seek, are, like the symbols we oppose, of two kinds. We make use, in the first place, of our institutions and our way of life—our freedoms, our individualism, our justice, and our accomplishments—and we are surprised and embarrassed by the fact that ambiguities are attributed to them, not unlike the ambiguities we censure in the symbols we oppose. Internally, we have not secured the objectives marked by the symbols that have guided the history of our development; our greatest differences are concerning the ways by which they can be secured—freedom and equal rights, economic security and social equality, equal opportunity and access to the means of satisfying our needs and our spiritual aspirations—and in the extremity of our differences concerning means we restrict our common symbols by calling those with whom we disagree un-American. Externally, our freedoms and individualism seem to others to be tradition-bound uniformity and conformism, our sense of justice parochial, and our accomplishments materialistic and exclusive of any concern with higher values. Since our external operations with other people are largely limited to a context of material needs and dangers of aggression, the symbols which lead us even to disinterested action seem materialistic and imperialistic.

Our difficulty with the primary symbols of our common life is enhanced by lack of common use of the symbols of religion, art, or philosophy. Religious leaders are convinced of the efficacy of a greater use of religious symbols; the "great books" movement has symbolic significance inasmuch as its spread would extend the scope and influence of common meanings and common associations based on a common literary and intellectual experience; our philosophies seek their symbols in the common experience of all men or in the construction of languages distinct from common language or in the hope that science or religion will provide the symbols. Inasmuch as we are engaged in the examination of symbols, our concern is not with the soundness of any of these programs, but rather with the peculiar problem we face in the construction and use of these secondary symbols, for they cannot be derived, if they are to be faithful to the primary symbols found in our institutions or established to stand for them, from a single philosophy nor from a single religious faith. They must be a coherent source of common action drawn from the variety of beliefs—religious, philosophic, social, economic, political—that have contributed to and that find a place in the evolution of our common living. The framework of such a system of symbols is suggested in the political philosophies of men like Jefferson, Madison, Hamilton, and Lincoln, in the humanistic and religious values that have conjoined in our culture, and in the influence of science, industry, and technology on its development.

The problem of symbols has been traditionally a problem, on the one hand, of communication and, on the other hand, a problem of unification and motivation to common action. It has, however, assumed a new guise and a new importance in the world today which makes that simple opposition an inadequate and deceptive distinction. The use of symbols in communication consisted in the past in setting forth vividly a proposed or probable course of action; the use of symbols in motivating actions was to prepare a common response to situations and problems appropriate to the unity of the group. Communication by symbols had to do with action against somebody; and the unity achieved by symbols was unity in opposition to, or at least in distinction from, other groups and other symbols. Communication concerning action is defective today, not in the failure to use symbols of opposition, but in the inadequacy of symbols of concord and agreement; and unity of action has adequate symbolic basis in overt conflict and war, but that basis is almost totally lacking or is inoperative in the absence of hostile symbols employed in action or in the presence of hostile symbols ambiguously preparing for action. These two defects in the use of symbols by groups or nations are part of a new need for more comprehensive symbols appropriate to the whole of mankind, and the treatment of the problems of symbols suggested in this analysis must find its supplement and guidance in those symbols. Philosophers, poets, and prophets have indicated the primary symbols on which that unity and communication must rest—the sense of justice and right which all men share, the brotherhood of man, the community of men and gods. The secondary symbols are found in the works of art, religion, philosophy, and science in which common values are expressed in many disparate ways, for they supply common symbols when they are understood and used as expressions of common values and not as odd and different ways in which other men, influenced by other manners and customs, lead lives devoid of certain important or crucial values. These symbols will not themselves be widely effective in communication or as sources of action for a long time, and the way which leads to them is one in which the symbols of smaller groups—the nations and the peoples of the world assembled in external relations and interdependences—are improved both as means of communication, by the development of symbols of agreement to balance the symbols of opposition, and as sources of unity to provide effective motives for common action even in the absence of external threat and opposition. Symbols, developed and used to make common values richer by the diversity of approaches to them and to make differences compatible by common courses of action that solve common problems even when the problems are differently conceived, provide the one practicable alternative to the imposition by force of a single set of symbols in the form of a single set of institutions interpreted by a single philosophy.

Philosophy of Communications and the Arts

An international conference on the uses of philosophy exemplifies the problems which it treats. The problems presented and encountered by philosophies in confrontation with each other are problems of multiple perspectives. Each of the philosophies is used to reorient the perspectives of experience, action, and thought. An international discussion of philosophic problems presents the diversity of philosophies of the world as they have been determined in the long traditions of past speculations by the new circumstances of present problems, while the uses of philosophies of the world are oriented to the future. New problems will be formed and presented by peoples philosophizing about common problems conceived and analyzed by use of divergent philosophic concepts. The perspectives of cultural space, in which the many philosophic traditions of mankind are lines of direction and orientation, take on a further dynamic dimension in the perspectives of temporal change, in which the problems, the nature, and the parts of philosophies have all undergone alterations.

The uses of philosophy have become its uses for all mankind and for today. What men mean by philosophy, how they use it, and whether or not they think it is useful, however, differ not only from culture to culture and from school to school but from man to man in each culture and in each school. Which philosophies are to be considered for use? How can their advocates make themselves intelligible to each other? Can they be moved to cooperate in understanding and in solving problems somehow recognized to be common in spite of differences of interpretation and specification? What is "philosophy" today; and how is "it" related to the philosophies of the past, and susceptible of adaptation to "uses" in the future?

Philosophers have always pretended to universality of a sort; and they have usually combined the quest for omnicompetence with strictures against the absurdity of assuming universal scope in the determinations of human knowledge or the applications of human power. From the beginning of speculation and inquiry, thinkers have justified reason and thought by its uses; and they have usually distinguished the thoughtful achievement of understood objectives and sought goods from unreasoning and unreasonable pursuit of dubious pleasures and questionable utilities. Names have been given to philosophies in past and present communications and controversies among philosophers from the subject-matters or immaterial forms in which they have sought universality and from the arts or unartificial skills by which they have developed uses. The parts of philosophy have been marked off, in like fashions, by names which indicate their uses by determining the subject-matters to which they apply. Traditional names, like "ethics," "aesthetics," and "logic" achieve this purpose by relating character and action, perception and presentation, and thought and speech, aided in the merging of matter and use by ambiguities of etymology and of shifting interpretations; and "metaphysics" could be named to indicate the location of a book in an edition of the works of a philosopher and then be interpreted to signify a subject matter and to indicate the speculative method appropriate to it. The process is clearer in English names constructed to set up new differentiations of parts of philosophy, freed from old ambiguities of designation and use, because the uses of philosophy are indicated by attaching the word "philosophy" with the preposition "of" to a name designating a field. Sometimes the field is another established discipline, as in "philosophy of education," "of religion," "of science," or "of history"; sometimes it is an activity or instrumentality of action, as in "philosophy of practice," "of belief," "of language," or "of mind." These traditional parts and applications of philosophy, ancient and modern, do little to clarify the uses of philosophy and of its parts. The arts developed in discussion of philosophy and its subdivisions are semantic arts which depend on giving the ambiguous field or activity a fixed definition; and in the practice of these semantic arts any consideration of alternative definitions of the subject-matter, developed by alternative arts, becomes a dispute concerning whether or not the expression "metaphysics," or "epistemology," "philosophy of science," "philosophy of history," or "philosophy of man" has any significance which bears on real problems susceptible of meaningful solutions.

Discussion, in philosophy or in general, depends no less on the richness and suggestibility of the theme explored than on the precision and testability of the consequences traced by different methods of inquiry and proof; the uses of theoretic and practical arts wander from field to field. There can be no discussion without a recognizable common subject-matter or without an identifiable common problem; discussion is likewise impossible when there is complete agreement about what is in question and about the nature and origin of the problem to be considered. It has frequently seemed wise in the past to depart from traditional divisions and applications of philosophy, and to divide and organize philosophy in newly conceived parts. The emergent parts of the philosophy of an age are found in the orientations of actions and interests: they are neither fixed by the nature of an independent subject-matter nor imposed by the inventive art of an arbitrary inquirer. If our interest is in the uses of philosophy in the future, our investigation of them should not be tied down to the classifications of philosophy in the present. Fortunately, in speculating on the evolution of the uses of philosophy, it is not necessary to have the gift of foresight or the art of prediction at each point of the changing uses in order to find indications of possible directions of reorientation. In any age some terms have a prominent place in philosophic discussion and acquire a like place in general discussion of problems of life and action. In both philosophic and common discussions these terms usually take on meanings and are put to applications which are justified by use or mention of devices and conceptions borrowed, by analogy or by heterogeneous substitution, from well-known and widely practiced skills and disciplines. It is possible, therefore, to make a dead-reckoning of the uses of philosophy in the future by mapping directions indicated by current combinations of fashionable ambiguous terms and of esteemed traditional or newly discovered arts.

The subject of a "philosophy of communications and the arts" is indicated and marked off by combining two such terms. "Experience," "existence," "language," and "communication" are familiar ambiguous general terms employed to focus the analysis of philosophical and of practical problems on unambiguous issues and concrete facts. Their meanings are developed by use of distinctions from "arts" and "sciences" transformed to explore concrete problematic circumstances in search of precise determinations for use in further inquiry and action. The arts and their subject-matters have had continuous histories; but arts which are for a time arts of knowing become arts of doing, and are then transformed into arts of making, and then repeat the cycle; the subject-matters of the arts are sought in turn among things, thoughts, action, and language, sometimes on the supposition that thoughts, actions, and discourses take their character from and conform to things, sometimes on the supposition that things are the products and creatures of thoughts, or deeds, or words. The arts and sciences by which we explore experience and existence, language and communication today are arts of discourse and arts of making. The arts of discourse borrow from the long history of the liberal arts, but they have been made arts of language and communication primarily, that is, the liberal arts have been reformulated in terms of grammar and rhetoric; the arts of making borrow from the long history of the fine and the mechanical arts, and transform the arts of knowing and doing into operational devices applied in mathematics, technology, and communications, but they too have been made primarily arts of rhetoric or communication and of grammar or construction. The arts of doing have been transformed into a rhetoric of demonstration, deliberation, and judgment; the arts of knowing have been transformed into a grammar of construction and interpretation of structures. The subject-matter of the arts of communicative discourse and of technological making is existence and experience, and ontological or epistemic principles and consequences are detected in that subject-matter only by statement and operation.

Experience and existence are mutually explanatory. Experience has ceased to be an epistemological grounding in ideas and their combinations for the certainties of knowledge and action, and has become instead a framework of cultural conditions and natural circumstances for the determination and statement of the facts of existence. Existence has ceased to be a metaphysical grounding or sign for the discovery of the principles of being, and has become instead the phenomenal immediacy of encountered nature and experienced art. Logic is freed from ontological commitments and dialectic from mentalistic or spiritualistic forms. In the arts of discourse and making, "demonstration" has been made a manifestation—poetic, practical, or theoretic—rather than an argument; "deliberation" has been made a balance of incitations, in which "decision" is a spontaneous pronouncement, adapted to forming groups in support of policies or opposed to policies, rather than a rational consideration of alternatives, in which decision is a reasoned choice among them; "judgment" has been made individual approval based on self-justification secured by self-representation or image-making rather than the assemblage of particulars in universal combinations and ordering relations.

The unity of philosophy as art and as subject-matter today is as illusive as any of the unities which philosophy has exhibited or professed at any other period of history when new philosophic arts have been devised in renaissances and revolutions to investigate new subject-matters and to treat new problems. There are many modes of communication in which philosophers and philosophically inclined inquirers explore experience and disclose existence; and there are many arts of communication in which the sequences and structures of invention and disclosure are developed and used. The uses of philosophy present a double question as a result of these transformations: (1) What is *philosophy* when it is viewed and practiced as an art of communications? and (2) What are the devices and skills of the particular *arts*—the transformed arts of poetry, of politics, and of rhetoric—when the method of communication is the method of all arts joined and ordered in a philosophy of the arts? The two questions are related to each other reflexively, for the subject-matter of philosophy can be indicated, delimited, and justified only by use of the philosophic arts, and the acquisition and judgment of the arts of philosophy are produced by the practice of the arts on an appropriate and recognized subject-matter. The subject-matter and arts of philosophy today are both fixed by common words of universal generality like "experience," "existence," "language," and "communication": they are synonymous in their scope when they are used to define a single universal subject-matter; they mark off different structures and isolate different elements when they are used to differentiate the devices of operation and statement.

1. The subject-matter and problems of a philosophy of communications and the arts.

Like other forms of communication, philosophy is a limited communication of shared words defined in partially shared meanings and attached to partially shared designations. The ambiguity of "communication" affects both the method and the subject-matter of a "philosophy of communications and the arts." The methods of communication range through dialogue, disputation, controversy, and monologue, each of which becomes philosophic by means of devices of "discussion" designed to clarify meanings and determine applications. Discussion and philosophy tend to arise today from controversy concerning meanings dependent on actions (including operations prescribed in languages and in games) rather than from disputation concerning meanings dependent on thoughts or from dialogue concerning meanings dependent on things. This tendency affects the subject-matter of philosophy, for philosophic discussion proceeds by establishing a universal scope within which it delimits proper ranges. It extends the shared meanings of "language" by equating them with "experience," "existence," and "communication," which in the process become comprehensive of all that is and all that is intelligible, and it delimits the specific proper meanings of anything that is experienced, exists, and is communicated in controversial opposition to meaningless statements of unverifiable resolutions of unreal problems. The subject-matter of philosophy was never thought to be unqualified reality or unquestionable things: it has been variously conceived as things certified and warranted in thought, action, and expression. The arts by which such a subject-matter is defined and investigated adapt their devices to all dimensions of their subject-matter by placing primary emphasis on one: they have been at various periods of philosophic discussion arts of essence, of thought, of action, and of discourse adapted to structures of being, sequences of what is, facts of experience, and elements of existence. The subject-matter and problems of philosophical discussion set the requirements of the arts of philosophical discussion; and the arts of being, thought, action, and expression, the arts of dialogue, disputation, controversy, and discussion determine the subject-matter of philosophical inquiry.

The antipathies expressed for subject-matters considered in past discussions of philosophy and for the arts developed to treat those subject-matters provide a key to the shifting subject-matters and altering arts which determine what is the case and what is significant and true about it. We are dubious about the arts of discourse conceived as arts of being based on the nature of things, because metaphysics raises questions about everything, and knowledge of the whole of things is impossible. We are dubious concerning the arts of discourse conceived as arts of thought based on the nature of reason and the passions, on the forms of thought and the association of ideas, because epistemology raises questions about thought and judgment as complexes to be analyzed and about ideas and feelings as simples to be synthesized, and entitizes thoughts, or psychologizes the objects of thought, or separates things thought and things sensed, things willed and things desired into disparate realms. In the place of discredited arts of being and of thought we construct arts of discourse conceived as arts of action in which we test what is presented as that which is or as that which is thought by considering that which is said and that which is done, and by seeking in statement and action the marks and warrants by which to determine and certify being and thought in what is said and done and in consequences discerned in statement and occurrence.

The subject-matter of the arts of being disappears in the use of the arts of communication and construction; but the structure of being is rediscovered in formulating and forming the structure of existence. Uneasiness with metaphysics has arisen periodically from doubts concerning things possessed of fixed essences and natures antecedent to our knowing, doing, or saying them. The arts of being by which they are treated and by which their consequences are explored cannot be applied to the contents of thought, action, or statement as they are in themselves. What is, and what it is, do not provide grounds for distinguishing knowing, doing, or making; the basic distinctions of changeless and changing, of known and perceived, and of natural and artificial have ceased to be necessary, self-evident, or primary, and have come to be probable, dubious, or derived. But metaphysics is not only a science of being qua being; it is also a science of first principles, and the arts of communication and construction must establish and use "principles" which serve a function among the facts of discourse and occurrence not unlike the function of metaphysical principles ordering the structures of actuality and of truth.

Our periodical metaphysical doubts might be resolved once and for all if some clear and indubitable criteria could be found to determine how we know before questions are raised concerning what is and whether it is, concerning how it is qualified and characterized and why. But uneasiness with epistemology has arisen periodically when critical examinations of knowing have uncovered complexities and contradictions reminiscent of the antinomies and paralogisms of metaphysics: it is obviously impossible to conceive elements, modes, or forms of thought ungrounded in reality, unexpressed in language, and inoperative in action. The subject-matter of the arts of knowing disappears, as had the subject-matter of the arts of being, in the arts of communication and construction; but the structure of thought, like the structure of being, is rediscovered in formulating and forming the structure of experience. The subject-matter of the arts of knowing cannot be modes of knowing and their judgmental consequences considered in themselves, unexpressed in language and unembodied in action; and they cannot be applied to the data of experience or the facts of existence objectively segregated from subjective presumptions and associations. The arts of the intelligible, the desirable, and the pleasurable are not arts of thinking or feeling, or laws of theoretical, practical, or productive thought, or manifestations of genius, sagacity, or taste. The sequences and associations of ideas and feelings do not provide methods of distinguishing, determining, or judging the forms or the processes of thought and feeling, or of perception and judgment in themselves, or in knowing, doing, or making; the basic distinctions of knowledge and opinion, intelligibilia and sensibilia, honesta (or the good) and utilia (or the useful) have ceased to be fundamental, sharp, and simple, and have come to be disputable, merged, and complex. But epistemology is not only a science of the elements and forms of human understanding; it is also a critique of methods, and the arts of communication and construction must develop and formulate "methods" of discourse and operation adapted to facts and to the formation and statement of relations among facts.

The subject-matters of the arts of being and the arts of thinking have been abandoned for the subject-matters of the arts of expression and communciation and of experimentation and construction, but it has been argued that the change has not been a retrenchment but an abandonment of old errors concerning what is and what is intelligible, which led, sometimes, to diremptions and dichotomies of a homogeneous world into unrelated parts, like the realms of being and becoming, or of soul and body, or of reality and appearance, and alternatively, to mergings and confusions of processes which are distinct and complementary, like knowledge and belief, or cognitive, emotive, and persuasive uses of language and action, or facts and values, or observed facts and a priori assumptions, or accounts of what is the case and themes of recurrent connections. Such arguments illustrate and demonstrate both the continuity of the philosophic arts and the novelty of the philosophy of communications and the arts, for no real subject-matter of inquiry has been lost, and yet more adequate arts of inquiry have turned to other characteristics as subjects for inquiry and have wholly changed the subject-matter.

Philosophers are able to continue to use the methods of philosophic hermeneutics by which the arguments of earlier philosophers are interpreted in meanings and with applications previously unsuspected. They also make use of the methods of philosophic controversy by which the conclusions attributed to other philosophers, earlier or contemporary, are shown to express errors and nonsense previously undetected about the nature of things and of knowledge. The subject-matter of the philosophic arts continues to be universal in scope, but the universality of the arts is exercised and exhibited in exploring structures of experience and existence, while the structures of being and of thought have become constructions grounded on inference from concrete facts and encountered data or designed to satisfy deep-seated cravings for generality and universality. Whatever is, and what it is, can be brought to light and examined by the arts of communication and construction, of expression and experimentation; and indeed being, and essential properties, can be certified only by such arts since they make possible the repetition of events and experiences in other circumstances and by other people. What is eliminated by the arts of communication and construction cannot be said to be in any respect, for it eludes expression adapted to experience and existence, while "fictive" beings and "eternal" objects, since they are expressed and presented clearly, provide models for seeing and judging other pretenders to being and essence. Whatever is thought and felt can be set forth and examined by the arts of communication and construction, of expression and experimentation; and indeed the only evidence that something has been thought or felt, and the only intimation of what it is, are embodied and conveyed by expression and action. What is eliminated by the arts of communication and construction is not conceivable in any respect, for it slips from experience and existence by eluding expression, like unformulated thoughts and unmanifested emotions; while "imaginary things" and "*entia rationis,*" since they are apprehended and comprehended clearly, provide models to clarify the subject-matters of direct experience and of empirical knowledge.

The arts of communication and construction are arts of language and action. They provide remedies for false pretensions to universality of knowledge and to universality in determinations of being by seeking objective generality and universality in experience and determining the whole of existence by the scope of experience. They eliminate false divisions and separations by seeking principles of individuation and generalization in occurrences and in law-like formulations of possibilities and consequences in occurring. They serve as bridges between "experience" in the broad sense in which any immediate experience is infinitely rich in aspects on which attention may be fixed and in interpretations by which facts may be specified, and "experiences" in the particular sense in which any fact of experience is fixed and irresistible and is stated unambiguously and precisely in true propositions. They serve as bridges between "existence" in the broad sense in which whatever happens and is perceived exists, including what is thought, said, and done, what is planned, imagined, and desired, and "existences" in the particular sense in which what is thought to exist and what is said to exist are considered not with respect to their existence as actions or statements but with respect to the existences they indicate and signify. They are arts of *inquiry* by which the tangled knots of occurrences and the recurrent themes of connections are undone and arranged in the ordered sequences and consequences of defined events and analyzed statements; and they are the arts of *semantics* by which the divergent accounts of an experience or an existence, worked out by different methods, are set in opposition or in accord, in controversy or disputation, in which the differences are contrarieties or contradictions, or in dialogue or debate, in which they are translatable, one into the other, as verbally different literal statements of the same thing, or as analogous statements of the same thing, or as literal or analogical statements of related things.

The continuity and innovations, the universality and specifications of the philosophic arts and their subject-matter reflect contact between the open, indeterminate problems of inquiry which can be stated and treated only in the closed, precise formulations of a structured semantics. The subject-matter and problems of philosophy change with changes of semantic schemata. Language and action, existence and experience are not discoveries of the arts of communication, but existence and experience assume priority in an examination of the concrete and the factual; and *clarity*, such as is available in a perception or a presentation, is a precondition to the determination of an inquiry or proof or the testing of its presuppositions or conclusions. The arts of thought provide a basis for language and action and an account of existence and experience, but the specification of what is and how it is qualified assumes priority; and *distinctness*, such as is manifested in an unambiguous account of connections and sequences, provides the test for dubious clarities and dogmatic certainties. The possibility and the structures of existence and experience and the establishment of principles of being depend on a critical epistemological investigation of the forms and elements of knowing. The revolution from the arts of thought to the arts of communication, despite the retention of names like "logic" and "rhetoric" and words like "inference" and "persuasion," and despite controversies between the "old" and the "new," involve a change of subject-matter and of problems which transform semantic questions of definition and method to ambiguous, substantive questions of inquiry and invention. The arts of being provide a basis for language, action, and thought and an account of existence, experience, and knowledge, but determination of why and principles of being provide the grounds of method, interpretation, and formulation; and *adequacy* assumes priority as it did in the search for clear, distinct, and adequate ideas by seventeenth-century metaphysicians. The principles of all sciences, all actions, and all productions are principles of being. The subject-matters change with the changes in the arts, and the arts of language and action, of expression and communication form different devices for the treatment of different problems when language and action determine thought and being than when language and action, together with being, are conceived as determined by the forms of thought or when language and action, together with thought, are conceived as determined by the structure of being. The nature and consequences of the changes in the subject-matter and problems of philosophy are elucidated best by examining the philosophic arts as arts of communication.

2. The Methods and Principles of the Arts of Communication and Construction.

The arts by which we come into contact with the facts of existence and the arts by which we explore the data of experience and uncover the sequences of changes in what is the case must have universality (that is, they must apply to whatever is as it is without distortion due to characteristics intruded or neglected or colored by the operation of the arts) and objectivity (that is, they must use methods and devices which indicate and delineate testable factual constructions and not simple fictive fabrications). All arts of communication and construction are universal, that is, apply to everything; and each of them is particular, that is, serves specific purposes and discovers or actualizes specific aspects of its universal subject-matter. There has always been a tendency to controversy among the arts in which the universality of established arts or of arts passing into desuetude is shown to be a dubious universality or a covert particularity, and their objectivity is shown to be subjective or abstract. The arts of being, which deal with matters of communication as aspects of being, are said to have fallen into the rigidities of metaphysicalism and the relativities of skepticism. The arts of thought, which deal with forms of communication as aspects of thought, are said to have fallen into the formalities of epistemologism and the variabilities of psychologism. The arts of communication and construction are arts of conjoining form and matter in the concreteness of experience and the individuality of existence. In the practice of those arts the dangers and errors of the arts of being and of thought are recognized as consequences of separating form and matter. The arts of communication and construction, on the contrary, are arts which move from ambiguity to precision by relating the problems of philosophic inquiry concerning experience and existence, which are infinitely rich in possibilities and aspects, to the problems of philosophic semantics concerning facts and elements, which are determinate in actuality and in formulation.

There are continuities as well as innovations in these transformations of the arts and their subject-matters. A sign of the continuities is in the retention of the names and the vocabulary of the liberal arts in altered meanings and functions. The liberal arts are arts of language and opinion, when philosophy is based on metaphysics as an architectonic science. They provide the techniques of presentation and construction, discussion and debate, refutation and rectification as *instruments* of formal presentation to supplement and complete the methods of inquiry into the nature of things and the processes of change. The liberal arts are arts of language and action, when philosophy is based on epistemology and an architectonic of the sciences as ways of knowing. They provide the laws of thought and expression, induction and deduction, community and communication, paradox and paralogism as *schemata* of material connection to provide criteria and foundations for necessary laws of nature and morals. The question of the priority of the theoretical or the practical and the consequent opposition of basic arts of knowing to basic arts of doing are recognized to be spurious questions when the arts of communication and construction assume the architectonic functions, previously attributed to metaphysics or epistemology, for when the basic arts are arts of saying and making, they are arts of the uses of reason, and the same or comparable devices of rational statement and construction are found to have theoretical and practical uses. Each of the traditional arts is broadened to a universal subject-matter, and the terms of art are adapted to more inclusive functions. They are frequently set in controversial opposition by their imperialistic pretensions to unique suzerainty in treating all problems, but they exercise different functions with respect to different aspects of experience and existence; and recognition of those interrelations provides the possibility of developing a new philosophy of communications and the arts.

Rhetoric is the art of persuasion and debate. When the philosophic arts are conceived of as arts of being or of thought, rhetoric is not treated as a philosophic art, although it is used extensively in the controversy and refutation which constitutes communication among philosophies. When the philosophic arts are arts of communication and construction, rhetoric is made into a universal and architectonic art. Cicero reports the position of rhetoricians who considered it the art of resolving all questions, general and particular, and did not distinguish rhetoric from philosophy by limiting rhetoric to particular questions about individual persons and fixed times and places and reserving general questions for philosophy. In the Renaissance rhetoric was used as the method of the new metaphysics. In the twentieth century rhetoric has assumed new rhetorical names and descriptions and has moved from the adjudication of law-court and the administrative committee, the debates of the legislative assembly, and the harangues of the market place and crossroads, from the new fine arts of presentation and creative audience participation, the new arts of scientific discovery, and the renewed arts of philosophical semantics, to mass communication, advertising, and technological innovations.

Rhetoric is an art of invention and disposition: it is an art of communication between a speaker and his audience, and it is therefore an art of construction of the subject-matter of communication, that is, of anything whatever that can be an object of attention. What is, is established by the convictions and agreements of men, and the rich potentialities of experience and existence are examined and developed by devices of discrimination and of opposition and adjustment in expression and communication. As an art of invention rhetoric has developed and used "topics" or "commonplaces": they were designed to be "seats" of invention and "sources" of new arguments; in the history of their use they have been extended to all fields and their example has inspired philosophers like Francis Bacon to seek "places" for the discovery not only of words and ideas but of things and of arts, while at the opposite extreme the word "commonplace" has come in its common usage to mean a repeated opinion rather than an instrumentality of novelty and invention.

As an art of communication rhetoric has been designed to make use of all means of persuasion—the character of the speaker, the preconceptions of the audience, and the structure and distortion of argumentation; in the history of their uses the devices of rhetorical argumentation have been extended to all fields, because all subject-matters, whatever else they are presented as, are "objects" of communication and are isolated and formed in a communication and by a communicator who uses data and attitudes previously communicated to him or to his audience to fashion what he presents in further communication. The devices of rhetorical argumentation are devices of "demonstration" in the sense of "manifestation" and "presentation" rather than of deductive "proof" or logical "inquiry." A position or a policy is established by manifestation or assertion of oneself and of what one is saying or doing, of what has been said and done by others, and of what will be said and done; it is not established on the nature of things or by use of the laws of thought, and it is an irrelevance or an impertinence to ask whether the communicator knows what he is talking about or the consequences of what he is doing, because his communication is judged by his success in making or generating the object of his communication—a position or a policy, a habit, skill, or attitude, leading to further statements or actions. The arts of communication and construction are arts of *innovation* and *tradition*; accepted facts and recognized objects are the products not the preconditions of the arts of communication and construction.

The new rhetoric or art of selection is the art of coping with new problems. It is sometimes confused with older or distorted forms of rhetoric in which the business of advancing novel or adapting traditional solutions to new problems is indistinguishable from propaganda, public relations, force, or deception, which employ arts of extending adherence to an opinion already formed, or arts of creating support or disapproval in common opinion for a person or a mode of action attributed to him or to the groups with which he is associated, or arts of lobbying for the passage of a law to enforce a policy or initiate a course of action or change an image. The unknown is the subject-matter of invention and creativity in the transition to the known from the unknown. The unknown is found in experience and in creation, once it can be named and identified after the discovery of the known. The arts and the sciences use what has been done and what has been said, on the frontiers of knowing and making, to explore the new, which at the moment of invention is that which is not yet and nonetheless is the subject-matter of the arts and sciences conceived and developed as arts of communication and construction. The new art of rhetoric is the art of *discovery*. It is not a heuristic *method* or radical *interpretation* but an art of topics or a *selection* of elements which opens the way to the recognition of new facts and to the perception of unnoticed structures and sequences. There is a fundamental rhetoric of all elements which enter into the perspective of everything communicated relative to what has already been done and said, for in the perspective of language and action, taken universally as formative of our worlds, man is the measurer and maker of what is and of what is not. There are also derived rhetorics of pleasing, teaching, and moving: a constitutive-hedonic rhetoric in which communication and construction are rendered effective by pleasing; an epistemic-dispositional rhetoric in which congruous knowledge and emotions are joined to prior knowledge and feelings by teaching; and a pistic-concupiscent-irascible rhetoric in which convictions are changed and perspectives are raised in scales of reality and value by arousing and moving.

Grammar is the art of statement and interpretation. The Greeks used the same word for a letter of the alphabet and an element of physical matter; and we have talked about grammars of language, of science, and of reality, both in the sense of formative rules of construction and in the sense of hermeneutic devices of interpretation. When the philosophic arts are conceived as arts of being or of thought, grammar is not treated as a philosophic art, although it is used extensively to set forth the elements of philosophical formulations and the rules of combination or syntax by which they are formed, and philosophers frequently seek "elements" from which to construct their philosophies in atoms, simple ideas, or undefined terms. Universal or speculative grammars have dealt with modes of being and understanding as well as with modes of signifying.

Grammar is an art of composition and division, or construction and interpretation: it is an art of communication which focuses on the communication itself and on what is communicated, and it is therefore an art of construction in which the nature of language and communicator and the nature of the circumstances and environment of language and man enter, both as matter and as conditioning form of communication. Whereas the object of communication in rhetoric emerges as an invention constructed in communication between communicator and audience, the object of communication in grammar emerges as a construction in discourse as a statement of fact and as an interpretation of the statement. Whatever is, is a nature or a situation; and the nature of communication and communicators is determined and known by consideration of like statements of fact and situation.

As an art of composition, grammar has distinguished and used parts of speech and structures of syntax; in the history of their use they have been extended from the modes of signifying to the modes of being, that is, to factual properties and structures of situations; and they have been extended to the modes of understanding, that is, to ideas and structures of judgment. Statements, situations, and judgments of fact are inseparable from each other and materially identical with each other, that is, they have to do with the same object; but formally they differ, for their composition depends respectively on the nature of things, the nature of thoughts, and the nature of language. "Hypotheses," which are the foundations or suppositions of statement, judgment, and of situation, have undergone the same variabilities between generalization and minimalization as "commonplaces" in rhetoric: they are sometimes used as unifying conceptions in science; they are sometimes avoided as figments of the imagination, unrelated to what is the case or to scientific knowledge. As an art of communication grammar has been designed to decompose any sentence, and therefore any situation or experience, any thought or sentiment, into the elements in which it is grounded, and in turn to compose sentences, situations, and judgments from their elements. The devices of grammatical analysis have been extended to all fields, and the words "elements" or "grammar" have been used in the title of fundamental works in all fields, as in the "elements of geometry" or the "grammar of science." The rules of syntax become, in this broadened analysis, conventional rules which are grounded in and express values: the proposition expresses a judgment of the true or the probable, the good or the useful, the beautiful or the pleasing and signifies a qualified situation. The arts of communication and construction are arts of *facts* and *values*; states of affairs, situations, and facts are recognized and judged relative to their elements and their composition by the arts of communication and construction.

The new grammar or art of interpretation or hermeneutics is the art of interpreting objective evidence, that is, of interpreting what is the case as what is the case. Its subject-matter is all things already known, expressed, and recorded, that is, all communications. Interpretation may focus primarily on statement, thought, or situation, but whatever its focus, each interpretation takes into account statements, judgments, and situations, and from them constructs a possible world and interprets it as one construction among possible worlds. The sciences and the arts are bodies of communications already achieved and recorded, and they provide the materials for the interpretation of facts and values as they have been found to be and present the evidence already available concerning what they are. The new grammar is the art of *recovery*. It is not an art of topics or a *selection* of elements, but an art of hypotheses or an *interpretation* of situations and facts. The subject-matter of the fundamental grammar is all situations and all that is known to be the case. The subject matters of derived grammars emerge when what is the case, situation, judgment, and statement are treated as language and symbol in exegetical grammars of analysis, or as thought and hypotheses in normative grammars of usage, or as things and facts in descriptive grammars of use.

Logic is the art of presentation and analysis, of inquiry and proof.

Logical and rational arts, *logoi* and *rationes*, are employed to analyze or resolve problematic situations and to discover or create sequential connections. We find a logic in the flow of statements, of ideas, of occurrence, and of feelings; and we develop and transmit arts and methods for the rational treatment of problems of discourse and discursive sequences, problems of thought and rational illations, problems of experience and factual consequences, and problems of feeling and emotional involvements. When the philosophic arts are conceived as arts of thought, logic provides the structure or essence of philosophy in all its branches, applications, and consequences; and Kant therefore is able to find in transcendental logic an order for the concepts and the problems of theory, practice, and judgment proper to each and relative to each other, and Russell is able to argue that logistic or mathematical logic becomes the "essence of philosophy" by providing a mathematical symbolism for deducing consequences from premises. But logic has a broader sense and scope, and applies to more kinds of discursive sequences of statement, than those of the forms of inference and judgment which fall under Boole's Laws of Thought or even of the forms of reason and judgment which fall under Kant's Aesthetics, Analytics, and Dialectics. There are narrative, descriptive, lyrical, rhetorical, communicative, and expressive as well as inferential and demonstrative consequences; and poetry or politics or rhetoric may become the essence of philosophy as facilely and persuasively as logic or grammar. There are different ways of conveying the same message, account, or proof; and there are different analyses of a single presentation or argument—formal or material, intentional or circumstantial, epistemic, pistic, or constitutive, demonstrative or heuristic.

Logic is an art of connection and conclusion, of inquiry and proof, of question and analysis, of problem and resolution. In Aristotle's logic, the forms of inference and the establishment of principles were treated in two "analytics" (which were sometimes called "*resolutoria*" in Latin), while in the Euclidean tradition principles were established by "analysis" and conclusions were derived by "synthesis." The two movements—from what is sought to what must be assumed, and from what is assumed to what is concluded or what is constructed—may be traced in all the varieties of meaningful connections of discourse, ranging from expressions of ideas and feelings, descriptions of things and situations, creations of artistic wholes through expositions of what is known and inquiries concerning what is not known, to the forms of valid inference and true demonstration. Conclusions are, with a change in the mode of analysis, denouements, consummations, ends, fulfillments, climaxes, or achievements. The rational or logical arts or methods are employed to establish the hypotheses and facts of interpretation and to trace their antecedents and conclusions. The sequences may, moreover, be considered in the forms of community established by communication as well as in the forms of connected statements, thoughts, and things. *Homiletics* reflects *analytics*, for homiletics is communication which forms an assembly or communion (*homilía*) by establishing likenesses or contacts (*homós*) in a crowd (*íle*), and analytics is communication which relates effects to causes.

The object of communication in logic broadly conceived emerges in connections set forth in the "themes" which are traced in their complications and resolutions of actions and their consequences. Themes and structures of connection recur with variations in particular accounts and analyses; and they are transposed from region to region, from science to science, from art to art, and from art to science and back again from science to art. Sequences of events and arguments are particular; formulations of the laws of sequences are universal. The devices of "demonstration" have been broadened in rhetorical argumentation from devices of deduction and proof to include all devices of manifestation, and the devices of "judgment" have been broadened in grammatical argumentation from the devices of forming and interpreting propositions to include all devices of forming and interpreting hypotheses and facts in situations, sentiments, and sentences. The devices of rational or logical argumentation are the devices of "deliberation," broadened from presentation of alternatives in practical actions and choice among them, to include all devices of analysis and decision-making. Homiletics, analytics, and methodologies establish and formulate that which is as it is found in connected subject-matters, in communities associated in common convictions, and in communications about subjects and between associated communicators. The arts of communication and construction are arts of *inquiry* and *presentation*;

connections of occurrence, thought, and statement provide the warrant and the framework for what are presented and accepted as the elements of existence and the facts of experience.

The new logic or analytic or art of method is the art of relating, that is, of relating occurrences and reactions in accounts which induce sensitive awareness and consequential judgment. Accounts of sequences and consequences examine and recount recurrent themes in specific or singular variations. An analytic of particular connections uncovers universal relations in individual embodiments of universal laws of connection. It is a method of knowing, doing, and making that which is, by organizing situations and problems, movements and resolutions into a unified, compendent whole or field, and by constituting its particularity in processes and accounts. By uncovering themes it moves from field to field. The new logic is the art of *presentation*. It is not an art of topics or of hypotheses, but an art of themes or a *method* of connections and accounts. The subject-matter of the fundamental logic is all that can be conceived or said to be and all connections which constitute possible worlds, possible laws of thought, and possible modes of statement and expression. The subject-matters of the derived logics emerge when basic connections are established as mapped spaces and loci which reproduce laws of natural occurrences and structures of matter, or as formed inferences and judgments which reproduce laws of thought and definitions of conception, or as expressed implications and variables which reproduce laws of syntax and determinations of vocabulary.

Dialectic is the art of dialogue and insight, of systematization and objectification, of assimilation and division. When the philosophic arts are conceived as arts of being, dialectic is the art of testing first principles, causes, and elements of knowledge, action, and construction. The principles of dialectic ground the compendent sets traced in the connections of things, thoughts, actions, and statements by logical inference or narration. The grounding is provided by establishing coincidences or identities of principles or beginnings of occurrences with principles or beginnings of analytic thought, of reasoned action, or of rational statement; that is, by establishing the compendent sets reflexively on each other in objective systems of identities and differences. Dialectic, as an art of being, makes metaphysics an architectonic science; as an art of thought it seeks connections in spirit or matter, and the architectonic ordering tends to come from practical reason; finally, the arts of communication and construction may transform dialectic and seek architectonic ordering in the dialogue of cultural communication and political construction.

Dialectic is the art of dialogue and insight, of reflexivity and individuation, of principle and encompassing order: it is an art of communication which focuses on the organization and circumstances of communication, and therefore on the cosmos as the model and ground of world order, mutual understanding, and common humanity. It is the system of the arts and sciences, the encyclopaedia of facts and suppositions, the compass of the actualities and potentialities. It is the encompassing dialogue in which "theses" are encountered and enunciated and are tried as principles constitutive of universes or systems of things, of thoughts, of communities, and of communications. In a dialogue which centers on theses and principles, on wholes and parts, self-sufficient parts are constructed into wholes and render them intelligible, and encompassing wholes are distinguished into parts which derive their properties and intelligibility from the wholes in which they function; and systems are transformed by change of principles. The arts of communication and construction are arts of *unification* and *transformation*; perceived or proferred connections are fantastic, subjective, or abstract unless they present evidence of their connection with what is the case and unless their reasons are tied down to the principles and causes of the connections they represent and present.

The new dialectic or systematics or art of principles is the art of structuring action and knowledge, that is, of bringing what we think, and say, and do into relation to what we are and the circumstances in which we find ourselves by forming them into encompassing wholes by reasoned, deliberative, and responsible integration. Principles of knowledge, action, and presentation are theses of being, thought, fact, value, and existence which are accepted and credited after having been tested in the actions which constitute inquiry, proof, discovery, and expression. It is a dialectic of principles and of the transformation of principles operating by an exchange and interpenetration of arts used as architectonic. It is a method of knowing, doing, and making tied to being by postulation of relations among all relevant fields in a system of interdependence. The new dialectic is the art of *action*. It is not an art of topics or of hypotheses or of themes, but an art of theses or *principles* proposed for arts and sciences and their interrelations. The subject-matter of the fundamental dialectic is the total framework of things to be done. The subject-matters of the derived dialectics emerge when it is postulated that metaphysics, or politics, or poetics, or rhetoric are architectonic sciences. The arts of communication and construction may take their ordering principles from models in structures of being or knowing; or the arts of communication and construction may provide the architectonic structures for knowing, doing, making, and saying and for the structures of being that are produced by action in accordance with those structures.

The philosophic arts have always been arts of communication and construction. As arts of forming statements constructed to be true and presenting arguments communicated to convince, they have been designed to achieve objectivity and universality. Yet the frequent changes of philosophic positions and philosophic problems in the history of philosophy have been expressions and manifestations of changes in the philosophic arts, and changes in the arts have brought with them changes in the subject-matter and data of discussion. Subject-matter and arts change from philosophy to philosophy, and communication among philosophers is more frequently ideological controversy concerning methods of determining what is the case than substantive discussion concerning what has been or might be alleged to be the case. Differences in subject-matters are differences concerning what the facts are and whether, once they have been stated clearly, they are indeed facts; they are differences concerning the contexts or universes which facts or occurrences constitute, and by which they are conditioned, and concerning how facts or occurrences are related to, and influence, each other. Differences in the arts are differences of method applied to the problems of knowing, doing, making, and saying, and to the intermingling of those problems which results from changes in subject-matters; they are differences which have been used to separate dialectic, logic, grammar, and rhetoric, to transform and revolutionize them in the history of their development, to delimit or expand the scope of their operation, and to establish the architectonic determination they assume relative to each other. There has been a continuity of structure and purpose in the philosophic arts which may serve as a mark by which to gauge progress in philosophical inquiry in any effort at dead-reckoning the uses of philosophy; but progress in inquiry by use of the philosophical arts has been obscured by semantic changes in the devices of the arts and in the consequent selection of data of existence or interpretation of facts of experience. But inquiry into the problems of existence and experience are inseparable from semantic selection and interpretation of categories and modes of statement, and semantic controversy and refutation has both obscured progress in philosophical inquiry, since an opposed position becomes opaque and meaningless when interpreted according to the assumptions and methods of the opposing philosophy, and has also contributed to the advance of philosophical inquiry, because the diversity of approaches revealed in controversy, once the ardor of debate has cooled, opens up the richness of common problems which are the subject of philosophical inquiry. Common experience and objective existence lie beyond, and exceed, the fixities of judgments in which facts are stated and interpreted and of categories in which terms are selected and defined. The subject-matter and the problems of the philosophic arts find their universal generality in experience and existence, in language and communication, which are the common sources of concrete facts and data, law-like structures and sequences; the assumptions and the devices of the philosophic arts find their neutrality and objectivity by adapting and merging the methods of traditional arts to the concrete specifications of a common subject-matter.

Debate and controversy are functions of the art of rhetoric. Communication among philosophies takes a rhetorical turn in the incidental references which philosophers pause to make to the errors of predecessors or contemporaries. Every philosophy has a place for rhetoric, large or small, positive or pejorative; and judgments about rhetoric, good or bad, as well as rhetorical judgments, prejudiced or judicial, have bases in the principles and methods of philosophy. Statement and interpretation are functions of the art of grammar.

Interpretation of philosophical statements in the citations of other philosophers made in the course of philosophic argument uncover a grammar of composition and make use of a grammar of interpretation to disclose meanings, and even in sympathetic interpretations the vocabulary and syntax of the interpreter affects the meaning of the cited words and statements. When the arts of communication and construction assume an architectonic function, the arts of logic and dialectic are practiced by devices borrowed from rhetoric and grammar, and the characteristics of things and thoughts are derived as subject-matter from the concrete data and facts of existence and experience. The fixities and distortions of semantic controversy are rigidified since the refutations and interpretations of rival philosophies are given a putative basis in concrete experience and existence in the statement and construction of each philosophy, but the transition from arbitrary determinations of semantics into structures of closed statements, to ongoing developments of inquiry into opening problems is rendered possible by the broadening and merging of the arts of communications in concrete applications and situations.

The arts of communication and construction give promise of constituting a new philosophy in which the pluralism of arts and philosophies makes use of semantic differences for diversified treatment of the common problems and subject-matters of philosophical inquiry rather than setting the different arts and philosophies in controversial opposition in which semantic differences mark off the rival possibilities of unique statement of truth and determination of values. The new rhetoric may be broadened from persuasion to include all elements of existence and to use commonplaces or topics for discovery of the unknown. The new grammar may be broadened from the composition of statements to include all facts of experience and to use hypotheses of semantics for recovery of the known. The new logic may be broadened from inquiry and proof to include all discursive sequences and all sequential series stated in discourse and to use the themes of the arts for presentation of connections. The new dialectic may be broadened from systems of thought and being to include all ordering principles, elements, and causes and to use the theses of inquiry to unify and transform possible world orders and human orders. The new philosophy can not be a monolithic inclusive shared ideology, but it may oppose the dogmatisms of partial and divisive universalisms to become a philosophy of communications and the arts.

Rhetoric in the Middle Ages

Medieval and Renaissance rhetoricians and philosophers, following the example of Cicero, seldom omit from their treatment of rhetoric some consideration of the subject matter, nature, and end of the art. Long before Cicero, rhetoric had become one of the focal points of the differences of philosophic schools, and the practice and application of the art had long wandered from field to field, reflecting and sometimes even affecting the complexities of philosophic discussions. Yet in histories which touch upon it, rhetoric is treated as a simple verbal discipline, as the art of speaking well, applied either as it was in Rome in forensic oratory and associated with the interpretation of laws or, more frequently, as it was in the Renaissance in the interpretation and use of the works of orators and poets and associated with, or even indistinguishable from, poetic and literary criticism. The history of rhetoric as it has been written since the Renaissance is therefore in part the distressing record of the obtuseness of writers who failed to study the classics and to apply rhetoric to literature, and in part the monotonous enumeration of doctrines, or preferably sentences, repeated from Cicero or commentators on Cicero. Scholarly labors have reconstructed only a brief and equivocal history for rhetoric during the Middle Ages. The development consists of slight and original increments of erudition in the compendia composed from the fourth to the ninth century—derived largely from the *De inventione* of Cicero and the *Ad Herennium*—and in later commentaries and treatises to the elaboration of coherent and complex doctrines in the twelfth century based on Quintilian and the later rhetorical works of Cicero, the *Orator*, the *De oratore*, and the *Topica*. The sequence of development is fortuitous and even implausible, for the treatment of rhetoric becomes more perfunctory as erudition in the works of rhetoricians increases, and rhetoric disappears abruptly when knowledge of it is at a maximum, particularly from the works of the authors who acknowledge the influence of Cicero and Quintilian. The translation of the *Rhetoric* of Aristotle, of the pseudo-Aristotelian *Rhetorica ad Alexandrum*, and of the *De elocutione* of Demetrius in the thirteenth century would seem to have had, by this account, no effect comparable to that of the other translations of the century in stimulating interest in its subject; and the return of rhetoric to prominence during the Renaissance is explained only on the supposition that men's minds were turned once more, after a long interval, to literature and life.[1]

1. Valla, Vives, Ramus, and other Renaissance rhetoricians who treat the history of rhetoric pass over the intermediate period separating them from antiquity, to criticize, refute, and occasionally approve of the doctrines of Aristotle, Cicero, Quintilian, and Boethius. In early works of erudition and philology the scope of the history of rhetoric is no broader than the scope of contemporary controversy. D. G. Morhof makes the transition from Cicero, Quintilian and their predecessors, who are considered in the first nine of the thirty-two paragraphs headed *De scriptoribus rhetoricis* in his *Polyhistor, literarius, philosophicus et practicus* (vi. 1 [3d ed.; Lubecae, 1732], I, 941–56), to the Renaissance rhetoricians treated in the last twenty-three paragraphs with the remark, "Nos vero, missis nunc veteribus, ad recentiores sparsim enumerandos progredimur." J. Clericus carries the *Historia rhetorica* down to the Church Fathers in his *Ars critica* (Pars II, Sectio I, cap. 17 [Leipzig, 1713], I, 336–52). The history of rhetoric has more recently been extended to the Middle Ages, but it is always rhetoric in some particular sense, applied to some particular subject, and the history is usually negative or at least deprecatory. J. B. L. Crevier thus traces the history of rhetoric in education by noting the absence of any provision for rhetoric in the regulations of the University of Paris until the restoration of letters (*Histoire de l'Université de Paris* [Paris, 1761], I, 299, 307, 376, 479; II, 450; IV, 190, 243–44, 249, 330, 349, and *passim*). The pattern of rhetoric had, incidentally, not changed from the Renaissance to the eighteenth century in the important respect that Crevier found little use in his own writings on rhetoric for any authors between the ancients and his contemporaries, and the imperfections of Aristotle, Cicero, and Quintilian are his excuse for writing: "Aristote me paroit trop philosophe, Cicéron trop orateur, Quintilien trop scholastique" (*Rhétorique françoise* [Paris, 1808], I, xix). E. Norden treats rhetoric primarily in terms of style and is able, therefore, to dispose of the entire period from the ninth century to the time of Petrarch briefly in terms of the opposition of the study of authors to the study of the liberal arts, of classicism to scholasticism (*Die antike Kunstprosa vom vi. Jahrhundert v. Chr. bis in die Zeit der Renaissance* [4th ed.; Leipzig, 1923], II, 688–731); cf. the treatment of rhetoric and poetic (ibid., pp. 894–98). According to C. S. Baldwin, the fate of rhetoric is determined by shifts in the interrelations of the arts of the trivium: rhetoric was dominant

There is little reflection in the histories of rhetoric of the differences concerning the subject matter and purpose of rhetoric by which rhetoricians thought to distinguish and oppose their doctrines; and only occasionally and opaquely do some of the consequences of basic philosophic differences appear in the place given to rhetoric in the enumerations and classifications of the arts and sciences. The theoretic presuppositions which underlie the shifts and alterations of rhetorical doctrines are readily made to seem verbal and arbitrary preferences, for in the course of discussion all the terms are altered in meaning, and the contents and methods of each of the arts are transformed when grammar, rhetoric, poetic, dialectic, and logic change places or are identified one with another, or are distinguished from one another, or are subsumed one under another. Yet the confident readjustments of Renaissance rhetoricians, their redistribution of technical devices among the arts, and their correction of the confusions of the ancients seem no less whimsical and haphazard, if their reasons and criteria are ignored

---

until the fall of Rome, grammar during the Carolingian period, dialectic during the Middle Ages (*Medieval Rhetoric and Poetic* [New York, 1928], p. 151). Rhetoric was crowded into medieval education between grammar for boys and dialectic for men, and Baldwin is therefore at pains to find reasons which explain "why there was no medieval rhetorician who really advanced the study" (ibid., p. 182). The history of rhetoric during the Middle Ages is consequently the account of its misapplications and extensions: poetic is a misapplication of rhetoric to style (ibid., pp. 185 ff., esp. 191–95); the dictamen is a development of rhetoric, but without need of perversion (ibid., pp. 208 ff., esp. 214–15); and preaching in the absence of political and forensic oratory makes use of epideictic or occasional oratory, the third of Aristotle's genera (ibid., pp. 229 ff.). According to P. Abelson (*The Seven Liberal Arts: A Study in Medieval Culture* [New York, 1906], pp. 52 ff.), rhetoric consisted of a practical training during the Roman period; then of the technical rules of a science; and, finally, when this theoretical and logical form of rhetoric fell into obsolescence, of the practical rules for writing letters and documents. In the account of N. Valois (*Guillaume d'Auvergne* [Paris, 1880], pp. 224 ff.) rhetoric was taught as a liberal art until the end of the twelfth century and then fell into discredit except as a practical discipline applied to preaching and prayer. The judgment of C. H. Haskins (*The Renaissance of the Twelfth Century* [Cambridge, Mass., 1928], p. 138) is no less concise in statement: "Ancient rhetoric was concerned with oratory, mediaeval rhetoric chiefly with letter-writing," and is illustrated with detailed evidence. More simply, if rhetoric is viewed as a form of literary criticism and associated with poetic, the decline of rhetoric is a symptom of the eclipse of the study of ancient literature (cf. L. J. Paetow, "The Arts Course at Mediaeval Universities with Special Reference to Grammar and Rhetoric," *University of Illinois Studies*, III (January, 1910), esp. 67 ff.; and D. L. Clark, *Rhetoric and Poetry in the Renaissance* (New York, 1922), pp. 43 ff.

and only the repetition of enumerations of the disciplines and their parts is recorded. Rhetoricians from Cicero to Ramus have in common a persistent care in defining their art, and it seems plausible that a history of rhetoric traced in terms of its matter and function, as specified at each stage, might give significance and lively interest to the altering definitions, the differentiation of various conceptions of rhetoric itself, and the spread of the devices of rhetoric to subject matters far from those ordinarily ascribed to it. Such a history would not treat an art determined to a fixed subject matter (so conceived, rhetoric is usually found to have little or no history, despite much talk about rhetoric and even more use of it, during the Middle Ages), nor, on the other hand, would it treat an art determined arbitrarily and variously by its place in classifications of the sciences (so conceived, the schemes of the sciences would be arbitrary in their alterations and uncontrolled by philosophic principles or material content). The history of rhetoric should have as subject an art which, although it has no special subject matter according to most rhetoricians, nonetheless must be discussed in application to some subject matter: rhetoric has been applied to many incommensurate subject matters; it has borrowed devices from other arts, and its technical terms and methods have become, without trace of their origin, parts of other arts and sciences; its own devices have been bent back upon themselves in such a way that any part of rhetoric or any matter incidentally involved in it—words and style, character and passion, reason and imagination, the kinds of orations, civil philosophy, practical action—have been made basic to the definition of all technical terms and distinctions. Moreover, if the succession of subject matters and functions can be used to reduce the welter of changes in rhetoric to a significant historical sequence, the theories implicated in the shifts of its subject matter should emerge, not merely as philosophic or sophistic disputes, but in concrete application, each at least defensible and each a challenge to the conception of intellectual history as the simple record of the development of a body of knowledge by more or less adequate investigations of a constant subject matter.

I

Three distinct lines of intellectual development during the Middle Ages were decisively determined or strongly influenced in their initial stages by rhetoric: first, and most properly, the tradition of rhetoricians themselves, who found their problems assembled and typical answers discussed in the works of Cicero and Quintilian; second, and less obviously, the tradition of philosophers and theologians who found in Augustine a Platonism reconstructed from the Academic and Neo-Platonic philosophies (conscientiously reversing the process by which they were derived from Plato's doctrines) and formulated in terms refurbished and simplified from Cicero's rhetorical distinctions; and, finally, the tradition of logic which passed as "Aristotelian," yet which followed Aristotle only in the treatment of terms and propositions and resorted to Cicero in the treatment of definitions and principles. Whatever the estimate that critics and historians are disposed to make of Cicero's achievement, originality, and consistency, his choices and emphases fixed the influence and oriented the interpretation of ancient thought, Greek as well as Latin, at the beginning of the Middle Ages and again in the Renaissance; and we today are far from having freed ourselves from the consequences of that long tradition in scholarship, criticism, or taste. During the Middle Ages and Renaissance many of the oppositions and agreements of theology and dialectic, no less than problems internal to each, were stated in language borrowed from or influenced by rhetoric and reflected theories by which rhetoricians had in antiquity opposed philosophers and logicians; surprising parallels were disclosed in theology and dialectic as well as in other arts and sciences, and they were expressed in language familiar to the rhetorician; innovations and discoveries were made which seem to follow the dictation of nature if their pattern of statement is ignored; and mere equivocations were pursued into interminable and recurrent verbal disputes.

The rhetoricians of the Middle Ages followed Cicero or suggestions found in his works when they discussed civil philosophy as the subject matter of rhetoric or divided that subject matter according to the three kinds of oratory—deliberative, judicial, demonstrative—or when they sought to determine it more generally by means of the distinction between *propositum* and *causa* (or *thesis* and *hypothesis*, as the Greek terms were Latinized), or by consideration of the characteristics of controversies and the constitutions (or *status*) of questions.[2] Moreover, they could learn, even from the *De inventione*, that there had been controversy on most of these points; and, in particular, the brief history of three views concerning the matter of rhetoric—Gorgias holding that it is all things, Aristotle dividing it into three kinds proper to the three kinds of oratory, and Hermagoras distinguishing "causes," which are specific to persons, and "questions," which are without such specification—supplied the arguments by which to dissent from, as well as those to support, Cicero's version of Aristotle's solution.[3] Major alterations in the contents and doctrines of rhetoric attended these changes in subject matter, and they required for their elaboration only a little erudition, such as might be derived from study of the points of difference between the *Ad Herennium* and the *De inventione*, or from the information supplied by Fortunatianus concerning figures and the Greek technical terms of rhetoric, or, finally, from Quintilian's orderly enumerations of divergent views and his statement and rectification of inconsistencies attributed to Cicero.[4] Even apart from

2. Cf. Cicero *De inventione* i. 4. 5: "Sed antequam de praeceptis oratoriis dicimus, videtur dicendum de genere ipsius artis, de officio, de fine, de materia, de partibus." After determining that its *genus* is "civilis scientia," its *officium* "dicrere adposite ad persuasionem," and its *finis* "persuadere dictione," Cicero defines the matter of all arts, including the art of rhetoric (ibid. 5. 7): "Materiam artis eam dicimus, in qua omnis ars et ea facultas, quae conficitur ex arte, versatur."

3. Ibid. 5. 7–7. 9. Cf. ibid. 9. 12 for illustration of the process by which basic terms are altered and the distinctions of rhetoric are bent back on themselves: in this case the dispute is concerning whether deliberation and demonstration are the genera of "causes" or are themselves parts of a particular genus of "cause." Isidore's list of the "inventors" of the art reflects the influence of Cicero's history of the matter of rhetoric, since the inventors are clearly determined by this history, as is the testimony to the elusiveness of the distinctions; cf. *Etymologiae* ii. 2: "Haec autem disciplina a Graecis inventa est, a Gorgia, Aristotele, Hermagora, et translata in Latinum a Tullio videlicet et Quintiliano, sed ita copiose, ita varie, ut eam lectori admirari in promptu sit, comprehendere impossibile. Nam membranis retentis quasi adhaerescit memoriae series dictionis, ac mox repositis recordatio omnis elabitur."

4. Cf. *Institutio oratoria* iii. 5. 4ff. for an excellent statement of the problems involved in rhetorical "questions," and the disputes concerning "thesis" and "hypothesis," and esp. 14–15 for the development of Cicero's doctrine. For a brief summary of some of the characteristic statements of the definition and end of rhetoric, cf. ibid. ii. 15; for disputes concerning its matter, ibid. 21. Or again, in illustration of the bending-back of rhetorical distinctions, what one man holds to be the "parts

the influence of theology and even before the influence of dialectic was felt, the remnants of old and the seeds of new controversies were preserved in rhetoric itself.

Rhetoric influenced Augustine both in his reactions against it and in his assimilation and use of devices borrowed from it; he differentiated two eloquences and two arts, much as Plato had proved rhetoric a pseudo-art in the *Gorgias* and yet had illustrated the method of the true rhetoric based on dialectic in the *Phaedrus*. Augustine was first attracted to philosophy by Cicero's *Hortensius*, which he encountered in the course of his rhetorical studies, and he was put off in his further attempt to combine philosophy with the name of Christ by the contrast of the scriptural and Ciceronian styles.[5] That stumbling block was finally removed in part by the aid of a rhetorical device which Augustine learned from Ambrose's preaching—the analogical method of interpreting Scripture[6]—and, although thereafter he refused to answer questions concerning Cicero's *Orator* and *De oratore*, on the grounds that it was a task unworthy of a bishop distracted with ecclesiastical cares,[7] his statement of Christian doctrine was, in the terms of Cicero, sublimated to new meanings and transformed to new uses. When he wishes to enumerate the questions basic to all inquiry, he resorts to Cicero's three "constitutions of causes"—whether a thing is, that it is, and what sort; and when he enumerates the methods to be used in treating scriptural questions, they turn out to be two of Cicero's five parts of rhetoric—discovery and statement; moreover, these two sets of questions seem to him exhaustive, and all problems and doctrines are concerned, as in the manuals of rhetoric, with "things" or with

---

of rhetoric" another treats as the "work of the orator" (ibid. iii. 3. 11 ff.); the two positions are taken, respectively, by Cicero, *De inventione* i. 7. 9, and Fortunatianus, *Ars rhetorica* i. 1 (Halm, *Rhetores Latini minores* [Leipzig, 1863], p. 81; henceforth cited as "Halm").

5. *Confessions* iii. 3. 6–5. 9 (*Patrologia Latina*, XXXII, 685–86; henceforth cited as "*PL*").

6. *Confessions* v. 13. 23 and vi. 4. 5–6 (*PL*, XXXII, 717 and 721–22). Cf. also the conversion of Victorinus the rhetorician and the effect of *salus* and *fides* on his rhetoric (*Confessions* viii. 2. 5 [*PL*, XXXII, 751]).

7. *Epistola CXVIII ad Dioscorum* i. 2 and v. 34 (*PL*, XXXIII, 432–33 and 448).

"signs."[8] This rhetorical language has, however, been adapted to the statement of a theology: discovery has been qualified as discovery of "what should be understood" and statement as statement of "what has been understood," with the result that the classification of signs and their uses is dependent, as it had not been in rhetoric, on the classification of things. In the *De doctrina Christiana* the first three books are concerned with discovery, the fourth with statement. The treatment of discovery is based, in the first book, on the distinction of things into those which as final ends are loved or enjoyed (*frui*) and those which as intermediate ends are used (*uti*) for further ends; consideration of the former takes the form of a theological inquiry into the attributes of God and divine things; the treatment of the nature of things is supplemented, in the second book, by a philological inquiry into the nature of words in relation to the Scriptures and the arts and institutions of the pagans; and, finally, in the third book, the inquiry into means of removing verbal ambiguities requires appeal to two sets of rules—grammatical rules applied to the manner of statement and rhetorical rules to determine the circumstances of fact.[9] The treatment of statement in the

8. *Confessions* x. 9. 16–10. 17 (*PL*, XXXII, 786). Cf. Cicero *Orator* 14. 45: "Nam quoniam, quicquid est quod in controversia aut in contentione versetur, in eo aut sitne aut quid sit aut quale sit quaeritur: sitne, signis; quid sit, definitionibus; quale sit, recti pravique partibus—quibus ut uti possit orator, non ille volgaris sed hic excellens, a propriis personis et temporibus, si potest, avocat controversiam." The context and application of the questions are rhetorical in the *Confessions*, but cf. *De diversis quaestionibus LXXXIII* 18 (*PL*, XL, 15): "Ideoque etiam cum veritas quaeritur, plus quam tria genera questionum esse non possunt; utrum omnino sit, utrum hoc an aliud sit, utrum approbandum improbandumve sit." The tendency of these questions toward generalization beyond their specifically rhetorical meanings is assisted by some of the names attached to them: the pseudo-Augustine calls them "rational or logical" questions (*De rhetorica* 9 [Halm, p. 142]); Martianus Capella calls them "principal status" (*De rhetorica* 6 [Halm, p. 455]); Clodian names them "rational status" (*Ars rhetorica* [Halm, p. 590]). A fourth question or constitution or status is added by Hermagoras, is rejected by Cicero and Quintilian, and is mentioned by the pseudo-Augustine and Clodian. Concerning the variety and evolution of questions (or "status," as he prefers to call them), cf. Quintilian iii. 6. 29–85; his own decision is presented as one prescribed by nature and coincident with the doctrine of Cicero (ibid. 80): "Credendum est igitur his, quorum auctoritatem secutus est Cicero, tria esse, quae in omni disputatione quaerantur, an sit, quid sit, quale sit? quod ipsa nobis etiam natura praescribit." For Augustine's enumeration of scriptural methods and problems cf. *De doctrina Christiana* i. 1–2 (*PL*, XXXIV, 19–20).

9. *De doctrina Christiana* iii. 4. 8, and 12. 18 (*PL*, XXXIV, 68 and 72–73).

final book is therefore concerned not so much with the *precepts* of rhetoric, although some precepts can be found from analysis of the fashion in which the three styles of Cicero are applied to their appropriate matters by "ecclesiastical orators," as with an eloquence in which the words are supplied by the things and by wisdom itself and the speaker is unlearnedly wise.[10] The judgment expressed by Cicero at the beginning of the *De inventione*, that wisdom without eloquence is of little benefit to the state and eloquence without wisdom a great danger, is transformed by Augustine's dialectic, and all the terms take on two meanings. The wisdom and eloquence of the world are to be contrasted to eternal wisdom and eloquence; for there are not only two kinds of things, temporal and divine, but two kinds of words, the external words instituted and used by men which have no correspondence to things except by designation and no controllable influence on our thought except by way of the context of other words, and the internal words, by which a master speaking within us teaches the truth.[11] Whether things be treated as signs or signs as things, only the eternal meanings and realities are important; knowledge of temporal things and of the arts is chiefly useful for the interpretation of the language and symbolism of Scripture, and the Sacraments are signs adapted to the mutability of human sensibilities but immutable in their significance of the

10. *De doctrina Christiana* iv. 1. 1–7. 11 (*PL*, XXXIV, 89–94).

11. *De magistro* 3. 5–6 and 11. 36–12. 46 (*PL*, XXXII, 1197–98 and 1215–20). Cf. the excellent statement of the relation of language to thought by E. Gilson, *Introduction à l'étude de Saint Augustin* (Paris, 1929), pp. 87–103. Augustine's conception of rhetoric is developed most fully in the *De doctrina Christiana*, *De ordine*, *De catechizandis rudibus*, and *Contra Cresconium*. Cf. also J. Žůrek, "De S. Aurelii praeceptis rhetoricis," *Dissertationes philologae Vindobonenses* (Vienna, 1905), VIII, 69–109; M. Comeau, *La Rhétorique de Saint Augustin d'après le "Tractatus in Iohannem"* (Paris, 1930); G. Combès, *Saint Augustin et la culture classique* (Paris, 1927), esp. pp. 49–56, where true eloquence is distinguished from the oratorical art; H.-I. Marrou, *Saint Augustin et la fin de la culture antique* (Paris, 1938), esp. pp. 507–40 on Christian eloquence. The rhetoric of Cicero was moral and political in its applications, and the influence of rhetoric extended to political doctrine. The differentiation of things according to ends loved and means used had already entered Christian ethics in Ambrose's *De officiis ministrorum*, which was based on the distinctions of Cicero's *De officiis*; and Cicero's rhetorically conceived political theory supplies, by virtue of the same distinction, the terminology for Augustine's discussion of the City of God as well as the elements of the terrestrial city to which it is contrasted.

changeless things of God.[12] Once account is taken of the distinction of things and words into those which are temporal and those which are changeless, the influence of rhetoric is discernible in many traits of the Augustinian tradition: in the analogical interpretation of Scripture and in the numerous medieval encyclopedias prepared to facilitate such interpretation (for words are signs which are useful less to designate things than to express truths and persuade minds, and things therefore are useful to interpret signs, rather than signs to interpret things);[13] in the literal interpretation in which apparently contradictory texts were reconciled in canon law and theology by use of the rhetorician's "circumstances" of statement, that is, by consideration of "who" said it, "where, when, why, how, with what assistance";[14] in the organization of theological problems according to the distinction of things and signs; and in the place of rhetoric after dialectic in the enumeration of the liberal arts (since it supplies the means of stating truths, once they have been discovered) instead of before dialectic, as in the enumeration of an opposed tradition (since it achieves only probability and persuasion but falls short of truth).[15]

The discussion of logic during the Middle Ages may be divided into four periods. During the first period, the elements of logic were learned from simple treatises like the pseudo-Augustine's *Principia dialecticae* and *Categoriae decem* (which Alcuin recommended to Charlemagne as Augustine's translation of Aristotle's *Categories*) or the sections on dialectic in such handbooks as those of Martianus Capella, Cassiodorus, and Isidore of Seville. During the second period, after the curriculum instituted by Gerbert at the end of the tenth century the basis of instruction in dialectic was broadened to

12. *Epistola CXXXVIII ad Marcellinum* i. 7 (*PL*, XXXIII, 527): "Nimis autem longum est, convenienter disputare de varietate signorum, quae cum ad res divinas pertinent, Sacramenta appellantur. Sicut autem non ideo mutabilis homo, quia mane aliud, aliud vespere; illud hoc mense, illud alio; non hoc isto anno quod illo: ita non ideo mutabilis Deus, quia universi saeculi priore volumine aliud, aliud posteriore sibi iussit offerri, quo convenienter significationes ad doctrinam religionis saluberrimam pertinentes, per mutabilia tempora sine ulla sui mutatione disponeret."

13. Cf. Gilson, op. cit., pp. 151–53.

14. *De doctrina Christiana* iii. 12. 18–29. 41 (*PL*, XXXIV, 72–81).

15. For the fashion in which rhetoric follows and supplements dialectic according to Augustine, cf. *De doctrina Christiana* ii. 35. 53–37. 55 (*PL*, XXXIV, 60–61); *De ordine* ii. 13. 38 (*PL*, XXXII, 1013).

include the works and translations of Boethius, among them two of the six books of Aristotle's *Organon*, which together acquired the traditional name of the "Old Logic." During the third period, the translation of the remaining four books in the twelfth century set up the New Logic, constituted of the *Introduction* of Porphyry, the *Organon* of Aristotle, and the *Six Principles* of Gilbert de la Porrée; but the authority of the Old Logic continued strong, since the contemporaries of John of Salisbury found the *Posterior Analytics*, which treats of the principles of scientific demonstration, difficult or even unintelligible[16] (and, indeed, the first important commentary on that work was written in the thirteenth century by Robert Grosseteste, while as late as the fourteenth century William of Ockham prepared an *Expositio aurea et admodum utilis super artem veterem*). Finally, during the fourth period, the discussion of logic is determined less by Aristotle's *Organon* than by the *Summulae*, written in the thirteenth century by Petrus Hispanus, Lambert of Auxerre, and William of Shyreswood. The extent of the influence of rhetoric on the development of logic may be judged from the fact that—although Aristotle's logic is characterized not merely by the schemata of terms, propositions, and syllogisms set forth in the first three books of the *Organon* but even more by the differentiation of proof, in accordance with the principles on which it depends, into three kinds: scientific or demonstrative, dialectical, and sophistical, which are expounded in the last three books, the *Posterior Analytics*, the *Topics*, and the *De sophisticis elenchis*—only the first three books had much influence until the thirteenth century, while principles were treated by devices which Aristotle used in rhetoric and dialectic, and, even after the thirteenth century, scientific method was in constant danger of being assimilated to dialectic, the *Posterior Analytics* to the *Topics*.

The early treatments of dialectic in the handbooks and encyclo-

16. John of Salisbury *Metalogicon* iv. 6, ed. C. C. J. Webb (Oxford, 1929), p. 171: "Deinde hec utentium raritate iam fere in desuetudinem abiit, eo quod demonstrationis usus uix apud solos mathematicos est; et in his fere, apud geometras dumtaxat; sed et huius quoque discipline non est celebris usus apud nos, nisi forte in tractu Hibero uel confinio Affrice." In contrast to his brief and almost flippant treatment of the *Posterior Analytics*, John devotes more than half the third book (iii. 5–10; Webb, pp. 139–64) to praise of the utility of the *Topics*.

pedias run through a familiar sequence of subjects: the predicables of Porphyry; the categories of Aristotle; a brief treatment of propositions, in which the testimony of Aristotle's *De interpretatione* is mixed in small doses with that of the treatise by the same name attributed to Apuleius; an exposition of the categorical syllogism derived from the pseudo-Apuleius and of the hypothetical syllogism derived from the rhetorician Marius Victorinus; and, finally, in place of Aristotle's principles of demonstration, sections on definition and on "topics" or "commonplaces" derived from the Greek rhetoricians by way of Cicero and the lost works of Marius Victorinus. So direct is the descent of the principles of demonstration from rhetoric that Cassiodorus closes his consideration of the art of dialectic, having treated of topics, with "atechnical" arguments (which form part of the *Topics* of Cicero but figure in the *Rhetoric* and not the *Topics* of Aristotle) and memory (which, although one of the traditional five parts of rhetoric, is common, according to Cassiodorus, to orators, dialecticians, poets, and jurists),[17] while Isidore supplements his statement of topics with a section on opposites derived from Cicero.[18] The basic pattern of this logic was not crucially altered by the return in the second period to the more extensive logical works of Boethius. "Dialectic" is not distinct from "logic" in the tradition of the Old Logic; rather, dialectic or logic is divided on the authority of Cicero into two parts, one (called "analytic" by the Greeks, according to Boethius) concerned with judgment, the other (called "topic" by the Greeks) concerned with discovery.[19] Boethius translated and wrote commentaries on Aristotle's *Categories* and *On Interpretation*, but he also translated and wrote two commentaries on the *Isagoge* or *Introduction* of the Neo-

17. *Institutiones* ii. 3. 16–17, ed. R. A. B. Mynors (Oxford, 1937), pp. 127–28; cf. Cicero *Topica* 4. 24 and Aristotle *Rhetoric* i. 15. 1375^{a}22–1377^{b}12. Mynors argues from the manuscripts that the *Institutiones* went through two recensions by other hands than Cassiodorus, and in them Boethius was substituted as authority in dialectic for Marius Victorinus (pp. xxviii and xxxvii). The closing sections of the later versions of the treatment of dialectic included, in addition to the rhetorical subjects of the earlier versions, a treatment of rhetorical places, discovery, and circumstances (*PL*, LXX, 1196–1202).

18. *Etymologiae* ii. 31.

19. *De differentiis topicis* i (PL, LXIV, 1173); *In Porphyrium commentaria* i (*PL*, LXIV, 73).

Platonist Porphyry, which expounds, as introduction to the *Categories*, the predicables treated by Aristotle in his *Topics*; and this dialectical treatment of "the five words" appeared thereafter, even when the influence of Boethius was slight, in medieval, Renaissance, and early modern treatments of Aristotle's logic and editions of his *Organon*. Instead of Aristotle's treatment of syllogism, medieval philosophers had, until the twelfth century, Boethius' essays *On the Categorical Syllogism* (in which the doctrine of Aristotle is modified by the doctrines of Theophrastus, Eudemus, and Porphyry),[20] *On the Hypothetical Syllogism* (in which the authority of Theophrastus and Eudemus is invoked for seeking necessary premises in the forms of propositions rather than in the nature of things),[21] and *On Division* (which goes back to the "peripatetic" tradition, according to the opening sentence of the essay, but cites explicitly only Andronicus, Plotinus, and Porphyry, for treatment of a "scientia dividendi" in which Aristotle himself places little store).[22] The *De definitione* which went under Boethius' name is by Marius Victorinus, and it supplies one more channel for the influence of Cicero and rhetoric.[23] Finally, instead of a treatment of the differences of demonstrative, dialectical, and sophistical principles and proofs, Boethius left two works which had the effect, during the Middle Ages and increasingly during the Renaissance, of translating the problem of distinguishing principles into the problem of

20. For references to Theophrastus, Eudemus, and Porphyry cf. *De syllogismo categorico* ii (*PL*, LXIV, 813, 814, 815, and esp. 829): "Haec de Categoricorum Syllogismorum introductione, Aristotelem plurimum sequens, et aliqua de Theophrasto et Porphyrio mutuatus, quantum parcitas introducendi permisit, expressi." The *Introductio ad syllogismos categoricos* (*PL*, LXIV, 761 ff.) seems clearly another recension of Book i of the *De syllogismo categorico*.

21. *De syllogismo hypothetico* i (*PL*, LXIV, 843): "Necessitas vero hypotheticae propositionis et ratio earum propositionum ex quibus junguntur inter se connexiones, consequentiam quaerit, ut cum dico: Si Socrates sedet et vivit, neque sedere eum, neque vivere necesse est; sed si sedet, necesse est vivere. . . . Necessitas enim propositionis in consequentiae immutabilitate consistit." Cf. *De differentiis topicis* i (*PL*, LXIV, 1176), where such propositions are called *per se nota*. For reference to Theophrastus and Eudemus cf. *De syllogismo hypothetico* 831.

22. *De divisione* (*PL*, LXIV, 875–76); cf. Aristotle *Prior Analytics* I. 31. 46^a31–46^b37.

23. On the question of the authenticity of the *De definitione*, cf. H. Usener, *Anecdoton Holderi* (Bonn, 1877), pp. 59–66. For the effect of the *De definitione* in introducing rhetorical distinctions into the medieval discussions of logic cf. C. Prantl, *Geschichte der Logik im Abendlande* (Leipzig, 1855), I, 688–90.

discovering arguments or things: his *Commentary on the Topics of Cicero* and his treatise in four books *On Topical Differences*, in which the topical schemes or commonplaces of Themistius and Cicero are set forth and reduced to a single classification.[24] With the advent of the New Logic in the third period, during the twelfth century, however, logic was distinguished from dialectic; and rhetoric became the counterpart of dialectic, although logic continued to be divided into judgment and discovery. Finally, during the fourth period, in the *Summulae* of the thirteenth century the emphasis is again on the topics, as it is also in the reaction against logic during the Renaissance, when the *Topics* of Cicero and of Boethius were once more used (as John the Scot had used topics) as inspiration for a scientific method of discovering, not arguments, but things, and the scholastic logic was viewed as a verbal discipline inferior in precision and practical effectiveness to these devices of rhetoric.

The effects of this extension of the devices of rhetoric to logic became apparent, in turn, in the treatment of rhetoric, and it became important to contrast rhetoric and dialectic when both rhetoricians and dialecticians made use of "places" for purposes of discovery. Paradoxically, in this tradition in which the methods of rhetoric were similar to those of dialectic, rhetoric was subordinated to dialectic, while, in the tradition in which rhetoric was criticized and then transformed to theological uses, dialectic was subordinated to rhetoric. The fourth book of Boethius' *On Topical Differences*, which treats of the differences between dialectical and rhetorical places, was used as a textbook of rhetoric in the twelfth and thirteenth centuries, and two short treatises devoted to rhetorical places passed under his name, the *Speculatio de rhetoricae cognatione* (which is more probably a compilation derived from Book iv of *De differentiis topicis* than an independent work by Boethius)

24. Boethius refers to translations he has made of other books of the *Organon*, but no evidence has been found in medieval literature of their influence prior to the twelfth century; cf. C. H. Haskins, "Versions of Aristotle's *Posterior Analytics*," in his *Studies in the History of Mediaeval Science* (Cambridge, Mass., 1924), pp. 231 ff. For the rhetorical character and effects of the *De differentiis topicis* cf. Prantl, op. cit., I, 720–22.

and the *Locorum rhetoricorum distinctio*. Boethius finds the distinction between dialectic and rhetoric in their matter, use, and end: the matter of dialectic is "theses," that of rhetoric "hypotheses," and thesis and hypothesis are related as two kinds of "questions," the one universal, the other particularized to circumstances; dialectic uses interrogation and response, and its arguments are set forth in syllogisms; rhetoric uses continuous speech involving enthymemes; the end of dialectic is to force what one wishes from an adversary, that of rhetoric to persuade a judge.[25] Boethius takes over the early position of Cicero, as expressed in the *De inventione*, concerning the matter of rhetoric; but the whole question of end, function, and matter is raised in the context of a considerably longer list of questions, and in that context the other answers have changed. Boethius asks no fewer than nine questions about rhetoric: its genus, species, matter, parts, instrument, the parts of the instrument, the work and duty of the orator, and his end. The genus of rhetoric is no longer "civil science" (as it was for Cicero) but "faculty" (much as Aristotle had held it to be a δύναμις rather than a science). The matter of the faculty is all things suited to discourse, which, as Boethius puts it, is almost equivalent to the "civil question"; this matter of discourse is indeterminate until it is given specific form by the ends of rhetoric: the "civil question" is made into a judicial "cause" when the end considered is the just; into a deliberative "cause" when the end is the useful or the honorable; into a demonstrative "cause" when the end is the good. It is, as Isidore later observed, an elusive question, in which what one man considered the genus of an art can be transmuted by another into its matter; but that strange difference between the treatment of rhetoric as a faculty and as a social science is one of the slight remnants of the difference between Aristotle's conception of rhetoric and that of Cicero and the rhetoricians; and, from that remnant in Boethius' questions, medieval commentators were to reconstruct, with slowly increasing erudition, the full specifications of the old opposition.

25. *De differentiis topicis* iv (*PL*, LXIV, 1205–6). Cf. also ibid. i (*PL*, LXIV, 1177).

II

These were not technical questions which were discussed by a few learned men, but distinctions which entered into all parts of medieval culture and life. Christianity had grown up in the environment of a culture which was preponderantly rhetorical: indeed, the chief differences between Greek and Latin Christianity may be related to the differences between the Latin rhetoric of the Republic and early Empire (in which the arts and sciences had been put to the aid of rhetoric and civil philosophy had all but been reduced to the art of *forensic* pleading) and the Greek rhetoric of the Empire (in which philosophy itself had been displaced by display or *epideictic* rhetoric in the guise of sophistic, the rules of oratory had become the canons of literature, and Plato's and Aristotle's comparison of rhetoric and medicine had been made into a scientific method which rhetoric shared with medicine).[26] Since many of the

26. For Greek doctrinal developments which led to the opposition of civil and sophistic rhetoric and to the advancement now of one, now of the other, as the preferred or unique manner of rhetoric cf. C. Brandstaetter, "De notionum πολιτικὸς et σοφιστὴς usu rhetorico," *Leipziger Studien zur classischen Philologie*, V (1893), 128–274. For the oppositions of sophistic, rhetoric, and philosophy cf. H. von Arnim, *Leben und Werke des Dio von Prusa* (Berlin, 1898), pp. 4–114; H. M. Hubbell, "The Rhetorica of Philodemus," *Transactions of the Connecticut Academy of Arts and Sciences*, XXIII (September, 1920), 276–84; J. F. d'Alton, *Roman Literary Theory and Criticism* (London, 1931), pp. 153 ff. For the interpenetration of rhetoric and dialectic and the transformation of dialectic by rhetoric in Hellenistic and Roman thought cf. Prantl, op. cit., I, Abschnitt VIII, 505 ff. Philostratus includes in his *Lives of the Sophists* some of the ancient philosophers who approximated the rhetorical style of the Sophists, but he distinguished philosophy from sophistic (i. 481), since philosophers merely set snares for knowledge by their questioning but asserted that they had no sure knowledge, whereas Sophists of the old school professed knowledge of that whereof they spoke. Philostratus' enthusiastic account of the Sophists of the Empire is vivid indication of the spread and importance of epideictic rhetoric; its influence is likewise to be remarked in the Eastern church particularly among the Cappadocian fathers: cf. Norden, op. cit., II, 529 ff. and 550 ff.; T. C. Burgess, "Epideictic Literature," *University of Chicago Studies in Classical Philology*, III (1902), 89–251; L. Méridier, *L'Influence de la séconde sophistique sur l'oeuvre de Grégoire de Nysse* (Paris, 1906); M. Guignet, *Les Procédés épistolaires de St. Grégoire de Nazianze* (Paris, 1911); T. E. Ameringer, *The Stylistic Influence of the Second Sophistic on the Panegyrical Sermons of St. John Chrysostom* (Washington, 1921); J. M. Campbell, *The Influence of the Second Sophistic on the Style of the Sermons of St. Basil the Great* (Washington, 1922); A. Boulanger, *Aelius Aristide et la sophistique dans la province d'Asie au ii siècle de notre ère* (Paris, 1923). The crossing lines of rhetoric and medicine are apparent in Eunapius' *Lives of the Philosophers*; cf. particularly his accounts of Zeno of Cyprus, Magnus, Oribasius, and Ionicus (Secs. 497–99). Mag-

early converts who first wrote on Christian doctrine had been professional rhetoricians before their conversions,[27] the rhetorical distinctions which they used in the statement of their problems and the organization of their works emerged often as doctrinal differences and empirical observations in later speculation on their statements. This emergence of rhetoric in the materials of discussion in all fields brought new questions into the technical disputes of the art. The numerous technical distinctions which had entered the apparatus and discussion of rhetoric took on applications which echo or anticipate many of the positions of philosophers, which vary according to three conceptions of rhetoric distinguishable and in shifting opposition in their treatment of the materials to which rhetoric is applied.

Until the coming of the New Logic in the twelfth century, the pattern of that opposition is relatively simple: the rhetorician who professed to treat of subject matters accessible to the "common notions" of the mind, without need of technical competence, found himself opposed, on the one hand, by theologians who had learned from Augustine to use the distinction between words and things to attack the rhetoric of the schools while practicing a rhetoric devoted to divine eloquence and divine things, and, on the other hand, by rhetoricians who had learned from Boethius to use the distinction between thesis and hypothesis to limit rhetoric to probable reasoning concerning specifically delimited questions subordinate to the general questions of dialectic. To the Augustinian, the excessive use or extension of rhetoric or of dialectic was suspect; to the peripatetic follower of Boethius, limitation or criticism of dialectic, whether from the point of view of theology or of rhetoric, was an attack on

---

nus made a happy combination of rhetoric and medicine by persuading the patients of other doctors that they had not been cured and then restoring them to health, apparently also by talk and questions; Ionicus was master of philosophy and medicine as well as the arts of rhetoric and poetry. Cf. P. H. and E. A. De Lacy, *Philodemus: On Methods of Inference* (Philadelphia, 1941), pp. 130 ff., where the relations between medicine and rhetoric are discussed in terms of an "empirical" or "conjectural" method.

27. Cyprian (cf. Jerome *De viris illustribus* 67 [*PL*, XXIII, 714]), Arnobius (cf. Jerome *Chronicon* ad annum 329 [*PL*, XXVII, 675–76]), Lactantius (Jerome *Chronicon* ad annum 319 [*PL*, XXVII, 669–70]), Augustine (*Confessions* iv. 2. 2 [*PL*, XXXII, 693–94]). Most of the other early Christian writers in the West, even those who had not been teachers of rhetoric, had studied the art as part of their education.

the use of reason; and to the rhetorician, as such, limitation of rhetoric by the laws of logic or theology was unwarranted restriction of the scope of reason and visionary neglect of the practical exigencies of the problems of law and morals. The simple lines of this opposition appear even in the early discussions of rhetoric, and they are preserved after the appearance of the New Logic, beneath the surface of the more intricate distinctions made necessary by the Aristotelian differentiation of logic from dialectic, poetic, sophistic, and rhetoric. These three main positions with respect to rhetoric may be marked off into four historical periods during the Middle Ages, sharply distinguished by the authorities on which the discussion of the arts was successively based: a first stage extending to about the end of the tenth century, when the chief authorities were the pseudo-Augustine, Martianus Capella, Cassiodorus, and Isidore; a second period extending through the eleventh and the first half of the twelfth century, dominated by Cicero, Boethius, and the Old Logic; a third period comprising the latter part of the twelfth century and the greater part of the thirteenth century, in which the New Logic became to some degree effective and was applied after a manner in the interpretation of the Aristotelian corpus; and, finally, the fourteenth century and the Renaissance, in which Aristotle and the Greek rhetoricians, Cicero, Qintilian, and Boethius all had increasing influence.

During the first period, rhetoric was concerned—on the authority of Hermagoras, Cicero, and Boethius, of Fortunatianus, Augustine, and Victorinus, and of all the even more derivative authorities that depended on them—with civil philosophy.[28] According to Cassio-

28. Cf. Cicero *De inventione* i. 5. 6; *Ad Herennium* i. 2. 2; Boethius *De differentiis topicis* iv (*PL*, LXIV, 1207); Fortunatianus i. 1 (Halm, p. 81); pseudo-Augustine, *De rhetorica* 3 (Halm, p. 138); Fabius Laurentius Victorinus, *Explanationes in rhetoricam M. Tullii Ciceronis* i. 5 (Halm, p. 171). The authenticity of the *De rhetorica* attributed to Augustine was questioned by his Benedictine editors in 1679 (cf. *PL*, XXXII, 1439) and by most authorities since that time; cf. M. Gibert, *Jugemens des savans sur les auteurs qui ont traité de la rhétorique* (Paris, 1716), II, 98: "Mais pour peu qu'on connoisse le style du Saint, il est aisé de voir que l'Ouvrage n'est pas de lui"; and G. Saintsbury, *A History of Criticism and Literary Taste in Europe* (New York, 1900), I, 377. Its authenticity has been defended on philological grounds by W. Crecilinus, *S. Aurelii Augustini de dialectica liber* (Elberfeld, 1857), and by A. Reuter, "Zu dem Augustinischen fragment *De arte rhetorica*," in *Kirchengeschichtliche Studien Hermann Reuter . . . gewidmet* (Leipzig, 1888), pp. 324–41; but the arguments adduced have been answered by J. Žůrek (op. cit.). The pseudo-Augustine attributes the position taken by Fortunatianus to Hermagoras.

dorus, "The art of rhetoric is, as the masters of secular letters teach, the science of speaking well in civil questions"; and that definition is repeated in almost the same words by Isidore, Alcuin, and Rhabanus Maurus.[29] The occasion of the dialogue with Charlemagne in which Alcuin's doctrine is stated is a request made by the emperor for information concerning the art, since he thinks it ridiculous for one whose daily occupation is with civil questions to be ignorant of the precepts of the art; the dialogue, moreover, is frankly moral not only in its traditional title, *On Rhetoric and the Virtues*, but in purpose, since the transition from rhetoric to the virtues is accomplished by recognition that this "sermocinandi ratio" which is applied to civil cases and secular business must be supplemented by the other virtues. Yet, within this broad agreement among rhetoricians that rhetoric is concerned with civil questions, there are numerous differences of statement, which sometimes lead to changes in the devices thought proper to rhetoric and which seem often to entail major philosophic differences. The chief of these is the difference between the position (which seems to go back to Hermagoras and for which Fortunatianus is sometimes given as authority) which treats civil philosophy in terms of the "common notions" of mankind and therefore undertakes to differentiate the subject matter of rhetoric in terms of the questions treated, that is, the kinds of theses and hypotheses, and the position (which goes back to Cicero) which finds the subject matter of rhetoric in the three genera—deliberative, demonstrative, and judicial. The former has the effect of emphasizing the common bases of rhetoric in human knowledge while turning analyses to the peculiarities of the questions that can be asked, the other the effect of centering on the common qualities of the subject matter and directing inquiry to the peculiarities and virtues of the orator. The problems of rhetoric arise largely in the mixtures of the two traditions. Cassiodorus, citing Fortunatianus, defines civil questions as those which fall within the common conception of the mind, that is, which anyone can under-

29. Cassiodorus *Institutiones* ii. 2. 1 (Mynors, p. 97); cf. ii. Praef. 4 (Mynors, p. 91): "secundo de arte rhetorica, quae propter nitorem et copiam eloquentiae suae maxime in civilibus quaestionibus necessaria nimis et honorabilis aestimatur"; Isidore *Etymologiae* ii. 1 (Halm, p. 507); cf. i. 2. 1 and ii. 10, where law is treated as one of the subheads of rhetoric; Alcuin *De rhetorica et de virtutibus* 3 (Halm, p. 526); Rhabanus Maurus *De clericorum institutione* iii. 19 (*PL*, CVII, 396).

stand when it is a question of the equitable and the good; Sulpitius Victor as those which are proper to no art but common to the opinion of all; Alcuin as those learned questions which can be conceived by the natural power of the mind.[30] Victorinus, on the other hand, divides the possible matter of rhetoric into two kinds: that with which the art operates (*ubi fit*)—namely, deliberative, demonstrative, judicial—and that from which the art is formed (*unde fit*)—namely, the arguments which contribute the matter of those three kinds—then limits the consideration of rhetoric to the former and refutes Hermagoras' doctrine of thesis and hypothesis in favor of the Aristotelian and Ciceronian doctrine of the three genera.[31] Martianus Capella repeats this differentiation of two kinds of matter but goes on to the exposition of theses and hypotheses, confining his disapproval to a remark concerning the extremely subtle reasons of some of the sectaries of rhetoric who hold that all rhetorical questions are general or theses.[32] The difference is between a tendency to make distinctions with reference to a subject matter and arguments suited to that subject matter and a tendency to make distinctions—often, indeed, the same distinctions—with reference to the orator and his problems of discovering and stating arguments. The former emphasis tends to intellectualize the art and change its orientation to a subject matter and its peculiarities into problems of inquiry and understanding, as when Sulpitius Victor, having limited rhetoric to the civil question and having divided the civil question into two parts, thesis and hypothesis, finds three duties for the orator—understanding, discovery, and disposition (the first of which was neglected by Cicero but was adequately treated by the Greeks)—and then three genera of causes in the place of those long customary—the ethical, pathetic, and judicial. The latter emphasis leads to a series of questions, which were much discussed during the Middle Ages, concerning the relation of morals and eloquence, concerning the relation of art and wisdom, and concerning the defini-

30. *Institutiones* ii. 2. 1 (Mynors, p. 97); cf. Fortunatianus i. 1 (Halm, p. 81) and the pseudo-Augustine (*De rhetorica* 4 [Halm, p. 139]), who supplies the Greek term κοινὴ ἔννοια suggestive of Stoic origins. Sulpitius Victor *Institutiones oratoriae* (Halm, p. 314) and Alcuin *De rhetorica et de virtutibus* 3 (Halm, p. 526).

31. Fabius Laurentius Victorinus 5 (Halm, pp. 174–77).

32. Martianus Capella 5 (Halm, p. 454).

tion of rhetoric as a virtue or an art or a discipline.[33] Rhetoric was to come into conflict with dialectic as a consequence of this tendency, as it was to come into conflict with theology as a consequence of its tendency to annex the problems of morals and the interpretation of Scripture. Since its discipline was gradually limited by the transfer of the commonplaces, definition, and, finally, proof—even in the rhetorical formulations they had received from Cicero, Victorinus, and Boethius—to the domain of dialectic and since its subject matter was limited by the transfer of moral and political questions to theology, rhetoric developed during its second period along three separate lines: as a part of logic, or as the art of stating truths certified by theology, or as a simple art of words.

III

The subordination of rhetoric to logic was based usually on the greater particularity of its subject matter, that is, its concern with hypotheses rather than with theses. The terms of the discussion of the relation of rhetoric to dialectic were borrowed from Boethius. The doctrine is expressed, however, before the appearance of Boethius in the curriculum of the schools. According to Isidore of Seville, logic (Isidore adds that the Greek term λόγος means "rational") has two parts, dialectic and rhetoric.[34] John the Scot omits grammar and rhetoric from his treatise *On the Division of Nature*, first, because many philosophers think they are parts of

33. Sulpitius Victor *Institutiones oratoriae* 4 and 6 (Halm, pp. 315, 316). Cato's definition of the orator as *vir bonus dicendi peritus* (Quintilian xii. 1; Seneca *Controversiarum* i, Praef. 9) was frequently repeated before the Carolingian period—by Fortunatianus, Victorinus, Cassiodorus, Isidore (Halm, pp. 81, 177, 495, 507)—and one of the favorite etymologies of "art" derived it from the Greek word for virtue. In the twelfth century Aristotle's authority (cited from the *Categories*) is used to deny that rhetoric is a virtue (cf. Abailard *Dialogus* [*PL*, CLXXVIII, 1652]; Hermannus *Epitome theologiae Christianae* [*PL*, CLXXVIII, 1750]; *Sententie Parisienses*, ed. A. Landgraf, *Écrits théologiques de l'école d'Abélard* [Louvain, 1934], p. 52). In the thirteenth century Aristotle's authority (cited from the *Nicomachean Ethics*) could be quoted to place it, together with the other arts, among the intellectual virtues. In the Renaissance, one of the chief grounds for Ramus' violent criticism of Quintilian is found in his tendency to identify rhetoric with morals (cf. P. Ramus, *Rhetoricae distinctiones in Quintilianum* [Paris, 1559]).

34. *De differentiis rerum* 39 (*PL*, LXXXIII, 93–94).

dialectic; second, from considerations of brevity; and, finally, because, unlike dialectic, grammar and rhetoric do not treat of the nature of things but either of words significant by convention or of special causes and persons.[35] The pseudo-Rhabanus Maurus was one of the philosophers who divided logic into three parts: grammar, rhetoric, and dialectic,[36] and Remigius of Auxerre divides philosophers into four kinds: dialecticians, rhetoricians, Sophists who always come to false conclusions, and jurists who dispute concerning the status of law.[37] Gerbert, who used all the dialectical works and translations of Boethius in his teaching at Rheims and Paris (including Cicero's *Topics*, which, like Cassiodorus, he thought Cicero had translated from the Greek, and the *On Definition* of Marius Victorinus), likewise considered dialectic and rhetoric parts of logic and taught rhetoric after dialectic.[38] Fulbert, finally, who restored studies at Chartres in the eleventh century and who knew, in ad-

35. *De divisione naturae* v. 4 (*PL*, CXXII, 869–70): "Primum quidem, quia ipsae duae artes veluti quaedam membra Dialecticae multis philosophis non incongrue existimantur. Deinde brevitatis occasione. Postremo, quod non de rerum natura tractare videntur, sed vel de regulis humanae vocis, quam non secundum naturam, sed secundum consuetudinem loquentium subsistere Aristotles cum suis sectatoribus approbat, vel de causis atque personis specialibus, quod longe a natura rerum distat. Nam dum Rhetorica de communibus locis, qui ad naturam rerum pertinent, tractare nititur, non suas, sed Dialecticae arripit partes." Rhetoric is limited to hypotheses or finite questions determined by the seven circumstances, while the common conceptions of the mind have become the property of dialectic; cf. *De divisione naturae* i. 27 (*PL*, CXXII, 475): "Rhetorica est finitam causam persona, materia, occasione, qualitate, loco, tempore, facultate discutiens copiose atque ornate disciplina; breviterque definiri potest, Rhetorica est finitae causae septem periochis sagax et copiosa disciplina. Dialectica est communium animi conceptionum rationabilium diligens investigatrixque disciplina."

36. V. Cousin, *Ouvrages inédits d'Abélard* (Paris, 1836), p. 614.

37. B. Hauréau, "Commentaire de Jean Scot Erigène sur Martianus Capella," *Notices et extraits des manuscrits de la Bibliothèque Impériale*, XX, No. 2 (1862), 11. Cf. ibid., pp. 20–21, for his difference from the doctrine of John concerning the natural bases of rhetoric in human nature.

38. The sequence of studies, as directed by Gerbert, were: first, dialectic, which included the *Isagoge* of Porphyry (with Boethius' commentary), the *Categories* and *On Interpretation* of Aristotle, the *Topics* (translated by Cicero and with Boethius' commentary), Boethius' *On Topical Differences*, *On Categorical Syllogisms*, *On Hypothetical Syllogisms*, *On Definitions*, *On Divisions*; second, as preparation for rhetoric, the poets; third, rhetoric; finally, sophistic. He includes the entire program under the term "logic" (Richer, *Historiae*, III, 44ff. (ed. G. H. Pertz, *Monumenta Germaniae historica*, Vol. V: *Scriptores*, III, 617).

dition to the *De inventione* and the *Ad Herennium*, Victorinus' commentary on Cicero and the two treatises on rhetorical places attributed to Boethius, has left twenty-one verses on the differences between rhetoric and dialectic: they are the three differences that Boethius found between the matters, uses, and ends of the arts.[39]

The transition to the third period in this tradition of rhetoric determined relatively to dialectic is accomplished when the increased influence, or at least the increased repute, of the New Logic led to separation of scientific or demonstrative proof from probable proof and to the location of rhetoric with dialectic under the latter. It is a gradual transition, dependent as much on increase of erudition in logic as in rhetoric. In the comprehensive collection of texts in the liberal arts prepared by Thierry of Chartres under the title *Heptateuchon* about 1141, all of Aristotle's *Organon* except the *Posterior Analytics* and the second book of the *Prior Analytics* appears, while under rhetoric are included (in addition to the traditional sources of rhetoric—the *De inventione*, the *Ad Herennium*, and Martianus Capella—and Cicero's *Topics*, which with Boethius' *De differentiis topicis* is classified under dialectic) only Cicero's *De partitione oratoria* and Julius Severianus' *Precepts on the Art of Rhetoric*.[40] Yet Thierry of Chartres wrote a commentary on the *De inventione* in which a history of rhetoric is reconstructed to explain the opening paragraph of Cicero's work as a refutation of Plato and Aristotle: Plato had argued that rhetoric was no art, Aristotle that it was an art but a bad art, while Cicero contends, against both, that it is a good art.[41] A short Preface and an Introduction precede the fragment of the *Commentary* which has been preserved. The Introduction is devoted to asking ten questions concerning rhetoric—its genus, definition, matter, duty, end, parts, species, instrument, who the orator is, and why the art is so called—to which two specific questions are added—the intention of Tully in this work

39. A. Clerval, *Les Écoles de Chartres au moyen-âge* (Chartres, 1895), p. 115.

40. Ibid., pp. 222–23; cf. R. McKeon, "Aristotelianism in Western Christianity," in J. T. McNeill (ed.), *Environmental Factors in Christian History* (Chicago, 1939), pp. 215–19.

41. *Fragmentum scholiastae inediti ad Ciceronem De inventione rhetorica* (W. H. D. Suringar, *Historia critica scholiastarum Latinorum* [Leyden, 1834], I, 213–53), pp. 224–36. Thierry's reading in works of rhetoric was apparently more extensive than the contents of the *Heptateuchon*, since he quotes Quintilian (ibid., p. 219).

and the utility of the work. The genus of rhetoric is still civil science, it is not a part of logic, and its matter is hypothesis.[42] Nor is the position of Thierry an anachronistic piece of conservatism, for one of the works which was most influential in preparing the way for the new knowledge of the thirteenth century and which was eagerly consulted as a source of information concerning the Arabic learning, the *De divisione philosophiae* of Gundissalinus, contains a section on rhetoric which not merely asks the same ten questions as Thierry of Chartres but is identical, apart from slight variations, with the Introduction to his *Commentary*.[43] Gundissalinus differs

42. Ibid., p. 217: "Genus igitur artis rhetoricae est qualitas ipsius artificii secundum ejus effectum: hoc autem est, quod ipsum artificium est, pars civilis scientiae major. Nam civilis ratio dicitur quidquid civitas aut rationabiliter dicit aut agit; dicimus enim: ratio est hoc vel illud facere vel dicere. Item civilis ratio dicitur, scientia dicendi aliquid rationabiliter et faciendi. Et haec quidem ratio, scientia civilis dicitur, cujus quidem pars integra, vel etiam major, rhetorica est. Nam sapientia i.e. rerum conceptio secundum earum naturam, et rhetorica civilem scientiam componunt. Et enim nisi quis sapiens et eloquens fuerit, civilem scientiam habere non dicitur. Major vero pars civilis scientiae dicitur rhetorica, quoniam magis operatur in civilibus causis quam sapientia, etsi sine sapientia nihil prosit. Maximam enim virtutem habet eloquentia in civitate, si sapientiae juncta sit." Thierry then goes on to compare this solution with Boethius' doctrine that the genus of rhetoric is *facultas* and finds the two doctrines in agreement, since the same science is an *art* in the master who teaches its rules and a *faculty* in the orator. He is explicit in excluding rhetoric from logic: "Non est autem dicendum, rhetoricam aut logicam esse aut ejus partem, idcirco quod logica circa thesin solam i.e. circa genera agendi, tantummodo versatur." Cf. ibid., p. 219 for *materia*. Cf. Adelard of Bath, *De eodem et diverso* in *Beiträge zur Geschichte der Philosophie des Mittelalters* (henceforth cited as "*BGPM*"), IV, No. 1, 19ff.

43. Dominicus Gundissalinus *De divisione philosophiae*, ed. L. Baur (*BGPM*, IV, Nos. 2–3 [Münster, 1903], 63–69). For the strange history of scholarly inquiries into the commentary of Thierry cf. M. Grabmann, "Eine lateinische Übersetzung der psuedo-Aristotelischen Rhetorica ad Alexandrum aus dem 13. Jahrhundert," *Sitzungsberichte der Bayerischen Akademie der Wissenschaften, Phil.-hist. Abt.* (1931–32), No. 4, pp. 4–5. In spite of the fact that it was published by Suringar in 1834, the fragmentary *Commentary* was discussed as an unpublished document by Rohde in 1881, by Bücheler in 1883, and by Thomas in 1884; its author was supposed to have been a contemporary of Theodoric the Great until Thomas suggested that the document was medieval (and consequently of very little interest); finally, Manitius identified it as the work of Thierry or Theodoric of Chartres, and Klibansky pointed out its identity with the work published by Suringar. Grabmann does not notice that there is one further coincidence, viz., the identity of one of the three sections (Suringar, op. cit., pp. 216–23) with the section on rhetoric in Gundissalinus. Short of examination of the manuscripts—unfortunately impossible at this time—the question of priority is difficult to decide: some of the sections contained in Thierry but omitted by Gundissalinus seem rather in the nature of additions to, than omissions

slightly from Thierry in the classification of rhetoric; for, whereas Thierry would have it a part of civil science and not a part of logic, Gundissalinus classifies both rhetoric and poetic among the eight parts of logic, but he also classifies rhetoric and poetic as parts of civil science.[44]

Hugh of St. Victor, who was contemporary with Thierry of Chartres, follows the suggestion of the Aristotelian division of the sciences into theoretic, practical, and mechanical (which seems to be Hugh's substitute for Aristotle's productive science): logic is a fourth branch and not a part of politics, which falls under the practical sciences. Moreover, his classification of logic makes an excellent transition from the customary classification according to the trivium of grammar, rhetoric, and dialectic to the "Aristotelian" classification as parts of logic and according to the kinds of proof. Following Isidore of Seville, Hugh points out the double etymology of λόγος, i.e., *sermo* and *ratio*, and argues that logic can be called either a verbal or a rational science (*sermocinalis sive rationalis scientia*); rational logic (which Hugh also calls *dissertiva*) is divided into dialectic and rhetoric, while verbal logic is the genus of grammar, dialectic, and rhetoric, and therefore rational logic is con-

---

from, an original text, and the references seem better suited to the *Commentary* than to the *De divisione philosophiae* (as, e.g., where Thierry says [p. 220]: "Sed quid sit circumstantia, in sequentibus melius dicetur," Gundissalinus says [p. 66]: "Set quid sit circumstancia in Tullio dicetur," although no further reference is made to Cicero on this point); on the other hand, the supposition that the work of Thierry was prior runs into the grave difficulty that all the sciences in the *De divisione philosophiae* are treated by means of the same ten questions here applied to rhetoric.

44. This section on the genus of rhetoric in Gundissalinus (p. 64) is the same as the statement quoted above (n. 43) from Thierry, but stops short before the discussion of Boethius and the statement that rhetoric is not a part of logic. In the section on logic, Gundissalinus cites Alfarabi for the eight parts of logic (p. 71): "Secundum Alfarabium octo sunt partes logice: cathegorie, perihermenias, analetica priora, analectica posteriora, thopica, sophistica, rhetorica, poetica." He need not have gone to the Arabs for this doctrine, for the equivalent of the six books of Aristotle's *Organon* plus rhetoric and poetic constituted the logic taught by Gerbert (cf. above, n. 39). Gundissalinus gives as the genus of logic that it is a part and instrument of philosophy (p. 69) and denies that its matter is "thesis," arguing that it is the second intention of the understanding (pp. 70–71). The genus of poetic is the same as rhetoric (p. 54): "Genus huius artis [*sc.* poeticae] est, quod ipsa est pars ciuilis sciencie, que est pars eloquencie. Non enim parum operatur in ciuilibus, quod delectat uel edificat in sciencia uel in moribus."

tained under it.[45] This treatment of the traditional trivium is supplemented, however, by another division of logic into grammar and *ratio disserendi* or "dissertive" logic, which is concerned with words as understood (*de vocibus secundum intellectus*). "Dissertive" or rational logic is, in turn, divided into integral parts, i.e., parts shared by its kinds, which turn out to be the Ciceronian distinction into discovery and judgment, and divisive parts, i.e., demonstrative, probable, and sophistic; the two parts of probable proof are dialectic and rhetoric.[46] John of Salisbury, one of the pupils of Thierry of Chartres, who had studied the whole of Aristotle's *Organon* and who was widely read in Cicero and Quintilian, attributes to Plato the division of logic into dialectic and rhetoric; but he prefers, as more philosophic, the division into demonstrative, probable, and sophistic, with the further division of probable into dialectic and rhetoric.[47] William of Conches, on the other hand, whom John calls the finest grammarian after Bernard of Chartres,[48] divides eloquence, which the ancients called "logic," into grammar, *ratio disserendi*, and rhetoric.[49]

45. *Didascalicon* i. 11, ed. C. H. Buttimer (Washington, 1939), pp. 20–21; or i. 12 (*PL*, CLXXVI, 749–50). Cf. Isidore of Seville *Etymologiae* ii. 24. 7.

46. *Didascalicon* ii. 28–30; Buttimer, pp. 44–47; or ii. 29–31 (*PL*, CLXXVI, 763–66).

47. *Metalogicon* ii. 3, ed. C. C. J. Webb (Oxford, 1929), pp. 64–65. Baldwin complains (op. cit., p. 157) that rhetoric is barely mentioned in the *Metalogicon* and seems "to have no distinctive composing function"; the few references which he finds indicate that he was looking for rhetoric before the treatment of logic, whereas John treats it under the *Topics*. Cf. *Metalogicon* iii. 5 (Webb, p. 139), and esp. 10 (Webb, pp. 154–55): "Quia ergo exercitatio dialectice ad alterum est; pares, quos producit et quos rationibus muniuit et locis, sua docet arma tractare et sermones potius conserere quam dexteras, et tanta cautela imbuit, ut totius eloquentie precepta hinc tracta principaliter, uelut a primitiuo fonte originis sue, manare perspicuum sit. Indubitanter enim uerum est, quod fatentur Cicero et Quintilianus, quia hinc non modo rethoricorum adiumentum, sed et principium rethores et scriptores artium assumpserunt; postmodum tamen propriis dilatata est institutis." The matter of dialectic is still the "question" as distinguished from the "hypothesis," which is the matter of rhetoric (*Metalogicon* ii. 12 [Webb, pp. 83–84]).

48. *Metalogicon* i. 5 (Webb, pp. 16–17): "Willelmus de Conchis, grammaticus post Bernardum Carnotensem opulentissimus."

49. C. Ottaviano, *Un Brano inedito della "Philosophia" di Guglielmo di Conches* (Naples, 1935), p. 28.

IV

The translations of Aristotle affected the discussions of theology as well as philosophy, and the changes in rhetoric and in the relations of rhetoric to dialectic are reflected in the methods of theology. "Aristotelian" conceptions of the organization of logic with rhetoric as one of its parts were not, however, intruded into theology, since the opposition was between the Augustinian conception of a single body of theological and philosophic truth possessed of a single method and the conception of a philosophy independent in method and subject matter from theology; and therefore the simple organization of the trivium as three rational or verbal sciences continued in theology and even in philosophy under the influence of Augustine long after it became obsolete in the philosophy influenced by Aristotle. Even as early as the sixth century, when Cassiodorus wrote his *Expositio in Psalterium*, he could appeal, in his introductory chapters, "On the Eloquence of the Whole Divine Law" and "On the Proper Eloquence of the Psalter," to an impressive list of learned Fathers—Augustine, Jerome, Ambrose, Hilary—who had studied both the figures which are common to sacred and secular letters and the proper modes of divine speech which are not touched by grammarians or rhetoricians.[50] Divine eloquence is not formed of human words or involved in human ambiguities, but, since its purpose is to spread divine law to all the corners of the world, it makes many uses of modes of speech, and it is "succinct with definitions, adorned with figures, marked by the propriety of words, expedited by the constructions of syllogisms"; and, while these devices are certain and clear in the Scriptures, they stand in need of the liberal arts when they come into contact with the opinions and disputes of men.[51] His commentary consists largely of such

50. *Expositio in Psalterium*, Praef. xv (*PL*, CLXX, 21).

51. *Expositio in Psalterium* 19: "Eloquentia legis divinae humanis non est formata sermonibus, neque confusis incerta fertur ambagibus, ut aut a rebus praeteritis oblivione discedat, aut praesentium confusione turbetur, aut futurorum dubiis casibus eludatur; sed cordi, non corporalibus auribus loquens, magna veritate, magna praescientiae firmitate cuncta dijudicans, auctoris sui veritate consistit. . . .Eloquentia siquidem est ad unamquamque rem competens et decora locutio." Cf. ibid. 20: "Haec mundanarum artium periti, quos tamen multo posterius ab exordio divinorum libro-

aids to understanding, dotted with identifications of kinds of definition, figures of speech, and forms of arguments.[52] The evolution of this use of rhetoric consists, primarily, in the increasing formalization of the methods of interpreting Scipture and the rules of divine eloquence and, secondarily, in the recurrent application of the secular art to Scripture and the recurrent expressions of concern at the excesses of the liberal arts in such application. In the one line of development, Augustine's simple suggestion that things as well as words are signs was elaborated until the spiritual sense, which balanced the literal sense, was divided into three kinds—the allegorical, the moral, and the anagogic; and this theological development of rhetoric eventually, in turn, influenced mundane or poetic rhetoric.[53] In the other line of development, more suspect of

rum extitisse manifestum est, ad collectiones argumentorum, quae Graeci topica dicunt, et ad artem dialecticam et rhetoricam transtulerunt; ut cunctis evidenter appareat, prius ad exprimendam veritatem justis mentibus datum, quod postea gentiles humanae sapientiae aptandam esse putaverunt. Haec in lectionibus sacris tanquam clarissima sidera relucent, et significantias rerum utilissimis compendiis decenter illuminant."

52. Cf. *Expositio in Psalterium* i (*PL*, CLXX, 27), for identification of two kinds of definition according to the technical terms of Victorinus; (*PL*, CLXX, 33), where the figure is explained by means of the mathematical disciplines; vi. 1 (*PL*, CLXX, 61), where the fashion in which the divine eloquence has been enriched by the various arts and disciplines is illustrated by discussion of rhetorical *status*; xliii, 15 (*PL*, CLXX, 314), where the figure of *anaphora* is identified, and so *passim*.

53. Cf. Augustine *De utilitate credendi* 3, 5 (*PL*, XLII, 68) (historical, etiological, analogical, allegorical, senses); Gregory the Great *Moralia, epistola Missoria* (*PL*, LXXV, 510–15) (historical, allegorical, moral); Peter Abailard *Expositio in Hexaemeron* (*PL*, CLXXVIII, 731) (historical, moral, and mystic); Hugh of St. Victor *De sacramentis, Prologus* 4 (*PL*, CLXXVI, 184) (historical, allegorical, tropological); and Peter of Poitier *Allegoriae super Tabernaculum Moysi, Prologus*, ed. P. S. Moore and J. A. Corbett (Notre Dame, 1938), p. 1 (historical, allegorical, moral, anagogic); cf. P. S. Moore, *The Works of Peter of Poitiers* (Notre Dame, 1936), pp. 65–77. Cf. Thomas Aquinas *Summa theologica* i. q. 1, a. 10: "Respondeo dicendum quod auctor sacrae Scripturae est Deus, in cujus potestate est ut non solum voces ad significandum accommodet (quod etiam homo facere potest) sed etiam res ipsas. Et ideo, cum in omnibus scientiis voces significent, hoc habet proprium ista scientia quod ipsae res significatae per voces, etiam significant aliquid." The first of these significations is historical or literal, the second (in which things signify other things) spiritual, and the spiritual interpretation is further divided into allegorical, moral, and anagogic. Dante follows the division of Aquinas; cf. *Epistola X Domino Cani Grandi de Scala* vii. 98–116; *Convivio* ii. 1 (cf. ibid. 14 for rhetoric). The "four senses" are also used to explain the "form of wisdom" (cf. Bonaventura *In Hexaemeron, Collatio ii* [*Opera omnia*, ed. Quaracchi (1891), V, 336–42], i.e., uniform, multiform [allegorical, anagogic, tropological, each of which has two forms], omniform, and nulliform) and

error and more frequently condemned in one form by conservative theologians who practiced it in another form, which they found indispensable to the understanding of Scripture, rhetoric supplied devices to clarify the meanings and remove the ambiguities of scriptural statements. Abailard begins his *Commentary on the Epistle of St. Paul to the Romans* with the statement: "The intention of all divine Scripture is to teach or to move in the manner of a rhetorical speech," and derives his triple division of the Old and New Testaments from these two purposes.[54] The divine pages cannot be read and appreciated without grammar and rhetoric.[55] An anonymous commentary on Romans repeats Abailard's statement of the twofold rhetorical purpose of the Old and New Testament, after having specified that all the arts are servants to divinity: grammar, which teaches constructions; dialectic, which expounds by arguments; and rhetoric, which consists in persuasion.[56] Even theologians who, like Robert of Melun, opposed the excessive use of rhetoric in secular as well as in divine letters, repeated the same judgment of the rhetorical purposes of Scripture.[57]

---

to classify the sciences (cf. M. Grabmann, *Die Geschichte der scholastischen Methode* [Freiburg i/Br., 1911], II, 43, n. 1, where a quotation is given from an unpublished manuscript, dated broadly as posterior to Hugh of St. Victor, in which the sciences are divided into theoretic, practical, and logical; practical science, in turn, is divided into actual [ethics, economics, and politics] and inspective, which is divided into *historia* and *spiritualis intelligentia*; history simply states the order of things without any hidden meaning apparent from that conveyed by the words; the spiritual understanding is divided into the tropological, allegorical, and anagogic. Rational logic is divided into dialectic, apodictic [or demonstrative], and sophistic). Bonaventura also uses these distinctions as the fourfold division in the "light of sacred Scripture" (*De reductione artium ad theologiam* 5 [*Opera omnia*, V, 321]).

54. *Commentaria super S. Pauli Epistolam ad Romanos*, Prologus (*PL*, CLXXVIII, 783–84).

55. *Introductio ad theologiam* ii. 2 (*PL*, CLXXVIII, 1044): "At jam profecto nec grammaticam a Christiano legi convenit, sine documentis cujus nec divina intelligi pagina, nec scriptura aliqua. Sic nec rhetoricam, quae omnis eloquentiae tradit ornamenta, quibus maxime sacra Scriptura est referta, nec ejus decor nisi his diligenter assignatis elucere poterit."

56. *Commentarius Cantabrigiensis in Epistolas Pauli e Schola Petri Abaelardi: In Epistolam ad Romanos*, ed. A. Landgraf (Notre Dame, 1937), pp. 1–2.

57. Grabmann, *Die Geschichte der scholastischen Methode*, II, 349, n. 2. H. Denifle, *Die abendländischen Schriftausleger bis Luther über "Justitia" (Rom. 1. 17) und "Justificatio"* (Mainz, 1905), p. 76: "Ad erudicionem autem ipsius omnes scripture facte sunt, quarum partes sunt tam sacre scripture, quam ethnice. In ethnicis enim,

The method of rhetoric was, moreover, put to another and even more characteristic use in the interpretation of theological doctrine. The "scholastic method," as it came to be called, grew out of the assemblage of "sentences," which derived their name and their initial methods of treatment from rhetoric.[58] The early collections of canon law were collections of authorities—statements from Scripture, decisions of councils, decretals, opinions of the Fathers—which, because of the practical problems involved in direction of action, presented urgently the problem of bringing discordant or apparently discordant canons into concordance. When Peter Abailard assembled apparently contradictory texts in his *Sic et non*, the rules for interpreting them which he set forth in the Prologue are developments of the rules elaborated by a long line of canon lawyers—notably Hincmar of Rheims, Bernold of Constance, Ivo of Chartres—and involve such directions as careful consideration of context; comparison of texts; specification of time, place, and person; determination of original cause of statement; and differentiation of general measures from particular.[59] Although this method led to a further step in the dialectical resolution of the contradictions, the method at this stage is rhetorical rather than dialectical. The rules of interpretation of the Prologue of the *Sic et non*, thus, approximate the performance of Abailard's *Commentary on Romans*, which is grammatical and rhetorical; but the texts such as those assembled there serve him as a storehouse of quotations for

id est gentilibus, scripturis et sermonum compositio et rerum proprietas docet. Sermonum composicio in trivio, rerum proprietas in mathematicis disciplinis secundum extrinseca et intrinseca. . . . Intencionem vero more rethorice oracionis docere et monere."

58. Cf. G. Paré, A. Burnet, and P. Tremblay, *La Renaissance du XIIe siècle: Les Écoles et l'enseignement* (Ottawa, 1933), pp. 267 ff., for an excellent statement of the rhetorical beginnings of the *sententiae*.

59. Ibid. 286 ff., where, however, the method is stated as dialectical. Cf. Grabmann, *Die Geschichte der scholastischen Methode*, I, 234 ff., and P. Fournier and G. Le Bras, *Histoire des collections canoniques en occident* (Paris, 1932), II, 334 ff. In the more orthodox tradition, theology derived its customary organization, indirectly from rhetoric, in Augustine's division of all doctrine into problems of things and problems of signs (cf. P. Lombard, *Sententiarum liber* i, dist. 1, cap. 1). The other distinction which Augustine makes at the beginning of the *De doctrina Christiana*, of all treatment of the Scriptures into the mode of discovery and the mode of statement, served as basis of organization of treatises on preaching (cf. Bonaventura *Ars concionandi* [*Opera omnia*, IX, 8]).

his systematic works, the *Theologia "summi boni,"* the *Theologia Christiana,* and the *Introductio ad theologiam,* in which the method which Abailard calls "dialectical" is used to resolve their differences, not by consideration of contexts and circumstances, but by reduction to an orderly body of true propositions. The difference, far from being slight, was to grow into one of the marks of differentiation between the line of Christian theology which adapted itself to the Aristotelian philosophy and made use of logic and dialectic and the line of Christian theology and philosophy which continued the distinction of the trivium and subordinated dialectic to rhetoric. One of the numerous admirers of Abailard, who tried to remove the taint of unorthodoxy from his doctrines, made that readjustment by shifting the functions of the arts, assigning to grammar a concern with meanings, to dialectic the production of conviction, and to rhetoric, finally, the motivation of the will.[60] This is a doctrine, moreover, which need suffer no opprobrium because of its connection with Abailard, since the same domination of the trivium by rhetoric is expressed, partly in the same words, by Bernard Sylvester, the friend of Thierry of Chartres, in his commentary on Virgil's *Aeneid,* a context which seems safe from the danger of heresy.[61]

60. [Anonymous] *Ysagoge in theologiam,* ed. A. Landgraf, op. cit., p. 72: "Eloquentia vero est scientia ad congruam agnitorum prolationem suum formans artificem. Que, quia triplicem habet efficatiam, tres habet partes, respondentque efficatie partibus ut effectus causis. Est enim prima grammatica, que pertinet ad intellectum; secunda dialectica, que ad fidem; tertia rethorica, que ad persuasionem. Quod enim prima vocum attendit accidentia, ideo fit, ut secundum ea competens fiat earum contextus ad manifestandum conceptum loquentis vel ad constituendum consimilem in auditore. Sed quia, si pulsetur de veritate, intellectus, quem indicat et constituit, nequit fidem facere, succedit dialectica, que acceptis orationibus a prima componit ex eis argumentationem, qua fidem confert. Sed quia possumus intelligere et intellectum credere et tamen illud nolle, consummationem dat rethorica. Hec enim accipiens argumentaciones a logica, ut illa orationes a grammatica, ex eis per orationem [*read* perorationem] facit et, quod prima intelligere, secunda credere, ipsa facit velle."

61. *Commentum Bernardi Silvestris super sex libros Eneidos Virgilii* vi, ed. G. Riedel (Gryphiswaldae, 1924), p. 31: "Eloquentia est scientia formans suum lectorem ad congruam cognitorum prolationem. Haec autem Trivia dicitur quia [a] tribus artibus quasi tribus viis ad eam incedimus. Ut autem perfecte habeatur eloquentia, primo oportet scire loqui absque soloecismo et barbarismo quod per grammaticam habetur. Deinde sic loquendo oportet scire aliquid probare vel improbare quod fit per dialecticam. Adhuc necessarium [oportet] persuadere vel dissuadere: possunt

The two general tendencies which came to their culmination in the thirteenth century, that by which rhetoric was made part of logic and that by which rhetoric became an instrument of theology, are determined by the important methodological differences which separate the Aristotelians and the Augustinians. For Thomas Aquinas rhetoric is one of the parts of logic concerned with probable argumentation; for Bonaventura rhetoric is the culmination of the trivium. Thomas wrote a commentary on two books of Aristotle's *Organon*, and, since he separated the method and subject of the philosophic from those of the theological truth, he could use the devices of Aristotle in the a posteriori proofs of his systematic theology and those of Augustine in his commentaries on Scripture; Bonaventura wrote no work on logic but did compose an excellent *Art of Preaching*, which is useful for the interpretation of his theological treatises and commentaries as well as his sermons.

The translation of the whole of the *Nicomachean Ethics* (which was called the "New Ethics" in contrast to the truncated earlier translation) brought to further refinement the solution of questions concerning the relation of rhetoric to civil questions: according to

---

enim auditores grammatica oratione aliquid intelligere, dialectica probatione de eodem certi esse et tamen illud nolle: ideo necessaria rethorica persuasio. Itaque est grammatica initium eloquentiae, dialectica dicitur provectus, rethorica perfectio. Atque adeo dicitur eloquentia Trivia." Cf. also ibid., pp. 36, 38, 87–88. It would easily be possible to attach too much significance to the order in which the arts of the trivium are enumerated; yet many of the enumerations of the twelfth and thirteenth centuries underline the importance of the order; and even before that time authors tend to a consistency in their enumerations, which suggests that some degree of importance was attached to the enumeration. Dialectic appears third in the lists of Cassiodorus (*Institutiones* ii, Praef.; Mynors, p. 91), Isidore (*Etymologiae* i. 2), Alcuin (*Grammatica* [*PL*, CI, 853]: "Sunt igitur gradus, quos quaeritis, et utinam tam ardentes sitis semper ad ascendendum quam curiosi modo estis ad videndum: grammatica, rhetorica, dialectica . . ."), Rhabanus Maurus (*De clericorum institutione* iii. 18 [*PL*, CVII, 395]: "Prima ergo liberalium artium est grammatica, secunda rhetorica, tertia dialectica . . ."). Rhetoric is third in Augustine (*De ordine* ii. 13 [*PL*, XXXII, 1013]), Martianus Capella, and Gerbert. After the eleventh century the tendency is either to place the trivium, together with demonstration and sophistic, under logic or to list the three with rhetoric in the dominant position. The rule is far from being universal; e.g., Adelard of Bath, who was strongly influenced by the Platonism of Chartres, places dialectic third in his allegory (*De eodem et diuerso* [*BGPM*, IV, No. 1, 21]).

Aquinas, the matter with which rhetoric is concerned is civil,[62] but rhetoric must not be confused with politics.[63] In much the same fashion the terminology and conclusions of the earlier rhetorical discussion enter into Thomas' classification of the parts of logic. The parts of logic or rational science or rational philosophy are determined by the diversity of the acts of reason: they are three of which the first is an act of immediate understanding and the last two are acts of reason. The first is the operation of the mind called (by Averroës) "information of understanding" or "imagination through understanding"; the doctrine which Aristotle treats in the *Categories* is ordered to this act of reason. The second is the operation of composition and division, which results in truth or falsity; the doctrine which Aristotle treats in the *De interpretatione* is concerned with this act of reason. Finally, the third act, which is the proper function of reason, is discursive movement from one thing to another, from something known to the unknown: the remaining four books of the *Organon* are concerned with this operation of reason. It may take any of three forms in conformity to a threefold diversity in nature: in some cases nature acts from necessity without the possibility of divergence; in some cases it operates for the most part in a certain way but with the possibility of deviation from its proper act; and there are therefore, in addition to necessary operations, two additional kinds of natural acts, those which occur for the most part and those in which nature deviates from what is proper to it. Corresponding to these there are three processes of reason: those by which scientific certitude is acquired and in which no deviation from truth is possible; those which come to conclusions true for the most part but not necessary; and those in which reason deviates from the true because of some defect of principle. The part of logic which treats the first of these processes is called "judica-

62. *In decem libros ethicorum Aristotelis ad Nicomachum expositio* i, Lectio 3, ed. A. M. Pirotta (Turin, 1934), p. 12, n. 36. Infallible proof is impossible in human affairs, and therefore the conjectural probability of the rhetorician is adequate; cf. *Summa theologica*, i a, ii ae, q. 105, a. 2, ad 8: "Ad octavum dicendum, quod in negotiis humanis non potest haberi demonstrativa probatio et infallibilis, sed sufficit aliqua conjecturalis probabilitas secundum quam rhetor persuadet."

63. *In decem libros ethicorum Aristotelis* x, Lectio 16 (Pirotta, p. 689, n. 2173).

tive," since its judgment is made with the certitude of science, and this part is treated in the *Analytics*: the *Prior Analytics* is concerned with the certitude of judgment which is based only on the *form* of the syllogism; the *Posterior Analytics* with the demonstrative syllogism, in which the certitude depends on *matter* or on the necessary propositions of which the syllogism is composed. The part of logic which is subject to the second process of reason is called inventive, for discovery is not always with certitude. *Topic* or *Dialectic* treats of this process when it leads to conviction or opinion (*fides vel opinio*); *Rhetoric* treats of it when it leads only to a kind of suspicion without total exclusion of the contrary possibility; *Poetic* treats of it when estimation inclines to one of the two parts of a contradiction only because of the manner of its representation. Finally, the third process of reason is called *sophistic* and is treated by Aristotle in the *De sophisticis elenchis*.[64]

Bonaventura's conception of rhetoric and logic, on the other hand, is quite unaffected by the Aristotelian philosophy: they are ordered in the trivium, dominated by rhetoric, and they are treated, with the other arts, by reduction to theology, or as parts of the first vision of God, which is by natural intelligence, or as part of the gift of science, which is one of the seven gifts of the Holy Spirit. There are four lights by which we are illuminated in knowledge: the exterior light of the mechanical arts, the inferior light of sensitive knowledge, the interior light of philosophic knowledge, and the superior light of grace and Sacred Scripture. The interior light by which we are illuminated to intelligible truths is of three kinds—rational, natural, and moral, corresponding to the traditional division of the philosophic sciences into logic, physics, and ethics. Rational truth or the truth of words is of three kinds—the expression of concepts (treated by grammar), the movement to belief (treated by logic), and the movement to love or hate (treated by rhetoric).[65]

64. *In libros Posteriorum analyticorum expositio* i, Lectio 1 (Rome, 1882), I, 138–40.

65. *De reductione artium ad theologiam* 4 (*Opera omnia*, V, 321): "Et quoniam tripliciter potest aliquis per *sermonem* exprimere quod habet apud se, ut scilicet notum faciat mentis suae conceptum, vel ut amplius moveat ad credendum, vel ut moveat ad amorem, vel odium: ideo *sermocinalis* sive rationalis philosophia triplicatur, scilicet in *grammaticam*, *logicam* et *rhetoricam*; quarum prima est ad expri-

The actual reduction of rational philosophy to theology is accomplished by consideration of the speaker (his expression of the conception of his mind is dependent on the eternal Word), his statement (in the congruity, truth, and adornment of which is seen the order of living, for actions by virtue of these have measure [*modus*], beauty [*species*], and order [*ordo*]), and the hearer (in whom the ends of speech are expressing, teaching, and moving, which are accomplished, as Augustine shows, only by the one true doctor who can impress species, infuse light, and give virtue to the heart of the hearer).[66] Or again, the first vision of God, which is by natural intelligence, is divided into three rays, since the light which is the truth of the soul illuminates the truth of things, of signs, and of morals: the second irradiation of truth is divided into three parts: grammar, logic, and rhetoric.[67] The consideration of general and special forms of argument in necessary matter as well as the consideration of "topical places" (in which induction proceeds by probable rather than necessary arguments) and sophistical places falls within logic, while rhetoric is concerned once more with civil utility and is divided into demonstrative, deliberative, and judicial.[68] Or again, the fifth gift of the Holy Spirit is science, comprising the three philosophic sciences (rational, natural, moral), in all of which, including rational philosophy or verbal science, Solomon was adept.[69]

It is in the platonizing Augustinian tradition, moreover, that music and poetry assume a broad sense and dominant importance:

---

mendum, secunda ad docendum, tertia ad movendum. Prima respicit rationem ut *apprehensivam*; secunda, ut *iudicativam*; tertia, ut *motivam*. Et quia ratio apprehendit per sermonem *congruum*, iudicat per *verum*, movet per sermonem *ornatum*: hinc est, quod haec triplex scientia has tres passiones circa sermonem considerat."

66. Ibid. 15–18 (*Opera omnia*, V, 323–24).

67. *In hexaemeron*, Collatio iv. 18–25 (*Opera omnia*, V, 352–53).

68. Ibid. 20–21 (*Opera omnia*, V, 352–53).

69. *De septem donis Spiritus Sancti*, Collatio iv. 5–12 (*Opera omnia*, V, 474–75); esp. 8: "Impossible est, quod sapientia fiat doctrina nisi per sermonem. Sermo autem non est sufficiens ad docendum, nisi sit sententiosus. Et non loquitur homo sententiose, nisi sermo eius *discussivus*, *inquisitivus*, et *persuasivus*, scilicet quod habeat sermonem potentem ad loquendum omne illud, quod potest apprehendi vel nosci, vel ad quod affectus potest inclinari. Congrue autem exprimit quod dicit per *grammaticam*, rationabiliter investigat per scientiam *logicam* et efficaciter persuadet per *rhetoricam*. Ista igitur est pars philosophiae, scilicet scientia sermocinalis, quae triplex est, ut patet, quam adeptus est Salomon."

Roger Bacon assigns to music the function which Bonaventura ascribed to rhetoric, and then distinguishes both rhetoric and poetic into two kinds—a theoretic rhetoric and poetic (or *rhetorica docens* and *poetica docens*) which are parts of logic and an applied rhetoric and poetic (or *rhetorica utens* and *poetica utens*) which are parts of moral philosophy.[70] The opposed tendencies which led to the dominance of rhetoric in the Augustinian tradition and to the importance of logical demonstration in the Thomist tradition are integral with the total complexions of the two theologies as evidenced in the conclusion of Bonaventura that theology is neither theoretic nor practical but an affective habit midway between theory and practice, as opposed to the argument of Thomas that theology subsumes both theoretic and practical sciences and is itself more theoretic than practical.[71] It is a distinction which later historians have treated crudely by trying to differentiate "voluntarism" from "rationalism."

V

Separate both from the tradition of the rhetoric assimilated to dialectic and proof and from that of the rhetoric assimilated to theology and edification—and the object of suspicion and attack by both—a third tradition of rhetoric seems to have flourished, at least during the second and third periods of the other two traditions, indifferent alike to the logical differentiation of necessary and probable arguments and to the theological limitation of persuasion to profound or salubrious truths. Since the three traditions were engaged in a three-cornered dispute, there is no single statement of the issue, for

70. *Opus tertium*, cap. 75 (*Opera inedita*, ed. J. S. Brewer [London, 1859], pp. 303–8, esp. 306–7): "Nam moralis philosophus scit uti sermone suavi, et gestibus convenientibus orationi delectabili conformandis. Similiter logicus et grammaticus. . . . Grammaticus igitur utitur his pueriliter; sed logicus quantum ad formam arguendi quam constituit, in his procedit viriliter, et causas et rationes assignat. Sed quantum ad decorem et ornatum et suavitatem argumenti, certe non potest logicus, sicut nec grammaticus, causas et rationes assignare, sed musicus; sicut geometer causas linearum, et angulorum, et figurarum, quibus utitur carpentator, habet dare." Cf. *Opus majus* iii and iv. 2, ed. J. H. Bridges (Oxford, 1897), pp. 71 and 99–102.

71. Bonaventura *Proemium in librum primum sententiarum* q. 3, concl.; i. 13; Thomas Aquinas *Summa theologica* i, q. i, a. 4.

to logicians the practitioners of this new art seemed sophists, while theologians lumped them with the heretical dialecticians and garrulous ratiocinators; from the point of view of the new art, which professed an exclusive concern with practical issues and effective applications, that is, with actions or with words, the rules of logic were themselves open to question, and visionary theories and inapplicable generalizations were devoid of moral attraction. For the most part we know about the early members of this tradition from the violence of the attacks upon them and the bitterness of the satire in which they were portrayed, but gradually in the course of the twelfth and thirteenth centuries they limited their statements to figures and forms of words, accomplishing their practical objectives by that device in a fashion which met with little effective opposition from logicians or theologians; and, since they were unhampered by the need to consider things or thoughts, they were prolific in production of the "new" methods—they were fond of calling themselves *moderni*—which constituted one of the important guises in which rhetoric entered the fourteenth century and the Renaissance.

A few fragments of the works of Anselm the Peripatetic are the only remains of the "Drogonic" sect—followers of the philosopher Drogo—which Anselm would have us believe was numerous and influential. He calls his art rhetoric; he professes allegiance to that art along with Hermagoras, Tully, Servius, Quintilian, Victorinus, Grillius, and Boethius and thought to illustrate it in his treatise *De materia artis* (now lost) and in the examples of rhetoric set forth in his *Rhetorimachia*; he specifies that rhetoric demonstrates, not truths, but verisimilitudes disguised as truths.[72] The *Rhetorimachia* is divided into three parts, one devoted to each of the genera—demonstrative, deliberative, and judicial—and each example takes the form of an attempt to turn the arguments of an opponent against him. The bearing of Anselm's performance on logic is not far to seek, since his approach permits him to deny the principle of excluded middle,[73] while its relation to theology is no less apparent

72. *Epistola ad Drogonem phylosophum (Anselm der Peripatetiker, nebst andern Beiträgen zur Literaturgeschichte Italiens elften Jahrhundert,* ed. E. Dümmler [Halle, 1872], pp. 19–20).

73. *Rhetorimachia* i, p. 34; cf. *Epistola ad Drogonem magistrum et condiscipulos de logica disputatione in Gallia habita,* pp. 56–58.

from the allegory of the dream, related as part of his treatment of deliberative rhetoric, in which the embraces and arguments of three virgins named Dialectic, Rhetoric, and Grammar turn him from communion with the saints in Heaven.[74] A "sophist" named John seems in like fashion to have had a numerous following, of whom Roscelin of Compiègne alone is easily identifiable.[75] In the twelfth century John of Salisbury attacks the doctrine of a teacher whom he disguises under the name of "Cornificius" (allying with himself in the attack the most illustrious masters of the age—among others, Gilbert de la Porrée, Thierry of Chartres, William of Conches, Peter Abailard) who broke that union of wisdom and eloquence which is the foundation of philosophy, of society, and of morals and who made everything new in his teaching, innovating in grammar, modifying dialectic, despising rhetoric; his exclusive reliance on the precepts of eloquence apparently leads Cornificius to exploit the traditional puzzles of the sophists, which turn on the confusion of word and thing or the application of a word or statement to itself.[76]

This tradition of rhetoric took form, for the most part, not in controversy or theory but in a vast number of textbooks which grew in three distinct groups, differentiated according to the subject matters once treated by rhetoric but now concerned with verbal forms employed in those three fields in lieu of direct treatment of subject matter. First, rhetoric had contributed to the method of studying

74. *Rhetorimachia* ii, p. 42.

75. Cf. *Historia Francica* (quoted by J. Reiners, *Der Nominalismus in der Frühscholastik* [*BGPM*, VIII, No. 5], p. 33, n. 2): "In dialectica quoque hi potentes extiterunt sophistae: Joannes, qui eandem artem sophisticam vocalem esse disseruit, Rotbertus Parisiacensis, Roscelinus Compendiensis, Arnulfus Laudenensis. Hi Joannis fuerunt sectatores, qui etiam quamplures habuerunt auditores." Cf. J. A. Endres, *Forschungen zur Geschichte der frühmittelalterlichen Philosophie* (*BGPM*, XVII, Nos. 2–3), and *Petrus Damiani und die weltliche Wissenschaft* (*BGPM*, VIII, No. 3); also J. de Ghellinck, "Dialectique et dogme aux Xe–XIIe siècles," *BGPM*, Supplementband I, pp. 79–99.

76. John of Salisbury *Metalogicon* i. 1–6 (Webb, pp. 5–21, esp. 21): "Plane eloquentie precepta sapientiam non conferunt; sed nec amorem eius et sepissime quidem ei obtinende non conferunt. Res enim philosophia (aut finis eius, que est sapientia) querit, non uerba. Ex his itaque liquet quia precepta eloquentie ab operis suis philosophia eliminat." Cf. the confusion of the arts of the trivium reported by Hugh of St. Victor *Didascalicon* iii. 5; Buttimer, pp. 55–57. Cf. P. Mandonnet, *Siger de Brabant et l'Averroïsme latin au XIIIme siècle* (2d ed.; Louvain, 1911), I, 122–23.

law, but the substantive consideration of law had moved into theology and had taken with it most of the appurtenances which might have made the law a learned profession, leaving only the verbal rhetoric of the *dictamen*.[77] Second, the art of preaching, which had assumed in the Christian tradition an exhortative function approaching that of ancient deliberative oratory—once due allowance is made for differences between the terrestrial and celestial city—

77. For the voluminous literature on the *Ars dictaminis* and *Ars notaria*, cf. L. J. Paetow, *A Guide to the Study of Medieval History* (2d ed.; New York, 1931), pp. 448–52; for the relation of these arts to rhetoric, cf. N. Valois, *De arte scribendi epistolas apud Gallicos medii aevi scriptores rhetoresve* ("Bibliothèque de l'École de Chartres," Vol. XXII [1880]), pp. 161, 257; for the relation of rhetoric to the teaching of law, cf. Abelson, op. cit., pp. 60–66. The manner of the change, no less than the pride in the novelty of it, may be judged from the contents of Boncompagni's two works, the *Rhetorica antiqua* (arranged in six books according to the character of the letter to be written) and the *Rhetorica novissima* (arranged in thirteen books: "Primus est de origine iuris. Secundus est de rhetoricae partibus et causarum generibus. Tertius est de diffinitionibus. Quartus est de naturis et consuetudinibus oratorum. Quintus de causarum exordiis. Sextus de principiis conuentorum. Septimus de rhetoricis argumentis. Octavus de memoria. Nonus de adornationibus. Decimus de invectivis. Undecimus de consiliis. Duodecimus de colloquiis. Tertius decimus de conditionibus"). Boncompagni professes in the Prologue to the former work not to remember ever having read Cicero, but he adds that he never dissuaded anyone who wanted to read him; and in the latter work he gives three reasons why he undertook to find a new rhetoric after Cicero had compiled a rhetoric from the infinite precepts of rhetoricians: (1) according to Boethius, the rhetoric edited by the ancients consists solely of precepts, without doctrine or utility; (2) students in civil and canon law would not get a solid foundation in the liberal arts, and (3) Cicero's rhetoric is rendered void, according to students of law, because it never read in "ordinary" courses but is run through and taught like a mechanical art by stealth; to these he adds a fourth: that Cicero was mistaken about the origin of the law (cf. L. Rockinger, "Über die Ars dictandi und die Summae dictaminum in Italien," *Sitzungsberichte der Königl. Bayerischen Akademie der Wissenschaften zu München, hist. Kl.*, I [1861], 135–45). For the closely related art of pleading, cf. A. Wilmart, "L'*Ars arengandi* de Jacques de Dinant avec un appendice sur ses ouvrages *De dictamine*," *Analecta Reginensia* (Vatican City, 1933), pp. 113–51. The relations of rhetoric to law and logic are reflected satirically in the "battle of seven arts"; cf. "*La Bataille des vii ars of* Henri d'Audeli," ed. L. J. Paetow, in *Two Medieval Satires on the University of Paris* (Berkeley, Calif., 1927), pp. 43 and 51. Cf. H. Kantorowicz, *Studies in the Glossators of the Roman Law* (Cambridge, 1938).

gradually moved to a formalism in which doctrine was left to theology and attention was centered on three problems: propriety of division of the subject stated in the theme of the sermon, brevity of distinction, and utility of expansion.[78] Finally, the art of poetry came to be considered, after the twelfth century, not a branch of grammar but alternately a kind of argumentation or persuasion (and, as such, subordinate to logic or morals) and a form of composition (and, as such, to be treated in terms of style, organization, and figures borrowed from rhetoric).[79] In common, these three ten-

78. Cf. the anonymous *Art of Preaching*, portions of which are edited in the *Opera omnia S. Bonventurae* (IX, 6–7), in which four modes of preaching are distinguished: (1) that which concords really and verbally with the words of Scipture—used by "modern" doctors and expounded in this treatise; (2) that which employs only real concordance with Scripture—appropriate to those newly learned in theology; (3) that limited to verbal concordance; and (4) contrasted to the modern method, the ancient mode "quod observant antiqui Sancti, sicut Augustinus et Bernardus et multi alii, quorum sermones in Ecclesia recitantur, in quibus non proponitur aliquod thema, quod sit materia praedicandi, nec solent divisiones vel distinctiones fieri, quae postmodum concordentur, sed quasi narrative procedit." The modern doctors advise against following the ancient mode, for the curious reason that these Fathers were, in a manner, founders of the church (*quasi ecclesiae fundatores*), and therefore they avoided all curiosity concerning distinctions of themes, subdivisions of members, and concordances of both. Bonaventura likewise divides the problems of preaching into three parts, *divisiones, distinctiones, dilatationes* (cf. *Ars concionandi*, Prooemium, ix. 8). For an excellent exposition of the technique of the medieval sermon and review of the methods expounded in most important medieval handbooks, cf. E. Gilson, "Michel Menot et la technique du sermon mediéval," *Les Idées et les lettres* (Paris, 1932), pp. 93–154. Cf. H. Caplan, "Classical Rhetoric and the Mediaeval Theory of Preaching," *Classical Philology*, XXVIII (1933), 73–96; "Rhetorical Invention in Some Mediaeval Tractates on Preaching," *Speculum*, II (1927), 284–95; "Henry of Hesse on the Art of Preaching," *PMLA*, XLVIII (1933), 340–61. The treatises of Robert of Basevorn and Thomas of Wales are published in T.-M. Charland, *Artes praedicandi: Contribution à l'histoire de la rhétorique au moyen âge* (Ottawa, 1936), preceded by a survey of writers of *Arts* and the customary form of theory. Cf. the differentiation of the two modes most used by moderns, the French and the English (Robert of Basevorn, *Forma praedicandi* 7, p. 244). Cf. also M. M. Davy, *Les Sermons universitaires parisiens de 1230–1231* (Paris, 1931); G. R. Owst, *Preaching in Mediaeval England: An Introduction to Sermon Manuscripts of the Period c. 1350–1450* (Cambridge, 1926); and C. H. Haskins, *Studies in Mediaeval Culture* (Oxford, 1929), pp. 36–71.

79. In early treatments poetry, considered as metric, was a part of grammar, while as a form of argument it was a part of topic or dialectic. Thus Cassiodorus defines

dencies continue the terms and some points of the organization of the *Ad Herennium* and of Cicero's *De inventione*, but the commonplaces which have been put to so many uses are no longer devices for discovering arguments of things and their traits but devices for remembering, for amplifying, for describing, and for constructing figures.[80]

VI

Two translations of Aristotle's *Rhetoric* were produced during the thirteenth century, and there are also translations of the *Rhetorica ad Alexandrum*, Averroës' commentary on the *Rhetoric*, and Demetrius' *De elocutione*. The effect of the Aristotelian rhetoric and its variant interpretations (both Demetrius and Averröes passed as "Aristotelian") on philosophy may be judged from the fact that these works on rhetoric are frequently found in manuscripts which contain works on morals, politics, or economics, and, indeed, specific marks of the *Rhetoric* can be seen in Aquinas' analysis of the passions.[81] Yet there are relatively few early commentaries on the work itself: Aegidius Romanus in the thirteenth century and John

---

grammar (*Institutiones* ii. 1. 1; p. 94): "grammatica vero est peritia pulchre loquendi ex poetis illustribus auctoribusque collecta; officium eius est sine vitio dictionem prosalem metricamque componere," but he includes the poets among the artists to whom topical arguments are supplied by memory (ibid. 3. 17, p. 127; cf. ibid. 2. 2, p. 98, for the function of memory in discovery). Cf. Isidore of Seville *Etymologiae* i. 39; the Venerable Bede, *De arte metrica* (*PL*, XC, 149). John of Salisbury notes the tendency to make poetic an art by itself or to assimilate it to rhetoric rather than to grammar, but he is explicit in his own resolution of the problem; cf. *Metalogicon* i. 17, p. 43: "Profecto aut poeticam grammatica obtinebit, aut poetica a numero liberalium disciplinarum eliminabitur." Cf. C. Fierville, *Une Grammaire latine inédite du XIIIe siècle* (Paris, 1886), pp. 94–119. The transition is gradual from a consideration merely of the words, their character, and position to the consideration of the general conditions or places relevant to the choice and disposition of words; a further step is needed to carry it, during the Renaissance, from the figures of speech and the figures of doctrine to the rhetorical consideration of the thoughts of the author and the effects on the audience.

80. Cf. E. Faral, *Les Arts poétiques du XIIe et du XIIIe siècle* (Paris, 1924), esp. pp. 52 ff. and 77 ff.

81. M. Grabmann, "Eine lateinische Übersetzung der pseudo-aristotelischen Rhetorica ad Alexandrum," pp. 6 ff.; G. Lacombe, A. Birkenmajer, M. Dulong, and A. Franceschini, *Aristoteles Latinus* (Rome, 1939), I, 77–79; B. V. Wall, *A Medieval Latin Version of Demetrius' "De elocutione"* (Washington, 1937).

of Jandun and John Buridan in the fourteenth century are the only outstanding scholastics to have left such commentaries.[82] The old problem of the genus of rhetoric, whether it is a part of civil philosophy or logic, is resolved by Aegidius into the difference between Aristotle (who placed it under dialectic) and Cicero (who made it a part of politics).[83] The position of this pupil of St. Thomas is indeed almost a parody of Bonaventura's doctrine that theology is midway between the practical and the speculative sciences, for he locates rhetoric midway between the moral and the rational sciences.[84] The readjustment is striking illustration of the fashion in which unchanged analyses may in the context of altered philosophies take on contrary significances, for the effort of rhetoricians from Quintilian through the early Middle Ages was to claim consideration of general or indefinite questions or theses and to resist efforts to restrict rhetoric to determinate questions or hypotheses, lest rhetoric yield its place and importance as a science to philosophy: the difference between politics and ethics, on the one hand, and rhetoric, on the other, according to Aegidius, consists in the fact that a science is determined by its subject matter and that, whereas politics and ethics have a determinate genus, rhetoric is indeterminate, being concerned with knowledge of certain common notions which bear on moral questions. John Buridan divides all sciences into two kinds, the "principal" science, which deals with the proper things of the science, and the "instrumental" science, which is concerned with the mode of statement and teaching. The instrument of the theoretic sciences is logic or dialectic, but in moral science the problem involved concerns not only the doubtful and the true but also the need to stir desire as it bears on understanding, and a special moral logic or dialectic is required which is divided into two parts, rhetoric and poetic.[85] John of Jandun divides philosophy into non-

82. The commentaries of Jandun and Buridan are unedited; that of Aegidius was published in 1515 in Venice, but I have been unable to consult a copy.

83. *De differentia rhetoricae, ethicae, et politicae*, ed. G. Bruni in *The New Scholasticism*, VI (1932), 5–8.

84. Ibid. (Bruni, p. 2). Cf. *Expositio in artem veterem* (Venice, 1507), 2v–3r, where speculative science is divided into *principalis* (concerned with things) and *adminiculativa* (the three arts of the trivium).

85. *Questiones super decem libros ethicorum Aristotelis ad Nicomachum*, Prooemium (Paris, 1518), fol. 4r.

organic (practical and speculative) and organic, which includes grammar and logic, rhetoric being a subdivision of logic.[86]

The three main lines in which rhetoric developed during the Middle Ages—as they had grown out of philosophic oppositions in antiquity and as they had been continued by medieval writers under the compulsion of the circumstances and nature of the problems they treated—are extended through the discussions of the Renaissance, notwithstanding revolt against the scholasticism of the Middle Ages, alike by the weight of tradition and by the exigencies of the problems themselves. The tradition of rhetoric as a part of rational philosophy subordinate to logic had a long and honorable continuation, which included Zabarella, Campanella, Varchi, Robertelli, and many others.[87] The tradition in which rhetoric domi-

86. *Quaestiones subtilissimae super tres libros de anima*, Prohemium (Venice, 1519), fol. 2v.

87. According to Zabarella, *De natura logicae* ii. 13–23 (*Opera logica* [Cologne, 1597], pp. 78–100), rhetoric and poetic are instruments of civil discipline and parts of logic (the arts of demonstration, dialectic, and sophistic are also parts of logic); like logic, they are rational faculties, not verbal, like grammar. Logic is divided into two principal kinds, universal and particular; rhetoric and poetic are instances of particular logic. Campanella divided his *Philosophia rationalis* into four parts: grammar, dialectic, rhetoric, and poetic. Rhetoric is a part of rational philosophy, deriving its arguments from dialectic and its matter from morals; it does not treat of all questions but is limited to persuasion and dissuasion of good and evil; poetic has the same function, but it differs from rhetoric in its universality, since it presents all goods and all truths to all audiences (*Philosophia rationalis, pars tertia, rhetorica* 1. 1 [Paris, 1538], pp. 1–7; cf. *Pars quarta, poetica* 1. 1, pp. 89–93). B. Varchi follows the traditional division of philosophy into real, active, and rational; rhetoric and poetic are subdivisions of rational philosophy, although, strictly speaking, poetic is neither an art nor a science, but a faculty; dialectic, rhetoric, and poetic are essentially the same thing, differing only accidentally, and the dialectician, rhetorician, and poet can be put on the same level of nobility and honor; cf. "Della poetica in generale," *Opere di Benedetto Varchi* (Trieste, 1859), II, 684: "La filosofia razionale, la quale favellando di parole e non di cose, non è veramente parte della filosofia, ma strumento, comprende sotto sè non solo la loica (intendendo per loica la guidiziale) a la dialettica (intendendo per dialettica non tanto la topica, quanto eziandio la sofistica e la tentativa) ma ancora la rettorica, la poetica, la storica e la grammatica." Robertelli raises the question not in terms of the form of the art but in terms of its matter and end: poetic shares its matter, *oratio*, with four other disciplines: demonstration, dialectic, rhetoric, and sophistic; grammar is excluded from the list, since it does not involve the intellectual content of what is said. The five are easily and rapidly distinguished (*In librum Aristotelis de Arte poetica* [Basel, 1555], p. 1): "Ex his quaelibet facultas unum arripit genus. Demonstratoria verum. Dialectice probabile. Rhetorica suasorium. Sophistice id, quod probabilis, sed verisimilis habet speciem. Poetice falsum, seu fabulosum." The end of poetic (ibid. 2) is

nated the arts continued into the Renaissance not only in the methods and doctrines of theology but in a secular tradition which took one of two forms: either all philosophy and all subjects are assimilated to rhetoric, as in the doctrines of Majoragius and Nizolius,[88] or the method of discovery is refurbished and transferred from rhetoric to revitalize and revolutionize dialectic, as in the doctrines of Rudolph Agricola and Petrus Ramus.[89] The tradition in which rhet-

---

the "imitating word," as the end of rhetoric is the "persuading word"; it is (borrowing from Cicero) the imitation of life, the mirror of custom, the image of truth. Cf. H. Cornacchinus, *Indagatio verae et perfectae definitionis logicae*, Pars V, cap. 21 (Padua, 1606), p. 247: poetic and rhetoric are parts or offshoots of logic, or rather aggregates composed from logic, grammar, and civil philosophy, and (ibid., Pars IV, cap. 10, pp. 220–21) dialectic, sophistic, and rhetoric are midway between grammar and logic.

88. J. L. Vives (*De causis corruptarum artium*, Liber iv [Lugduni Batavorum, 1586], p. 239) reports the doctrine of philosophers who distinguish two rhetorics, one universal and applicable to all things, the other particular and suited to civil use; Vives interprets the position as being in opposition to the tendency to make rhetoric part of logic. The position is defended by M. A. Majoragius on the authority of Cicero (*De finibus* ii. 6. 17) against Aristotle (*Aristotelis Stagyritae De arte rhetorica libri tres cum M. Antonii Maioragii commentariis*, Liber i [Venice, 1591], p. 2). M. Nizolius holds, again on the authority of Cicero, that philosophy and oratory are not two separate faculties but one and the same art, composed of two arts which are imperfect when separated (*De veris principiis et vera ratione philosophandi contra pseudophilosophos* iii. 3 [Parma, 1553], p. 211); he quotes Laurentius Valla, with approval, when he argues that dialectic is a part of rhetoric, since it consists of only one of the five parts of rhetoric, namely, discovery (ibid. 5, p. 240); and, finally, he holds that rhetoric is a general art and science, under which are subsumed all other arts and sciences (ibid. iii. 8, p. 268). The distinction of the two rhetorics—the rhetoric of precepts and the rhetoric in use—is preserved by Riccoboni, who also adds "ecclesiastical" as a fourth genus to the traditional three, "deliberative," "demonstrative," and "judicial" (A. Riccobonus, *De usu artis rhetoricae Aristotelis commentarii vigintiquinque, quibus duplex, rhetorica strictim explicatus, altera, quae praecepta tradit persuadendi, altera, quae re ipsa persuadet*, etc. [Frankfurt, 1595]). The use of rhetoric in refurbishing scriptural interpretation is well illustrated in the *Heptaplus* of Pico della Mirandola (in which Moses emerges as the "Idea" of the writer, the exemplar of the prophet) and John Colet's *Enarrationes in Epistolas S. Pauli*.

89. Rudolph Agricola undertook to reinstate in dialectic the processes of discovery which had become part of rhetoric because civil philosophy came into prominence in Greece before the maturity of the other arts (*De inventione dialectica* ii. 18 [Cologne, 1538], pp. 538 ff.), and to correct the errors which Aristotle, Cicero, and Boethius had committed in treating and classifying the places. The function of rhetoric was limited to *ratio dicendi*. According to Petrus Ramus, logic or dialectic is a general art, the whole art of reason (*Scholae in liberales artes* [Basel, 1569], *scholae dialecticae* ii. 2, pp. 35–37). The parts of dialectic are discovery and judgment (ibid. 8,

oric had become a discipline of words, independent alike of philosophy and dialectic, finally established verbal distinctions which grew into doctrines of things: the long and subtle speculations of fourteenth-century philosophers on *insolubilia, obligatoria,* and sophisms laid the foundations for many of the early theories in physics and mathematics, and symbolic logic, though unconcerned with its past, still repeats the elements of this heritage; the analysis of the figures of the poet was made, without undue or violent alteration, into a theory of poetry, which dealt with imagination, passion, truth, and virtue; and political philosophy has never entirely lost the rhetorical turn from which its theories derived their modern concreteness and practicality.

Once the general movements in the arts, of which the variegated history of rhetoric is a symptom, have been set into some intelligible schema, the startling and revolutionary shifts of doctrines and of problems are more easily understood. Since the problems of the sciences and the arts are closely related and are often stated in almost identical language, a slight shift of theory or terminology may at a point bring an unsuspected richness from one art into the threadbare terminology of another. The three customary questions of rhetoric—*whether it is, what it is,* and *what sort*—merged readily with the questions of logic and influenced early modern attempts to formulate the scientific method. The customary rhetorical inquiry into the duty of the artist and into the matter and end of the art took on metaphysical generality when it was merged, in the thirteenth century, with the Aristotelian causes by the simple addition of questions of form to what were already questions concerning the efficient, material, and final causes; and, metaphysics apart, the four questions contributed to the foundations of philology in the inquiries into the four causes of books with which Aquinas and Bonaventura and other medieval writers opened their commentaries. The

---

p. 53); the parts of rhetoric are elocution and action (*Scholae rhetoricae*, i, p. 238). The logic of Aristotle abounded in errors, confusions, vain precepts, and altercations: Ramus professed to have supplied the missing virtues, removed the errors, and made the art usable. The error of Cicero consisted in transferring all the Aristotelian devices of dialectic to rhetoric and of having made one art of two; and Quintilian mixed rhetoric with all the other arts; Ramus undertook to correct both errors (*Rhetoricae distinctiones in Quintilianum* [Paris, 1559], pp. 3–8).

controversy concerning thesis and hypothesis merged with Plato's dialectical use of hypothesis and Aristotle's differentiation of thesis, hypothesis, and definition and contributed unsuspected commitments and implications in modern discussions of scientific method. Rhetoric is, at most, an unusually clear example among the arts and sciences of a tendency which appears in the history of rhetoric only because it is universal in intellectual disciplines. In application, the art of rhetoric contributed during the period from the fourth to the fourteenth century not only to the methods of speaking and writing well, of composing letters and petitions, sermons and prayers, legal documents and briefs, poetry and prose, but to the canons of interpreting laws and Scripture, to the dialectical devices of discovery and proof, to the establishment of the scholastic method, which was to come into universal use in philosophy and theology, and, finally, to the formulation of scientific inquiry, which was to separate philosophy from theology. In manner of application, the art of rhetoric was the source both of doctrines which have long since become the property of other sciences (such as the passions, which were considered in handbooks of rhetoric until Descartes proposed a "scientific" treatment of them different only in details) and of particular devices which have been applied to a variety of subjects (such as to the "commonplaces" which were sometimes techniques for inventing arguments, sometimes means for dilating statements, sometimes methods for discovering things, or to "definition" or "order," which may be determined entirely by consideration of the verbal conditions of expression, the psychological requirements of persuasion, or the circumstantial probabilities of fact). In theory or application, the art of rhetoric was now identified with, now distinguished from, the whole or part not only of grammar, logic, and dialectic (which were, in turn, distinguished from or identified with each other) but also of sophistic and science, of "civil philosophy," psychology, law, and literature and, finally, of philosophy as such. Yet, if rhetoric is defined in terms of a single subject matter—such as style or literature or discourse—it has no history during the Middle Ages; the many innovations which are recorded during that period in the arts with which it is related suggest that their histories might profitably be considered without unique attachment to the field in which their advances are celebrated.

Poetry and Philosophy in the Twelfth Century: The Renaissance of Rhetoric

The problems, the visions, and sometimes even the language of philosophy have served the purposes of poets; and philosophers have borrowed poetic modes of expression and have speculated on the nature and effects of poetry, on the criteria of poetic values, and on the fate deserved by poets. The variations of both poetry and philosophy have been so great, however, that no simple relation between them could continue long or in wide acceptance. At times and according to the precepts of some philosophies, poetry approximates closely to the subjects and problems of philosophy, and the relation of poetry and philosophy oscillates between identity and antithesis. The poet, who is often a philosopher, is then conceived as giving final expression to the fullest experience and the loftiest ideas that men have had about the actions and destiny of man and the nature and order of all things, while the philosopher, who is sometimes a poet, constructs an intellectual system in which the vain fictions of poets are among the chief sources of error and immorality. At other times and following the principles of other philosophies, the purest poetry is devoid of recognizable doctrine and often even of sense, and the investigations and conclusions of philosophy require distinctions and demonstrations for which the most ingenious critic would have had difficulty in finding poetic expression, if, indeed, there were any reason to undertake so unpromising an enterprise. It is a mistake to reduce this difference, as has been done,[1] to a distinction between the arduous methods of philosophic inquiry which are ill suited to poetic formulation and the sublime conclusions which the philosopher only touches by reason but which the poet grasps by passionate imagination. Despite the temptation to claim the scientific method for literary criticism, philosophy and poetry are not to be classified after the fashion of purely natural phenomena or things, precisely because they contain and are affected by the ideas used in defining and classifying them.

The period of the Middle Ages, which incloses within its limits examples of so many diverse things, affords an illustration of these two attitudes toward the relationships of poetry and philosophy, sharply separated in doctrine and yet closely related in time. During the twelfth century, philosophy reached a mature and characteristic form, Platonizing in manner and humanistic in tradition. Many of the major philosophers of the century expressed their philosophy in excellent poetry; and they continued in philosophy and poetry the paradox of Plato, who also used poetic devices and quotations from the poets to explore philosophic ideas and yet expelled poets from his second-best as well as his perfect state, retaining only carefully selected poetic forms for use in the education of the young. The poets and rhetoricians of the later Renaissance of the fifteenth and sixteenth centuries exemplified the same paradox when they borrowed philosophic problems from philosophers, not merely to seek more felicitous expression for solutions arrived at philosophically, but to attain to a fuller realization of truth than they thought possible by the technicalities and futilities of philosophic distinctions.

During the last half of the twelfth century and the first half of the thirteenth the translations of Aristotle and the Arabic philosophers changed the form and matter of philosophy. The tradition of the twelfth century was broken abruptly, and that break was accentuated by the fact that few of the philosophers who first struggled to assimilate the growing materials of the new translations were studied by their successors in the latter part of the thirteenth century or were recorded in later histories of philosophy. Great philos-

1. Cf. G. Santayana, *Three Philosophical Poets: Lucretius, Dante, and Goethe* (Cambridge, 1910), pp. 10–11.

ophers of the second half of the thirteenth century, as, for example, Thomas Aquinas and Bonaventura, continue to write excellent verse; but in their philosophies the ends and instruments of poetry are sharply distinguished from those of theory, and their poetry is not a device to express their basic or most characteristic philosophic doctrines, while Dante, the great philosophic poet of the period, is not a philosopher by the crucial test that, despite the philosophic doctrines that crowd his poem, scholars have been unable to agree concerning what his attitude toward the philosophers he uses is.

Bonaventura, seeking frankly to combine Plato and Aristotle after the fashion in which they had been combined by Plotinus and Augustine, assigns to Plato the realm of wisdom and the eternal and to Aristotle the realm of science and the changing. On the other hand, Aquinas, seeking to distinguish philosophy from theology, criticizes the Platonic method in philosophy and repeats Aristotelian refutations of the doctrine of Ideas, but retains Platonic devices in theology and even preserves Platonic Ideas by finding a place for them in the mind of God. Yet for both, as for Aristotle, poetry is distinct from philosophy, not an inferior but comparable discipline, rivaling the purposes of philosophy and endangering its ends. Dante, in like fashion, exhibits mingled traces of Platonism and Aristotelianism. His poetic use of the philosophic tendencies of his times is not in advocacy of a philosophic position or to sharpen philosophic differences but tends, rather, to reconcile the Aristotelianism of Aquinas with the Averroism of Siger of Brabant. His use of philosophy is not the expression of a philosophy, and it is difficult, if not impossible, to state his doctrines or place them among the schools of his time; yet, when he expounds the method by which his poem should be interpreted, he reverts to the devices of the twelfth century and requires, as had been customary, that his poem be placed under the proper part of philosophy, identifying that part as ethics.[2]

2. For the discussion of Dante's philosophy cf. B. Nardi, *Saggi di filosofia Dantesca* (Milan, 1930) and *Note critiche di filosofia Dantesca* (Florence, 1938); P. Mandonnet, *Dante le théologien: Introduction à l'intelligence de la vie, des oeuvres et l'art de Dante Alighieri* (Paris, 1935); E. Gilson, *Dante et la philosophie* (Paris, 1939). For Aquinas and Bonaventura on the relation of poetry and philosophy, cf. below, nn. 30, 31, and 32; for Dante's critical method, cf. *Epistola* X, to Can Grande della Scala, and n. 35, below.

An examination of the relation of poetry and philosophy during the twelfth century has therefore more than merely historical interest, since light is thrown on the problems of criticism and of philosophy by the theory and practice of poetry in any period. The nature of poetry and the criteria for its evaluation as well as the techniques of expression and interpretation in literal statement and analogy, in proof and persuasion, are treated in detail by the Platonizing philosophers of the twelfth century, and, in the manner of Platonisms, the dialectical shifts in doctrines complete a circle in which the reasons used by philosophers in criticism of poetry suggest poetic reasons for the criticism of philosophy by theologians.

The Platonic tradition had attracted the Greek and Latin Church Fathers, but it had also set them the puzzling task of explaining how skepticism and idealism, no less than logic-chopping and mysticism, had all been derived from the teachings of Plato. Modern scholarship has given us fuller materials concerning the paradox of Socrates, but Augustine explored the full range of its implications. The conversations of Socrates have been the source of many and highly diversified inspirations. We have records of them in the plain common sense of Xenophon as well as in the philosophic subtleties of Plato; and we have constructed a Socratic problem, sometimes by seeking in internal evidence and external information touchstones to differentiate the Socratic from the Platonic strand in Plato's dialogues, sometimes by using the Platonic philosophy to suggest a missing level of communication in the account of Xenophon, hinted with enigmatic and parabolic intent or omitted because it went unobserved. Moreover, Socratic dialogues were written by Megareans and Elean-Eretrians, Cynics and Cyrenaics; and the Socratic method was invoked by hedonists, skeptics, dialecticians, cynics, idealists, and mystics, whose writings have been lost and whose fragmentary history has been a puzzle to scholars and philosophers.

There is almost a consensus among the philosophers of the twelfth century that Plato was the greatest of philosophers, and he is frequently referred to, much as Aristotle was in the thirteenth and fourteenth centuries, as "The Philosopher."[3] Since little was known

3. John of Salisbury calls Bernard of Chartres "perfectissimus inter Platonicos seculi nostri" (*Metalogicon* iv. 35, ed. C. C. I. Webb [Oxford, 1929]), p. 205; *Patro-*

of Aristotle's philosophy, except a few books of his *Organon*, the materials for most of the philosophic controversies of the first half

---

logia Latina [cited henceforth as "*PL*"], CXCIX, 938C). Herman of Dalmatia dedicated his translation of Ptolemy's *Planisphere* to Thierry of Chartres, who was "the first and sovereign anchor of second philosophy [i.e., the quadrivium] in our times, the immobile support of studies tossed by every kind of storm, . . . in whom relives the soul of Plato descended from Heaven for the happiness of mortals, the true father of Latin studies" (A. Clerval, *Les Écoles de Chartres au moyen-âge* [Chartres, 1895], p. 190). Abailard calls Plato the greatest of philosophers: "Maximus omnium philosophorum Plato" (*Introductio ad theologiam* iii [*PL*, CLXXVIII, 1087D]); "ille maximus philosophorum Plato" (*Theologia Christiana* i [*PL*, CLXXVIII, 1144A]); "summum philosophorum Platonem" (*Th. Chr.* i [*PL*, CLXXVIII, 1155A]); "summus philosophus" (*Th. Chr.* i [*PL*, CLXXVIII, 1160D]); "Pluribus quoque sanctorum testimoniis didicimus Platonicam sectam catholicae fidei concordare. Unde non sine causa maximus Plato philosophorum prae caeteris commendatur ab omnibus, non solum a peritis saecularium artium verum etiam a sanctis" (*Th. Chr.* i [*PL*, CLXXVIII, 1159C]); Augustine's praise of Plato is quoted with approval (*Th. Chr.* ii [*PL*, CLXXVIII, 1176B–1177C]); "maximus omnium philosophorum Plato" (*Th. Chr.* v [*PL*, CLXXVIII, 1317B]); "Novimus etiam ipsum Aristotelem et in aliis locis adversus eumdem magistrum suum et primum totius philosophiae ducem, ex fomite fortassis invidiae aut ex avaritia nominis, ex manifestatione scientiae insurrexisse, quibusdam et sophisticis argumentationibus adversus ejus sententias inhiantem dimicasse, ut in eo quod de motu animae Macrobius meminit" (*Dialectica* Pars i, lib. 2; *Ouvrages inédits d'Abélard*, ed. V. Cousin [Paris, 1836], pp. 205–6). Adelard of Bath refers to him in terms of esteem and familiarity: "a principe philosophorum" (*De eodem et diverso*, ed. H. Willner, in *Beiträge zur Geschichte der Philosophie des Mittelalters* [henceforth cited as "*BGPM*"], IV, No. 2, 4); "familiaris meus Plato" and "meus Plato" (ibid., p. 13); "philosophus" (ibid., p. 15); and his nephew, who is his interlocutor in the dialogue, *Natural Questions*, detects in him a complete acceptance of Platonic principles: "Cum enim et in philosophicis contemplationibus et in physicis causarum effectibus ethicisque etiam consultibus Platoni te penitus consentire perceperim . . ." (*Quaestiones naturales* 24, ed. M. Müller [*BGPM*, XXXI], No. 2, 31]); "auctor huius divinae rationis Plato simil cum suis celebretur et ametur" (*BGPM*, XXXI, No. 2, 34); and he is referred to throughout the *Natural Questions* as "The Philosopher" (cf. *BGPM*, XXXI, No. 2, 6, 9, 30, 31, and *passim*). John of Salisbury, despite his admiration for Aristotle and Cicero, ranks Plato above all other philosophers: "Totius etenim philosophiae princeps Plato (si tamen Aristotilici adquiescunt) . . ." (*Policraticus* i. 6; ed. C. C. J. Webb [Oxford, 1909], I, 40 [*PL*, CXCIX, 401C]); "Totius denique ueteris philosophiae princeps Plato . . ." (*Polic.* ii. 26 [Webb, I, 141; *PL*, CXCIX, 460A]); ". . . et in tantam eminentiam philosophiae et uigore ingenii et studii exercitio et omni morum uenustate eloquii quoque suauitate et copia subuectus est ut quasi in trono sapientiae residens praecepta quadam auctoritate uisus sit tam antecessoribus quam successoribus philosophis imperare. . . . Porro tantae multitudinis dissidentiam Plato qua praeminebat auctoritate cohibuit et in se attentionem omnium diutius prouocauit et tenuit" (*Polic.* vii. 5 [Webb, II, 105; *PL*, CXCIX, 644A–B]); "Sol e celo uisus est cecidisse qua die philosophorum princeps Plato rebus excessit humanis, et quasi lucernam mundi extinctam defleuerunt qui ad thronum sapientiae, cui ille diu praesederat, sua arbitrabantur studia referenda.

of the century may be found in the opposed elements of Platonism, learned also at second hand but developed with great philosophic sensitivity and skill. The philosophers of the twelfth century accepted from Augustine the judgment that Plato's philosophy was most nearly of all philosophies in accord with Christianity. Some of them made this the basis of their plea for the preservation of humanistic culture, while others found the homogeneity of Christianity and Platonism in Neo-Platonic doctrines, which Augustine had found in Plotinus and which had been blended with Christian doctrine through the influence of the pseudo-Dionysius the Areopagite, and turned their speculations wholly to the return to God from the consideration of the world. Others learned from Cicero that both academic skepticism and stoic morality stem from Plato, and they found in Cicero's rhetoric a philosophic method and hints of a philosophic doctrine which harmonized with the logic and the logical realism taught by Porphyry and Boethius. Still others found

---

Sed cum ei Aristotiles discipulus, uir excellentis ingenii et Platoni impar eloquio sed multos facile superans, in docendi officium successisset, . . ." (*Polic.* vii. 6 [Webb, II, 111–12; *PL*, CXCIX, 647C]); "Licet autem nominum et uerborum turbator habeatur, non modo subtilitate, qua cunctis celebris est, sed et mira suauitate dicendi eualuit, adeo quidem ut Platoni merito proximus fuisse uideatur" (Webb, II, 113; *PL*, CXCIX, 648B). William of Conches repeats the preference of Augustine: "Si gentilis adducenda est opinio, malo Platonis quam alterius inducatur; plus namque cum nostra fide concordat" (quoted from the *Dragmaticon philosophiae* by C. Prantl, *Geschichte der Logik im Abendlände* [reprint; Leipzig, 1927], II, 129, n. 96). Alan of Lille sets above Aristotle's logical inquiries Plato's more divine investigations of the nature of the things, of the heavens, and of God: "Illic arma parat logico, logicaeque palaestram / Pingit Aristoteles; sed eo divinius ipsa / Somniat arcana rerum, coelique profunda / Mente Plato, sensumque Dei perquirere tentat" (*Anticlaudianus* i [*PL*, CCX, 491B]); Plato is in philosophy what Croesus is in wealth, Cyrus in power, Narcissus in beauty, Turnus in courage, Hercules in strength, Hippolytus in chastity (*De planctu naturae* [*PL*, CCX, 468C]); "Plato ingenii splendore rutilabat sidereo. Illic stellata cauda Tulliani pavonis rutilabat. Illic Aristoteles sententias aenigmaticarum locutionum latibulis involvebat" (*De planc., nat.* [*PL*, CCX, 479D]); he is referred to, as he frequently is in the twelfth century, as "The Philosopher" (*Contra haereticos* i. 5 [*PL*, CCX, 311C]). Finally, Alan of Lille set for himself the task of translating or expanding Plato: "His animadversis mens sese accingat ad illa, / Quae minime fiunt, sed sunt, velut ipsa Platonis / Verba canunt; . . ." (*A deo semper incipiendum et in eumdem desinendum* [*PL*, CCX, 576B]). Cf. C. Baeumker, "Der Platonismus im Mittelalter," *Studien und Characteristiken zur Geschichte der Philosophie insbesondere des Mittelalters* (*BGPM*, XXV, Nos. 1–2, 139–79); and R. Klibansky, *The Continuity of the Platonic Tradition during the Middle Ages* (London, 1939).

the beginnings of science and cosmology in Chalcidius' translation of a portion of the *Timaeus* and his commentary on it, and in Apuleius and Marcobius.

The discussion of poetry during the twelfth century exemplifies the doctrinal diversity possible in the development of the tradition of Platonism. Four distinct, and even contradictory, positions concerning the relation of poetry and philosophy were developed in excellent literary and poetic form, and each reiterated Plato's love of poetry and his suspicion of its effects. All four positions reflect the Platonic statement of the problems in terms of the opposition of opinion and belief, on the one hand, to dialectic and philosophy, on the other. Poetry as a form of opinion and belief is opposed to philosophy and is full of dangers to the truth which those other poets, the lawgiver and the dialectician, attain by means of knowledge; and yet it is possible for poetry to state right opinion and true belief, and, indeed, poetry and the interpretation of poetry may attain to truth by divine inspiration. Moreover, a further complexity had been introduced into Christian Platonism by the redefinition of belief or faith: for belief (πίστις), according to Plato, is that variety of knowledge which grasps *visible things*, and it is inferior, as empirical certitude, to the knowledge gained by understanding and reason, whereas medieval philosophers followed the Pauline definition of belief (*fides*) as the argument of things unseen, and belief or faith, defined as the knowledge of *invisible things*, assumed a place superior to reason in their classification of knowledge. The problem of the relation of poetry to philosophy or the liberal arts became, as a consequence, an extension or development of the problem of the relation of philosophy to religion or theology.

The position of Peter Abailard, renowned both as dialectician and as poet,[4] derives from Plato by way of Augustine. Abailard develops

4. Judgments concerning the poetic value of medieval poetry have undergone marked alterations during the last few decades. The prejudice against "didactic poetry" has not disappeared, but the present-day taste for speculative and metaphysical verse is reflected in the estimation of earlier poets. P. S. Allen (*Medieval Latin Lyrics* [Chicago, 1931], pp. 243–44) traces the history of the shift of his views in twenty-two years concerning Abailard's authorship of poems in the *Carmina Burana*. One reason for his hesitation in attributing poems from that collection to Abailard was his judgment of Abailard, revealed in his extant poetry as "the composer of a letter to Astrolabius, the author of cut-and-dried planctus on Old Testament subjects, the writer of ninety hymns and sequences that breathe but the lifeless excogitations of

arguments borrowed from Augustine to defend the study of secular letters both for their utility and for themselves, since the liberal arts and philosophy are essential to Christian doctrine and the interpretation of Scripture. He also argues on Augustinian grounds that poetic figments are wholly forbidden to Christians, not only because they expound errors and *a mouth that lieth destroyeth the soul* according to the Book of Wisdom (1:11) but also because the soul is enticed by cogitation on inane fables to desire the disgraceful things feigned in poetry and is abducted by them from the study of Sacred Scripture. Abailard is at pains, therefore, to interpret the numerous strictures against pagan letters, particularly those of Jerome, to show that they are directed exclusively against poetry and do not apply to the liberal arts or philosophy.[5] He defends the liberal arts strenuously on the ground that no knowledge, but only its improper use, can be evil, and no art should therefore be forbidden except on grounds of utility. But he can find no use for "poetic figments and inane fables." He refutes those who maintain that the study of the poets is essential to the arts of the trivium, arguing that Scripture supplies better material for grammar, rhetoric, and dialectic; and he points out that even Cicero, when he wished to set forth the art of discourse fully in his rhetoric, did not use poetic examples, but his own discourses, in which he said the art shone forth more fully. Will Christian bishops and doctors, Abailard asks, welcome to the city of God poets, whom Plato excluded from the city of the world? Yet misguided priests spend day and night on

---

a theological wit." F. J. E. Raby, on the other hand, places Abailard high among the great hymn writers of the Middle Ages and is impressed particularly by the novelty and skilful development of his verse forms (*A History of Christian-Latin Poetry from the Beginnings to the Close of the Middle Ages* [Oxford, 1927], pp. 319–26); he praises the *planctus* for their "rich variety of rhythmical schemes and their sureness of execution"; and he finds even the poem to Astrolabe not wanting in facility, although the execution of verses is not above reproach (*A History of Secular Latin Poetry in the Middle Ages* [Oxford, 1934], II, 5–7). Helen Waddell judges the meters exquisite and the treatment poignant (*The Wandering Scholars* [7th ed.; London, 1934], p. 196); and F. A. Wright and T. A. Sinclair characterize Abailard as "a scholar, a philosopher, a theologian, an orator, and above all a poet" (*A History of Later Latin Literature* [London, 1931], p. 296). For a general survey and estimate of Abailard's poetry cf. M. Manitius, *Geschichte der lateinischen Literatur des Mittelalters* (Munich, 1931), III, 109–10.

5. *Introductio ad theologiam* ii. 2 (*PL*, CLXXVIII, 1040–46).

solemn feast-days with troubadours and jongleurs—*joculatores, saltatores, incantatores,* and *contatores*—and reward them with recompenses stolen from ecclesiastical beneficies. Such actors (*histriones*) are a diabolical troup, and the devil himself has introduced theatrical obscenities (*scenicas turpitudines*) into the church of God.[6]

The position of the cosmological poets and philosophers, in the second place, derives from Plato by way of the *Timaeus* and the interpretations of Chalcidius and by way of the speculations of that mythical god and philosopher, Hermes Trismegistus, and the treatises of Macrobius and Apuleius. Poetry, in the allegorizing cosmological philosophy, may be joined with philosophy in the case of a poet like Virgil, and in the case of lesser poets it may be useful in education, although unsuited to mystical or allegorical interpretation, or it may be the statement of erroneous doctrines on questions concerning which the truth can be found only in the study of nature and God.

Bernard Sylvester, whose *De mundi universitate* is composed in prose alternating with poetry of great beauty,[7] takes the former of

6. *Th. Chr.* ii (*PL,* CLXXVIII, 1209–12); cf. Abailard's citation of Augustine's statements in approval of the expulsion of poets by Plato (*Th. Chr.* ii [*PL,* CLXXVIII, 1182–83]).

7. *Bernardi Silvestris De mundi universitate libri duo sive megacosmus et microcosmus,* ed. C. S. Barach and J. Wrobel (Innsbruck, 1876). The critical estimate of Bernard's poetic abilities has varied between very widely separated extremes. He is compared to Dante in the account of his work in the *Histoire littéraire de la France* (XII, 272), and Hauréau summarizes that judgment without stating dissent (*Histoire de la philosophie scolastique* [Paris, 1872], I, 417): "Il y a dans cet ouvrage, selon les auteurs de l'*Histoire littéraire,* des traits de génie. Il y a certainement de l'invention, et ce n'est pas trop louer certains passages du *Microcosme* que de les comparer à d'autres passages de la *Divine comédie.* Bernard n'avait pas seulement l'imagination ingénieuse et facile; il l'avait encore puissante: c'est vraiment un poëte." Gilson refers to the same authorities as prelude to his own more moderate praise (*La Philosophie au moyen âge* [2d ed.; Paris, 1944], p. 273: "Certains passages de cette oeuvre ne sont pas sans beauté, mais il est vraiment excessif de rappeller à leur occasion, ainsi qu'on l'a fait, le grand nom de Dante et le souvenir de la *Divine comédie.*" Charles Huit considers him the true philosopher-poet ("Le Platonisme au XIIe siècle," *Annales de philosophie chrétienne,* XXI [new ser., 1889–90], 169–70): "C'est un véritable poète philosophe, chez lequel l'éclat de l'imagination l'emporte sur la solidité du raisonnement, et qui a mérité de Charles Lenormant ce bien sincère éloge: 'J'étais attiré par un attrait irrésistible vers les écrits de Bernard: j'y trouvais un parfum littéraire, un sentiment de la belle antiquité, une intuition de la philosophie platonique (et pourtant Bernard n'avait à sa disposition que la traduction du *Timée*)

these alternatives. He finds occasion to discuss the nature and value of poetry when, in his allegorical interpretation of Virgil's *Aeneid*,[8] he expounds the pious hero's journey, at the beginning of the sixth book, to the temple of Apollo (interpreted as the philosophic or theoretic arts) near the vast cavern of the Sybil (interpreted as the profundity of philosophy) by way of a grove called Trivia (which suggests that the study of eloquence is preliminary to the theoretic arts). Science is divided according to Bernard into four parts: wisdom, eloquence, poetry, and mechanics. These are arranged in graded sequence: poetry is clearer and higher than mechanics, and eloquence has a like superiority over poetry, and wisdom or philosophy over eloquence. The study of eloquence, however, is pursued by instruction in authors, and the poets are therefore introductory to philosophy. But, although the amusing stories of authors and poets prepare for the arts of eloquence, and therefore for philosophy, they are not worthy to be interpreted mystically.[9] For this reason the priestess of Apollo and Trivia arouses Aeneas from the contemplation of the fables painted on the doors of the temple to invite him into the temple itself.

This judgment of poetry, however, is developed in a commentary on a poet; for Virgil in this form of the Platonic paradox is not merely a poet but a philosopher, and, as Macrobius pointed out, he taught philosophic truth without neglecting poetic fiction.[10] The

---

qui ne pouvaient, il est vrai, arrêter un grand mouvement comme celui de la scolastique, mais qui du moins maintenaient la chaîne des traditions du goût.' Ses vers sont remplis de peintures riches et brillantes, attestant le progrès qu'avait fait entre tous les arts l'art d'écrire pendant ce demisiècle privilégié." Like Victor Cousin, Helen Waddell compares Bernard to Giordano Bruno (op. cit., p. 115), and her praise of his *De mundi universitate* is enthusiastic (ibid., p. 118): "His book has two sources, the *Timaeus* of Plato and the comment of Chalcidius; but the driest of the Platonic dialogues is only the fuel for his fire. The poet in him never sleeps; the sheer mechanism, the skeleton of philosophy, stuff like the theory of the four elements becomes a succession of visions. . . . The very baldness of his argument . . . is the dream of the *Faerie Queene*, of *The Tempest*, of *Hyperion*. And of the Providence, his prose is the prose of Shelley's *Defense of Poetry*." According to Raby (op. cit., p. 297): "Bernard's verse, like his prose, is stiff and obscure, although he had read Horace, Virgil, and Ovid."

8. *Commentum Bernardi Silvestris super sex libro Eneidos Virgilii*, ed. G. Riedel (Gryphiswaldae, 1924), pp. 30–38.

9. Ibid., p. 37; cf. Bernard's citation of Plato's *Timaeus* in support of the doctrine that poetry is imitation (ibid., pp. 74–75).

10. Ibid., pp. 1–3. The citation from Horace is of *Ars poetica* 333–34.

purposes of poets, which Bernard repeats from Horace, are utility and delight. Satirists aim at utility; writers of comedy, at delight; epic writers, at both. Virgil, as poet, pleases with adornment of words and with the situations and deeds narrated; and he serves likewise a double utility, as model for imitation in learning the art of writing and by exhortation to prudence by examples of right action. As philosopher he treats of the nature of human life according to a parabolic mode of demonstration proper to poetry.

> In so far as he is a philosopher, he writes of the nature of human life. His mode of writing is this: he describes under concealment [*sub integumento*] what the human spirit does and suffers, situated temporally in the human body. And in writing thus he uses the natural order, and thus he observes both orders of narration, as a poet the artificial, as a philosopher the natural [i.e., the narrative begins literally *in medias res* and its temporal beginnings are supplied later in the tale related to Dido, but the six ages of man traced in the allegorical meaning follow their natural sequence through the first six books]. Concealment, moreover, is a genus of demonstration which enfolds the understanding of truth under a fabled narration, and therefore it is also called envelopment [*involucrum*]. Furthermore, man derives utility from this work according to his recognition of himself, inasmuch as it is of great utility to man, as Macrobius says, if he knows himself. Whence "From the heavens descends *notisheliton*," that is, *know thyself*.[11]

Poetry, though distinct from philosophy, may, nonetheless, coincide with it in a great poem; and together poetry and philosophy may deal in almost wholly pagan terms with a Christian theme, as the creation of the universe and man is treated in Bernard's *De*

11. *Commentum Bernardi Silvestris*, p. 3; the citation is from Juvenal xi. 27, quoted from Macrobius *Commentaria in Somnium Scripionis* i. 9. 1–2; cf. also Macrobius *Saturnalia* i. 6. 6. The line from Juvenal is quoted also by John of Salisbury, *De septem septenis* 6 (*PL*, CXCIX, 956B). For other references to the allegorical interpretation of poets and particularly to the poetic mode of demonstration by *integumentum* or *involucrum*, cf. Alan of Lille, *De planctu naturae* (*PL*, CCX, 454C); John of Salisbury, *Polic*. viii. 24 (Webb, II, 415; *PL*, CXCIX, 816D–817A); and Honorius of Autun, *Selectorum Psalmorum expositio* (*PL*, CLXXII, 269C): "Ideo autem mysteria hujus libri sunt per involucra et aenigmata texta, ne vilescerent omnibus aperta."

mundi universitate, to the confusion of later scholars who like to distinguish literally between pagan and Christian philosophy.

Alan of Lille, who also wrote excellent poetry on cosmological themes, took the second alternative of the cosmologists and argued in his poetry, with no less fidelity to the Platonic paradox, that poetry is committed to falsity. Cicero and Virgil are treated in sequence in the Alexandrian verses of the *Anticlaudianus*, and the poet suffers by comparison with the rhetorician: "Tully redeems his verbal poverty by the splendor of colors [i.e., figures] and gives lightning flashes of embellishment to his words. The muse of Virgil colors [i.e., glosses over] many falsehoods, and weaves cloaks for falsehood under the guise of truth."[12] In the *De planctu naturae*, the poet

12. *Antic*. i. 4 (*PL*, CCX, 491C). The judgments passed on Alan's verse are as various as those suffered by other poets of the century. Hauréau traces his transition from logical to poetical exposition of philosophic subjects and concludes (op. cit., I, 522): "C'est, en effet, le philosophe des mystiques et des poëtes." Charles Huit counts him in the number of the most brilliant poets of the century (op. cit., p. 178): "Si Jean de Salisbury est au premier range parmi les érudits du XIIe siècle, Alain de Lille compte au nombre de ses plus brillants poètes. Ses écrits attestent les progrès étonnants réalisés dès cette époque par la culture littéraire et le soin jaloux avec lequel, dans les classes lettrées, on étudiait pour les imiter les chefs-d'oeuvre survivants de l'antiquité latine, à commencer par les vers de Virgile, d'Ovide, de Sénèque et de Claudien. La poésie didactique et allégorique, en si grand honneur au moyen âge, n'a rien produit de supérieur à l'*Anticlaudianus*, où Dante a puisé l'idée première de maint épisode célèbre de la *Divine Comédie*." Gilson finds little poetry in the *Anticlaudianus* but some grandeur in the *De planctu naturae* (op. cit., p. 315). Raby finds Alan's philosophical poems less charming than his shorter *rhythmus* (op. cit., p. 15). Allen quotes the same *rhythmus* (*Omnis mundi creatura*) that was praised by Raby, as evidence that "lyric song," which he seems to identify with "poetry in the modern sense, romantic poetry at least," is unknown among the products of the twelfth-century humanistic schools (op. cit., p. 233). D. M. Moffat, who translated the *De planctu naturae*, has a particularly low opinion of the poetic quality of that work. After acknowledging the indebtedness of Chaucer and Jean de Meun to Alan, Moffat disposes of his poet in summary judgment (*The Complaint of Nature by Alain de Lille*, Preface [New York, 1908], p. 1): "The statement of Langlois that 'more than five thousand verses of the *Roman de la Rose* are translated, imitated, or inspired by the *De planctu naturae*' is excellent authority that this mysterious scholar of the Middle Ages, whose very identity is unascertained, was of those who beget kings in literature, though he himself were none." It would be difficult to gainsay Moffat's judgment on the basis of his prosy, though for the most part accurate, translation; but even Homer is not a poet in all translations. The differences of scholarly judgment indicate the need of a reanalysis of the intellectual poetry of the Middle Ages on other standards than those suggested by the romantic lyric.

converses with Nature concerning such imperfections of man as sodomy and stirs his interlocutor to a truly Platonic outburst against poets by asking about their accounts of like ignominious deeds by the gods. The dreamy fancies of the poets deserve no credence, according to Nature, and philosophy's saner treatment files away and erases by means of higher understanding what was learned in the child's cradle of poetic teaching. Among the distortions of the poets, those concerning love are most of all in error.[13] When Alan persists in his interest in things poetic and asks concerning the nature of Cupid, which various authors have depicted under the concealing envelopment of enigmas (*sub integumentali involucro aenigmatum*) without leaving us any vestiges of certitude, Nature reproaches his inattention to her high discourse and promises in her prose argument to demonstrate the indemonstrable and to extricate the inextricable, as she puts it, by describing in certain description or defining in legitimate definition. "The artful exposition of her doctrine, the theory of the art of love" stated in a "chastened loftiness of style" is an artful lyric on the nature of love.[14]

The position of the humanists and the moderate skeptics, in the third place, derives from Plato by way of Cicero and the Roman rhetoricians and poets. The condemnation which Abailard brought against poetry itself is reserved in their criticism for the errors of poets, and the praise of poetry is reflected in its use and interpretations by philosophers. Moreover, in this analysis, poetry is not separated, as it is according to Abailard, Bernard, and Alan, from the liberal arts, but it may be a part of one of the liberal arts and a useful tool of theology.

John of Salisbury, whose urbane verses treat problems suggested by the history of philosophy and the errors of philosophers, wrote that he did not blush to acknowledge himself an academic skeptic, for he was content to doubt concerning things of which a wise man

13. *De planctu naturae* (*PL*, CCX, 451A–452A).

14. Ibid., sexta quaestio (*PL*, CCX, 454C–456B). It should be observed that, since the purpose of the poem is demonstrative, it will naturally seem unpoetic to critics who dislike "allegorical" proof and the use of the "common-places." According to Raby (op. cit., II, 20), "the 'descriptio Cupidinis' is a school-exercise."

cannot be certain.[15] But this Ciceronian skepticism left him three sources of certain knowledge: the senses, reason, and faith. He is anxious to safeguard a modicum of culture from the ignorance of the illiterate masses, and he has no doubt that reading in the historians, orators, and mathematicians is essential to a liberal education. He can therefore repeat from Cicero both the condemnation of poets (since they are lauded in spite of the darkness they spread, the fears they engender, and the passions they inflame) and also the praise of poetry (since it is essential to education and philosophy).[16] John quotes Cicero's moral defense of poetry, probably from a portion of the *De re publica* which is no longer extant:

> He alone who does not fear to be the object of contempt makes the poets and the various writers of the arts and of history contemptible. For they both have the use of virtue and afford the material of philosophy; they note the vices, to be sure, but do not teach them, and they are attractive either because of utility or because of pleasure. They make their way thus through moral dangers only to establish a place for virtue.[17]

This journey through moral dangers to the pleasures of philosophy is to be found signified allegorically in the adventures of Ulysses; and John also repeats, in brief summary, Bernard Sylvester's allegorical interpretation of the first six books of the *Aeneid.*[18] According to John, Virgil intimates his philosophic conclusions under the cloak of his feigned invention (*sub involucro fictitii commenti*), and John quotes with approval the opinion of those expert in the interpretation of authors that Virgil makes use of a twofold instruc-

15. *Polic.*, Prologus (Webb, I, 17; *PL*, CXCIX, 388B–C); cf. *Metal.* ii. 20 (Webb, p. 106; *PL*, CXCIX, 882B). Since John is given to literal statement rather than to allegory, his poetry has fared better at the hands of modern critics. Raby admires his *Entheticus de dogmate philosophorum* as a medley of satire, philosophy, and moral counsel, and he exempts it from his favorite condemnation of intellectual poetry as school-exercises. Cf. op. cit., II, 91: "The seriousness and the soundness of his outlook are abundantly clear; his poem is no mere *tour de force* or school-exercise. It has preserved its freshness because it bears the impress of his keen and judicial intelligence, of his grave irony and his deep seriousness."

16. *Polic.* vii. 9 (Webb, II, 126; *PL*, CXCIX, 655C–656A).

17. Webb, II, 127; *PL*, CXCIX, 656C.

18. *Polic.* viii. 24 (Webb, II, 415–18; *PL*, CXCIX, 816C–818B).

tion, since he has enfolded the secrets of philosophic virtue in the vanity of poetic figment.[19]

The art of poetry, according to John of Salisbury, is to imitate nature, and poetic shares this function with grammar, the mother and nurse of the study of poetry. To be sure, grammar and rhetoric are not primarily natural; they are conventional, but nature has some control over them, since they imitate nature. He dismisses disdainfully the arguments of those who hold that poetic is a separate art and concludes that it must either be a part of grammar or have no place among the liberal arts.[20] Poetic is essential to philosophy, although, as Seneca pointed out, it is not sufficient to make a man good; but one who aspires to philosophy must lay hold of four things: reading, learning, meditation, and the practice of good works.[21] John states the relation of poetic to the liberal arts and the interrelations of the liberal arts in terms of an elaborate figure of speech derived from weaving, in which grammar and poetic furnish the background of the tapestry or brocatel.

> Grammar and poetic, indeed, pour themselves out entirely and occupy the whole surface of what is expounded. Logic, bearing its colors [i.e., figures] of proof to this ground, as it is wont to be called, sets off its reasons in a blaze of gold; and rhetoric emulates the brightness of silver with its places of persuasions and brilliance of style. Mathematics is borne on the wheels of its quadrivium and, following on the tracks of the others, weaves its own colors and charms in manifold ways. Physics, having explored the counsels of nature, brings from its storehouse numerous charms of colors. Moreover, that which rises above the other parts of philosophy—I mean ethics, without which not even the name of philosopher subsists—surpasses all the others in the grace of ornament that it brings. Examine Virgil or Lucan, and you will find in them, whatever philosophy you profess, adornment for it.[22]

John of Salisbury is one of our chief sources of information concerning the methods of literary instruction and interpretation prac-

19. Webb, II, 415, 417; *PL*, CXCIX, 816D–817A, 818A.
20. *Metal.* i. 17 (Webb, pp. 42–43; *PL*, CXCIX, 847A–D).
21. *Metal.* i. 22–23 (Webb, pp. 51–53; *PL*, CXCIX, 852B–853C).
22. *Metal.* i. 24 (Webb, pp. 54–55; *PL*, CXCIX, 854B–C).

ticed by Bernard of Chartres—"the most perfect Platonist of our times," as John calls him—in which the identity of poetic and grammar and the fundamental contribution of grammar to philosophy are both apparent. John was convinced, moreover, that the liberal arts were all organically interrelated, both with each other and with philosophy; and the portrait of Gilbert de la Porrée which he draws in the *Historia pontificalis*, in careful balance to Gilbert's great antagonist, Bernard, is concrete manifestation of the possible contribution of poetry and philosophy to theology:

> He used, as the matter required, the aid of all disciplines, for he knew that in these severally the whole rests upon mutual supports. He had connected the disciplines, and he made them serve theology, and he restricted the rules of all within the limits of the proper genera. For they are each adapted to their proper genera, and they are immediately vitiated when they have been transferred to another genus. He made clear the properties and figures of words even in theology by the examples not only of philosophers and orators, but also of poets.[23]

Within the interrelation of the arts, poetry has his proper place as one of the liberal arts and as support to philosophy and theology.

One final variant of the interpretation of poetry derives from Plato by way of mystical theology. Some of the great mystics of the twelfth century cultivated the liberal arts as one stage in the return of the soul from experience of things to self-knowledge and thence to God; and in their doctrine poetry is subordinate to the liberal arts and not wholly essential to them, while other great mystics were suspicious alike of all secular arts—the liberal arts as well as poetry—and they expressed their adumbration of the truth missed by the liberal arts in poetry comparable for its force and imagery to the poetic statement other mystics gave to their suspicion of poetry.

Hugh of St. Victor, whose careful differentiation of the arts in the *Didascalicon* presupposes the same kind of organic cohesion among them that John of Salisbury praised, finds only a secondary place for poetry.[24] There are two kinds of writings, one properly called

23. *Historia pontificalis* 12, ed. R. L. Poole (Oxford, 1927), p. 28.

24. *Didascalicon: de studio legendi* iii. 4, ed. C. H. Buttimer (Washington, 1939), pp. 54–55 (*PL*, CLXXVI, 768D–769C).

"arts," such as grammar, dialectic, and rhetoric, which furnish subject matter to philosophy, the other only appendages to the arts, which look toward philosophy but have some subject matter outside philosophy. The latter include all the songs of the poets, such as tragedies, comedies, satires, heroic and lyrical poems, and iambics and certain didascalic poems, likewise fables and histories and even the writings of men usually called philosophers now, who are wont to extend a brief matter in long involutions of words and to obscure an easy meaning with confused words or even to bring together divers things at once as if to make a single picture from many colors and forms. The distance between the arts and the appendages to the arts, Hugh characteristically measures by a quotation from Virgil's *Eclogues*, for it is as great as that between the willow and the olive or the reed and the rose. Sometimes the appendages to the arts touch on bits torn here and there in disorder from the arts; or when they engage in simple narration, they may prepare for philosophy. One may, however, become perfect in reading without the appendages to the arts, whereas no perfection whatever can be conferred by the appendages without the arts.

Honorius of Autun treats the liberal arts in a work entitled *On the Exile and the Homeland of the Soul*, for the exile of man is ignorance and the homeland, wisdom, to which he returns by a route which leads through the liberal arts as through cities. The first of these cities is grammar, in which there are certain subordinate *villae*, the books of the poets, which are divided into four kinds: tragedies, comedies, satires, and lyrics.[25] Tragedies are poems which treat of wars, as Lucan; comedies, those which sing nuptials, as Terence; satires, those which are concerned with reprehensible things, as Persius; lyrics, those which give voice to odes, that is, praises of gods and hymns to kings, as Horace.

Hildebert of Lavardin, finally, one of the great poets of the twelfth century, abandons philosophy as well as poetry as progressive stages in the return to Scripture. In one of his sermons he generalizes from what he has said about the Virgin to all interpretation of Scripture:

> For we have, for the most part, passed by the fictions of poets, who are compared to croaking frogs. We have sailed over the

25. *De animae exsilio et patria* (alias, *De artibus*) 2 (*PL*, CLXXII, 1243C–D).

pallid arguments of sophists, who are said to be hateful to God. We have bid farewell to the pompous opinions of philosophers, who have tried, while they were still among us, to raise their eyes above the heavens, among whom the more learned—I mean the academics—have confessed that truth is hidden in a bottomless well. We have given up magniloquent speech to follow veriloquent speech. For we sought wisdom, but behold it was not in the land of pleasantly speaking or living. *We heard of it in Ephrata,* that is, in a mirror or in a watchtower, that is, hidden in an image, but behold *we found it in the fields of the wood,* that is, in the manifestation of the New Testament and the obscurity of the Old Testament.[26]

26. *Sermo LX: in festo Assumptionis Beatae Mariae, et de laudibus, sermo secundus* (*PL*, CLXXI, 633A–B). For the reference to the Sophists cf. Ecclus. 37:23: "Qui sophistice loquitur, odibilis est." For the reference to "the land of pleasantly speaking or living" (*sauviter loquentium seu viventium*) cf. Job 28:13: "Nescit homo pretium eius [i.e., sapientiae], nec invenitur in terra suaviter viventium." Cf. Jerome *Comm. in Job* (*PL*, XXVI, 701A): "Et ideo suaviter dicti sunt vivere illi, qui nullo jugo disciplinae tenentur, et effrenes ac praecipites in labem prorumpunt vitiorum." Hildebert has apparently connected Jerome's reference to "disciplines" with the "disciplines" in the sense of the liberal arts and particularly the arts of speech. The Septuagint does not contain a term equivalent to "discipline" or, indeed, to the *terra suaviter viventium* which lacks discipline, but has merely οὐδὲ μὴ εὑρεθῇ ἐν ἀνθρώποις, and Jerome in his translation from the Greek (*Lib. Iob. Altera versio ex Graecis exemplaribus sive ex Originis Hexaplari editione* [*PL*, XXIX, 94B]) renders the passage "nex invenietur in hominibus." The interpretation of Ps. 132 (131):6, "Lo, we heard of it in Ephrata: we found it in the fields of the wood," which had taken a traditional form in the twelfth century, composed of elements which go back to Jerome and Augustine, is an excellent example of the allegorical and etymological interpretations. "Ephrata" is a name applied to the region of Bethlehem and to the town of Bethlehem itself (cf. Gen. 35:16 and 19, 48:7; Ruth 4:11; Mic. 5:2). Jerome was the source, for medieval writers, of both the literal explanation and some of the allegorical meanings. "Ephratha, regio Bethleem civitatis David, in qua natus est Christus. Est autem in tribu Juda (licet plerique male aestiment in tribu Benjamin), juxta viam ubi sepulta est Rachel quinto milliario ab Jerusalem, in eo loco qui a Septuaginta vocatur Hippodromus" (*De s'tu et nominibus locorum Hebraicorum* [*PL*, XXIII, 939]). Cf. *Commentaria in Jeremiam prophetam* vi. 21 (*PL*, XXIII, 877A–B) (this passage is repeated by Rhabanus Maurus, *PL*, CXI, 1035); *Commentaria in Abdiam* (*PL*, XXV, 1116C); *Commentaria in Micheam* v (*PL*, XXV, 1198B). Among the meanings attached to the word by Jerome are *uberrima, ubertas, furorem videt.* "Ephratha vero et Bethlehem unius urbis vocabulum est, sub interpretatione consimili: siquidem in *frugiferam* et in *domum panis* vertitur propter eum panem qui de coelo descendisse se dicet" (*Liber Hebraicarum quaestionum in Genesim* [*PL*, XXIII, 1042B]). He interprets it *uberrima* (*Epistola* cviii [*PL*, XXII, 885]), *ubertas sive pul-*

The language is close to that which Bernard and William of St. Thierry employed to condemn the intellectual audacity of Abailard, and the reasons are not unlike those which Abailard alleged to condemn the vain figments of the poets. The error of philosophers consists in raising their eyes to, or poking their noses into, things above the heavens[27] and in submitting faith to the manipulations of reason. Abailard had criticized the poets because of the discrepancies

---

verulenta (*Liber de nominibus Hebraicis* [*PL*, XXIII, 822]), *frugifera sive equidem (furorem?) vides* (*PL*, XXIII, 872). Augustine, however, seems to have been the source of the tradition in the Latin Middle Ages in which it is interpreted *speculum* (*Enarratio in Psalmum CXXXI* [*PL*, XXXVII, 1720]). Prosper of Aquitaine makes the two parts of the verse signify the mirror of the prophets and the lofty but erroneous achievement of the Gentiles: "Ephrata nomen Hebraeum interpretatur Latine speculum, in quo propheticae significationis imago precessit. Per speculum enim prophetiae, annuntiata haec sedes vel habitatio Dei, de qua dicitur, *Ecce audivimus eam in Ephrata*, id est, in eloquiis prophetarum. *Invenimus eam in campis silvae*, hoc est, in altitudine gentium, in quibus fuerunt vepres idololatriae, concretiones errorum, et silvestres incultarum mentium feritates" (*Expositio in Psalmum CXXXI* [*PL*, LI, 379A–B]). Much the same interpretation is put on the verse by Cassiodorus: "*Ephrata* lingua Latina significare memoratur speculum. *Campi* vero *silvae* indicant corda gentilium, quae ex peccatis quasi silvestribus ac dumosis, mundante Domino, campestri puritate patuerunt. *Campi* siquidem a capacitate et spatio diffuso dicti sunt. Facti sunt enim ex hispidis nitidi, ex agrestibus mansueti, ex sterilibus fructuosi, ex cubilibus daemonum templa Dominantis. Et ideo in campis silvae, id est, in gentibus dicit esse compertum, quod in imagine prophetiae Judaeis fuerat repromissum" (*Expositio in Psalterium* [*PL*, LXX, 949A–B]). Cf. Christianus Druthmarus *Expositio in Matthaeum* (*PL*, CVI, 1280D); Walafridus Strabus *Glossa ordinaria*, Genesis 35:16 and Ruth 1:2 (*PL*, CXIII, 162D, 533A–B); and Rupertus Tutiensis *De Trinitate et operibus ejus* xlii, *in Genesim* lib. ix (*PL*, CLXVII, 548B). Paschasius Radbertus emphasizes the interpretation *furorem videns*, which he reconciles with *frugifera* (*Expositio in Matthaeum* ii. 2 [*PL*, CXX, 131C–134B). Petrus Comestor has a plausible explanation to bring the three meanings together: "Ephrata, id est *furorem vidit*, id est experimento iram Dei cognovit. Vel interpretatur *speculum*, quia plaga ejus omnibus est posita in exemplum; sed tunc primo propter incredibilem ubertatem sibi [cibi?] reditam cepit vocari Bethlehem, quod est *domus panis*" (*Historia scholastica, historia libri Ruth* [*PL*, CXCVIII, 1293C]).

27. Hildebert describes philosophers in general with the characterization, "qui dum adhuc essent apud nos, conati sunt attollere oculos super coelos"; St. Bernard turns the same conception into an attack on Abailard in his letter to Innocent II: "Qui dum omnium quae sunt in coelo sursum, et quae in terra deorsum, nihil, praeter solum Nescio, nescire dignatur; ponit in coelum os suum, et scrutatur alta Dei, rediensque ad nos refert verba ineffabilia, quae non licet homini loqui: et dum paratus est de omnibus reddere rationem, etiam quae supra rationem, et contra rationem praesumit, et contra fidem" (*Contra quaedam capitula errorum Abaelardi, Epistola CXC seu Tractatus ad Innocentium II Pontificem* 1 [*PL*, CLXXXII, 1055A]).

between their poetry and their faith, but he had held that reason and philosophy cannot be contrary to faith. Bernard criticized Abailard's dialectic because of the discrepancies between his philosophy and his faith, but in so doing he reproaches Abailard for trying to see all things face to face and for making no use in his philosophy of the device, familiar to poets, of seeing truth in a mirror and enigma. Bernard's criticism of philosophy and poetry thus accomplishes a complete reversal of literary criticism and philosophy; for it employs in defense of faith both the poetic devices of allegorical interpretation, which permit Bernard to criticize even the "profane novelties of words and senses" which Abailard introduced into his theological works, and also the philosophic arguments concerning self-knowledge and love, which echo the words of Socrates and prepare the matter, in prose and verse, of immortal poetry.[28]

28. Cf. *Epistola CXCII ad Magistrum Guidonem de Castello* (*PL*, CLXXXII, 358C–D): "Magister Petrus in libris suis profanas vocum novitates inducit et sensuum: disputans de fide contra fidem, verbis legis legem impugnat. Nihil videt per speculum et in aenigmate; sed facie ad faciem omnia intuetur, ambulans in magnis et mirabilis super se. Melius illi erat, si juxta titulum libri sui, se ipsum cognosceret, nec agrederetur mensuram suam sed saperet ad sobrietatem." The last reproach refers to the title of Abailard's moral treatise, *Scito teipsum*. Abailard, on the other hand, accuses Bernard of introducing novelties, without authority and contrary to custom, into ecclesiastical matters, such as prayers, ritual, and the singing of hymns (cf. *Epistola X ad Bernardum Claraevallensem abbatem* [*PL*, CLXXVIII, 339]): "Si haec vestra novitas aut singularitas ab antiquitate recedat aliorum, quam rationi plurimum et tenori regulae creditis concordare: nec curatis quantacunque admiratione super hoc alii moveantur, ac murmurent, dummodo vestrae, quam putatis, rationi pareatis. Quorum ut pauca commemorem, pace vestra, hymnos solitos respuistis, et quosdam apud nos inauditos, et fere omnibus Ecclesiis incognitos, ac minus sufficientes, introduxistis. Unde et per totum annum in vigiliis tam feriarum quam festivitatum uno hymno et oedem contenti estis, cum Ecclesia pro diversitate feriarum vel festivitatum diversis utatur hymnis, sicut et psalmis, vel caeteris, quae his pertinere noscuntur: quod et manifesta ratio exigit. Unde et qui vos die Natalis, seu Paschae, vel Pentecostes, et caeteris solemnitatibus hymnum semper eumdem decantare audiunt, scilicet, *Aeterne rerum conditor*, summo stupore attoniti suspenduntur; nec tam admiratione quam derisione moventur." Despite his differences from Bernard's interpretation of its significance for philosophy, Abailard recognized the subordination of eloquence and philosophy to the wisdom of Christ (cf. *Hymnus LXV, Ad laudes et ad vesperas* [*PL*, CLXXVIII, 1805]): "Stulta seculi, mundi infima / Christus eligens sapientia / Quaeque conterit et sublimia. // Nil urbanitas his rhetoricae, / Nil verbositas [valet] logicae, / Sed simplicitas fidei sacrae. // Eloquentia cessit Tullü, / 'Tace' dictum est Aristoteli; / Leges proferunt mundo rustici. // Perpes gloria." For the discussion of the conceptions of love developed by Abailard and Bernard and their possible influences on the "courtly love" of poetic tradition, cf. E. Gilson, *La Théologie mystique de Saint Bernard* (Paris, 1934), pp. 183–89 and 193–215.

All four of these conceptions of poetry, despite the oppositions among them, echo the judgment of Plato by which poets are condemned because philosophers are engaged on a more truly poetic enterprise. In the thirteenth century, poetry is no longer so close to philosophy or so dangerous a rival to it. Even after the translation of Aristotle's works, the influence of Platonism continued strong, particularly in the form in which the arts and philosophy serve as subordinate and preparatory stages to theology. Thus, for Bonaventura, poetry seems to have become one of the mechanical arts. There are four lights by which the mind is illuminated: the exterior light of the mechanical arts, the inferior light of sensitive knowledge, the interior light of philosophic knowledge, and the superior light of grace and the Sacred Scriptures. The mechanical arts are concerned with the production of artificial things, which are classified, following the distinction made by Horace in the *Ars poetica*, as the useful and the delightful. Only one of the seven mechanical arts, the theater, is concerned with the delightful,[29] and under the theater Bonaventura includes all arts of play, whether of songs, instruments, figments, or gesticulations of the body. Grammar, logic, and rhetoric fall under the rational arts of philosophic knowledge, concerned, respectively, with apprehensive, judicative, and motive reason, and rhetoric therefore finds its function in moving to love or hate by means of ornate words. The treatment of the mechanical arts consists of three parts, which take account of the arts of the artificer, the quality of his effect, and the utility of his product or fruit; and Bonaventura concludes from such considerations that the illumination of the mechanical art is on the way to the illumination of Sacred Scripture and that nothing in it is not pertinent to true wisdom.[30]

The influence of Aristotle, on the other hand, had led in the thirteenth century to the establishment of a philosophy independent of theology in method and subject matter, and that philosophy likewise is not in opposition to poetry. Thomas Aquinas, thus, treats poetic not as the science of a product or process of production but as a subdivision of logic. Logic or rational science consists of eight

29. *De reductione artium ad theologiam* 1–2 (*S. Bonaventurae opera omnia*, ed. Quaracchi, V [1891], 319–20).

30. *De reductione* 11–15 (*Opera omnia*, V, 322–23).

parts, six of which correspond to the matter treated in the six books of Aristotle's *Organon*, to which rhetoric and poetic are added. Besides the parts of logic which treat of the certitudes of science and which are called Judicative, there are three parts which treat of the processes of discovery, often short of certitude, and which are called Inventive. Poetic is one of these. Dialectic treats of the process of discovery when it leads to conviction or opinion (*fides vel opinio*); rhetoric treats of it when it leads only to a kind of suspicion without total exclusion of the contrary possibility; poetic treats of it when estimation leads to one of the two parts of a contradiction only because of the manner of representation, as a man may be led to hold a certain food in abomination because it is represented to him under the likeness of something abominable. The specific function of the poet is to induce to virtue by fitting representation.[31]

What philosophers say about poetry might have little bearing on the nature of poetry or of philosophy, if the grounds and consequences of their judgments were not clearly apparent in both. The repetitions in the twelfth century of Plato's moral criticisms of the poets, adapted to Christian theology and expressed with undiminished poetic force, suggest to the critic and the scholar several lines of inquiry in which the historical relations between poetry and philosophy may serve to elucidate some of the qualities and problems of poetry.

The approximation and rivalry of poetry and philosophy—one of the great commonplaces of Platonism which was, in its next recurrence during the Renaissance of the fifteenth and sixteenth centuries, to yield the victory to the poets—throws some light, in the first place, on the subject matters appropriate to poetry and philosophy. The twelfth century was a period in which poets and philosophers were engaged on the same themes, and the poetic expression of philosophy as well as the philosophic criticisms of poetry reflect the basic theological problem of the relation of reason and faith. This problem recurs in the great development of the liberal arts worked by philosophers like Bernard of Chartres, Thierry of Chartres, Abailard, Hugh of St. Victor, and John of Salisbury. But the liberal arts

31. *In libros Posteriorum analyticorum expositio* i, Lectio 1 (*Opera omnia*, I [Rome, 1882], 138–40).

also furnished subject matter for poetry as various as the *Fons philosophiae* of Godefroy of St. Victor (in which the seven liberal arts are derived as streams from a single source, theology) and the numerous poems of Alan of Lille: the *De planctu naturae*, in which the arts of the trivium are considered in relation to the schools of Venus; the *Anticlaudianus*, in which the liberal arts construct a chariot for Prudence; and the mystic *rhythmus*, *On the Incarnation of Christ*, in which the seven liberal arts are applied to the Word of God. The methods of the liberal arts underlie the great cosmological speculations in which philosophers like Thierry of Chartres, Adelard of Bath, and William of Conches followed pagan inspirations related only occasionally to the account of Genesis. The same cosmological materials serve as subject matter for the poems of Bernard Sylvester and Alan of Lille, while enthusiasm concerning the creation of the world and of man is tempered by the recurrent theme *De contemptu mundi* in poets and philosophers like Bernard of Morlas, John of Salisbury, Hildebert of Lavardin, Alan of Lille, and Bernard. The same liberal arts are employed in the moral speculations to which twelfth-century philosophers returned, after the model of Socrates: the studies of passions and motives which Abailard develops in his ethical treatise *Scito teipsum* recur as poignant poetic subjects in his hymns and planctus; and Hildebert of Lavardin can turn from the collection of excerpts from moral philosophers, which constitute his *Moralis philosophia de honesto et utili*, to the vigorous verses in his *Libellus de quatuor virtutibus vitae honestae*.

The Platonic influence in the twelfth century, manifested in cosmological speculations inspired by the *Timaeus* and in Socratic inquiries into morals and method, runs through diversities which may be recapitulated in the interpretation of the Socratic dictum, "Know thyself." The concreteness of imaginative innovation and the richness of emotional antithesis developed in the interpretation of that dictum illustrate the use of philosophic issues by which they are made poetry, while the theoretic scope and opposition of the positions to which it was attached make it subject to numerous moral, cosmological, and mystic implications. Peter Abailard entitled his treatise on morals, *Know Thyself*; and for him self-knowledge is found in the specific analysis of actions, intentions, and sins, which constitute the abstract arguments of his ethics and are reflected in the concrete emotions of his lyrics and which lead, in turn, to his moral condemnation of poetry. Bernard Sylvester justified his allegorical interpretation of Virgil on the ground that it would assist man to know himself; and for him self-knowledge is attained through the analogies of literature, in which the career of a hero signifies the ages of man, and of nature, in which man is microcosm and the universe megacosm. "Know thyself" is the recurrent injunction of the mystics, of Bernard, William of St. Thierry, and Richard of St. Victor, for whom perfect self-knowledge was never attained by the philosophers, since man is the image of God, whom philosophers ignored. All these themes and issues are reflected finally in the philosophic analysis and poetic development of the concept of love, which is pervasively Platonic and persistently poetic, for it is the object of philosophical disputation and the source of poetry from the dialectical analyses and love songs of Abailard to the mystical developments of Bernard and William of St. Thierry and of Victorine and Cistercian poets.

The continuity of the subject matter of poetry and philosophy suggests a second inquiry into the methods and forms, which makes possible the transition from the interpretation of nature, art, and thought to the constructions of poetry and the demonstrations of philosophy. The common method is rhetoric, which assumes many forms and uses in the twelfth century. Abailard borrowed a method for philosophy from the procedures of canon law and laid the foundations of theological inquiry by assembling opposed authorities whose contradictions could be resolved by rhetorical devices, such as consideration of the circumstances under which the antithetical statements had been made; he was convinced, furthermore, that the intention of all divine Scripture is to teach and move in the manner of a rhetorical speech.[32] Matthew of Vendôme, in one of the earliest of the medieval treatises on the art of poetry, includes an analysis of poetry in a conversation between Philosophy and her four companions: Tragedy, Satire, Comedy, and Elegy. Elegy teaches Philosophy that the charm of poetry consists in three things: the content of the thought (*venustas interioris sententiae*), the form of the

32. Cf. *Sic et non*, Prologus (*PL*, CLXXVIII, 1339–49), and *Commentaria super S. Pauli Epistolam ad Romanos*, Prologus (*PL*, CLXXVIII, 784).

words (*superficialis ornatus verborum*), and the quality or rhetorical color of the expression (*modus dicendi* or *dicendi color*);[33] and the discussion of the "content of thought" consists in examining the verbal means of treating as subject matter of poetry such distinctions of character and emotion as might enter into their moral aspect into the philosophic discussions of virtue. Conrad of Hirschau, in one of the earliest histories of literature, the *Dialogus super auctores*, says that the treatment of ancient writers should consist of seven parts: author, title of work, quality of the poem, intention of the writer, order, number of books, and explanation, specifying that explanation is fourfold, with respect to letter, meaning, allegory, and morality. The explanation of modern writers, however, requires only four parts: the matter of the work, the intention of the writer, the final cause or fruit derived from reading the work, and the part of philosophy under which what is written falls; and the parts of philosophy are logic, physics, and ethics, the liberal arts being distributed under logic (the trivium) and physics (the quadrivium).[34]

The method of resolving differences in canon law, of posing theological and philosophical problems, and of interpreting poetry, finally, does not differ radically from the method expounded in the early treatises on the art of preaching; for Guibert of Nogent undertakes to justify the differentiation of the historical, allegorical, tropological, and anagogic modes of interpretation,[35] while Alan of Lille devotes himself to the consideration of the nature and subject

33. *Ars versificatoria* ii. 4–11; iii. 1–2, ed. E. Faral, *Les Arts poétiques du XIIe et du XIIIe siècle* (Paris, 1924), pp. 152–54, 167–68.

34. *Conradi Hirsaugiensis Dialogus super auctores sive Didascalon*, ed. G. Schepss (Würzburg, 1889), pp. 27–28, 74–84. Dante follows a similar conception of criticism in the sixfold division which he makes of his Introduction to the *Paradiso* in his letter to Can Grande della Scala (*Epistola* X, 7): "Sex igitur sunt, quae in principio cujusque *doctrinalis Operis* inquirenda sunt, videlicet *Subjectum, Agens, Forma, Finis, libri Titulus*, et *Genus philosophiae*." The kind of philosophy under which the *Divine Comedy* falls is ethics; cf. ibid. 16: "*Genus* vero *philosophiae*, sub quo hic in Toto et Parte proceditur, est *morale Negotium*, sive *Ethica*, qui non ad speculandum, sed ad opus inceptum est Totum. Nam, etsi in aliquo loco vel passu pertractatur ad modum speculativi negotii, hoc non est gratia speculativi negotii, sed gratia operis; quia, ut ait Philosophus in secundo *Metaphysicorum*, 'ad aliquid et tunc speculantur practici aliquando.'"

35. *Liber quo ordine sermo fieri debeat* (*PL*, CLVI, 22–32, and esp. 25–26).

matter of sermons, the quality of preachers, and the kinds of audiences; and he differentiates preaching from poetic composition by the fact that the preacher has no need for scurrilous or puerile words or melodies of rhythms and consonances of meters, such as might be suited to theatrical or mimic predication.[36] In the art of preaching, subject matter is found and examined in the nature and origin of the virtues and vices, in the contempt of world and of self, and in the kinds of men and the means by which they are moved; and the fourfold method of reading is applied by the writers of the twelfth century to the interpretation of nature, which is an image of God, as well as of poetry and Scripture. Rhetoric is the connecting link not only among such divergent matters but also between Platonism and the increasing knowledge of the Aristotelian logic. The Aristotelian logic and the Platonic dialectic are at cross-purposes, but the Aristotelian and Platonic conceptions of rhetoric are homogeneous; for, according to Aristotle, rhetoric is characterized by its figurative language, while logic requires univocal terms and dialectic distinguishes among definitions, and, according to Plato, rhetoric, unless it is identified with dialectic, is imperfect dialectic based on insufficient knowledge of subject matter and expressed in language uncorrelated with fact. In the mystic theology, in which matters of faith are beyond the scope of reason and all things and all words have allegorical and mystical significances, the method which joins poetry to philosophy and Plato to Aristotle passes beyond all such matters to serve as surrogate for all techniques of inquiry or literal statement.

Questions of matter and form, however, suggest the third and basic question of poetic value. The philosophers of the twelfth century speculate about and write a kind of poetry whose subject matter—apart from love lyrics, drinking songs, and a few satires—has seemed by later standards unpoetic. Their poetry often employs allegorical devices of exposition and, whatever the style, is designed to be read according to an allegorical interpretation, whereas the modern reader, even when he can recognize allegorical meanings,

36. *Summa de arte praedicatoria* 1 and 39 (*PL*, CCX, 111–12, and 184). Chap. 39 states the threefold division of the treatise which reduces the fivefold scheme announced in the Praefatio along lines reminiscent of Aristotle and Cicero: "Dicto, quorum debeat esse praedicatio, et quales esse oporteant praedicatores, restat ostendere, quibus proponenda sit praedicatio."

seldom employs them as a means of discerning and appreciating poetic values. The poetry of the Middle Ages, like all great poetry, can be appreciated by other critical standards than those according to which it was conceived. Yet the poetic qualities on which the different interpretations fix seem to be the same, despite the differences of meaning attached to them. Modern readers find a literal trait of character or emotion or a concrete episode among unnoticed allegorical, moral, and anagogic significances, and they savor vague didactic allusions without feeling a temptation to determine what part of philosophy the poem falls under. What they find in medieval poetry is the ingenious and colored language, the concrete confrontation of emotion and intention which is the outer surface of the Socratic self-knowledge, the passionate moral aspiration, the partially understood didactic intention, and the grandiose mystic definition of the relation of man and God. The transformations of value and the continuities which make possible the discovery of values in related or identical qualities by different modes of analysis and criticism serve to isolate some of the basic problems of aesthetics. They are problems which are underscored for us by the poetry and philosophy of the twelfth century; for poetry is related to philosophy today in methods and matters as different as those of existentialism, Marxism, and pragmatism, and it has again returned to themes similar to those of medieval poetry and to echoes of philosophical and theological discussion which recall that man is in a grave predicament, that words are ambiguous, and that the church or its apostle is a hippopotamus and God is mysterious. A language which echoes folklore and religion has been constructed for poetry; subject matter is found in the motives and confusions of man set forth in simple unresolved oppositions; moral problems are made poetic by obscuring suggestions of resolution; and poetry may be didactic if its lessons are vague, or metaphysical if it is without commitment to a philosophy, or religious if religion furnishes a restraint to sentiment in the construction of figures. Philosophers and poets in the twelfth century were engaged on a single set of problems; poets in the twentieth century convey a sense of treating philosophic problems, but their philosophy has become little more than a play with the colors of language which medieval poets employed to express a philosophy.

A Philosopher Meditates on Discovery

Novelty and discovery are subjects which elude analysis and discourse, for novelty, in the degree that it is intelligible, is familiar, and processes of discovery, if they could be reduced to rule, would differ little from customary actions guided by precept or habit. The inspiration which led the artist to a new form is reduced to technique or banality when he tries to explain how the idea occurred to him in any way other than by another artistic or poetic creation as mysterious as the first. The discovery of new scientific principles is lost in the accounts of antecedent ideas and attendant circumstances which explain neither the occurrence nor the novelty of the discovery. New insights in religion, even when they do not appeal to the operation of supernatural powers, are not reducible to formulas within the voluntary control of human agencies. Mathematics is the only field in which heuristic principles can be stated in a precise, abstract form and can be given practical application in the solution of problems, and it is possible there only by use of knowledge of an underlying order. In general, the discussion of discovery and of the occurrence of new ideas and insights must take the form either of a psychological examination of what goes on in the mind (and the crucial moment of discovery must then be assigned to the subconscious), or of a sociological study of influences (and the novelty of the discovery must then be found in the peculiarity of one man's response to what is common), or of a formal statement of guiding principles (and the discovery must then be sought in the possibly vacuous region surrounded, and progressively delimited, by those principles). During periods in which logicians have been concerned with problems of discovery and proof rather than with language and modes of expression, controversies in logic have often turned on the paradoxes of discovery, as when Mill criticized Whewell's "logic of discovery" on the grounds that discovery cannot be reduced to rules, and Whewell criticized Mill's inductive logic on the grounds that it only verified what had been discovered and omitted the problems of greatest importance to the scientist and the logician.

Discovery in philosophy is involved in the same paradoxes as a discovery in art, natural science, mathematics, and religion. Yet the universal scope of philosophy, and the divergent forms which philosophic speculation takes under the influences of analogies borrowed from art, science, mathematics, politics, and religion makes the profession of a new philosophical discovery at once more presumptuous (since the field is so large and the ground so well explored) and more modest (since the discovery of the new is scarcely distinguishable from the rediscovery and restatement of the changeless). Philosophy is a form of personal expression, of social integration, of scientific formulation, and of insight into fundamental values. In each of its forms, the approach of any philosopher is novel and the statement of his philosophy is a discovery, yet it is determined by conditions and circumstances which include the statements of other philosophers, the habits and institutions of men, the knowledge of scientists, and the underlying values that assume different forms in great varieties of expression, institution, and knowledge. Any given discovery is a function at once of the psychological experiences of one man and of the patterns accessible to all men whose experiences evolve in the common setting. Viewed as a personal expression of values, philosophy is an activity in which all men engage: we are all, willy-nilly, philosophers, and our originality is part of our character and individuality. Viewed as a social adjustment to times and circumstances, philosophy expresses shared attitudes, common cultures, and accepted values: we are all philosophers in a sense which transcends personal and esthetic differences in so far as we are sensitive and sympathetic to the values of those with whom we are joined in association and community. Viewed as a form of knowledge, philosophy is a systematization or integration of experience, science, and values: any one who reflects on his situation and his actions, his origin, nature, and destiny, is a philosopher in a sense which transcends personal and social differences in so far as he seeks common principles governing the interrelations in his life and in his understanding of what he perceives and what he knows, what he undergoes and what he seeks. Philosophers who aspire to that name as their particular designation (if only in the catalogues of universities in which they carry on their speculations or in the names of learned societies which they join) differ from these more numerous philosophers primarily in the fact that they relate their philosophic activities in personal expression, in social communication, and in scientific formulation explicitly to the basic values which they seek to realize. The peculiar psychological processes by which the philosopher is led to novelty of form or content takes place, therefore, on a background of historical, cultural, and intellectual constants.

The claim of novelty and discovery is frequent and recurrent in the history of philosophy. In a sense, the same thing has always been discovered, if we are to believe the claims that have been made—and the claims that are being made—and yet the novelty is in each case genuine. This pattern of reiterative novelty was set at the very beginning of the history of philosophy in the West. Socrates, according to Aristotle, was the first to apply the scientific method, which had previously been used only in physics, to the affairs of men—or, as Cicero repeated the novelty of Socrates's achievement, he first brought philosophy down from the heavens and gave her habitation in the cities of men. Both of the persistent elements of philosophic novelty are present in these statements of discovery—the use of science and the concern with values. Aristotle professed to have continued the task where Socrates left off, and Cicero acknowledged his effort to renew the method of Socrates, but without giving undue prominence in his philosophy to the new sciences which Aristotle thought had resulted from a like effort in his own works. The coming of Christianity brought new tidings concerning values, concerning the origin, relations, and destiny of men. The Church was established in the Roman Empire three hundred years after the beginning of the Christian era, and Christianity received philosophic systematization in the works of St. Augustine in the course of another hundred years. Augustine had postponed his conversion until he found the instrument for the interpretation of Scripture in the analogical method of Philo and in the rhetorical method of Cicero. Rhetoric, which had become the science of the practical for the Romans, provided the means by which to set forth Christian values, and the use of rhetorical devices disclosed a structure in the philosophy of Plato on which to organize them. The biographies deposited for the canonization of St. Thomas Aquinas, fifty years after his death, stressed the novelty of his philosophy and of the arguments which he brought to the exposition and defense of Christian truths. During the thirteenth century the philosophic works of Aristotle had become available again in the West, and Aquinas's great achievement was to have reconciled the vast corpus of that scientific doctrine and the subtleties of that scientific method with the body of Christian theology and to have saved Christian theology from the dangers of contradiction and heresy which followed from the similarities of Augustinism to Averroistic Aristotelianism. With the beginnings of modern science in the seventeenth century, philosophers renewed their efforts to apply the scientific method to the problems of man: Hobbes was convinced that the science of politics began with his treatise *De Cive*; Descartes, Spinoza, and Locke conceived ethics to be the central trunk of the tree of philosophy and sought, in varying ways, to formulate a science of human behavior; Hume took new inspiration from Newton in his inquiries concerning human understanding and concerning the principles of morals. Kant thought of Copernicus when he sought an analogy to explain the revolution he had worked by making man the center of his philosophy; and John Dewey devoted a great part of his intellectual energy to bringing the method of science to bear on human affairs and on human actions, thinking that in so doing he had accomplished a second Copernican revolution based on the experimental method, not by reorienting the world to the knower, but by indicating the possibility of "naturalizing" knowledge in the life of society.

At each step the novelty is the same; it is the use of science and knowledge—and usually of a specific method which is presented as scientific and practical—for the achievement, preservation, and understanding of values. Yet what is discovered at each step is different, and the discovery not only affects the whole of what is viewed as reality and the whole of what is accepted as knowledge, but also reveals without need of further inquiry the errors of other methods and the illusions of other discoveries. The history of discoveries in philosophy is self-rectifying, for the new truth can seldom be expressed without excursions into a new interpretation of the history of philosophy, of the insights and inadequacies of previous philosophers, of their anticipations of the truth, their tangential excursions into unreal problems which can henceforth be disregarded, and their misguided commitment to false distinctions which delayed the use of the true scientific method and the discovery of the truth. We have made progress in the development of sciences of man and of society, but we have found no means of applying science, even the new "science of values," to human actions even in problems which involve the use of the sciences and which reflect the effect of science on civilization and behavior. We have made progress in the study of values and of their cultural embodiments and interrelations, but we have found no means of making explicit and effective the underlying common values which would save values from the relativism into which they fall when they are naturalized and localized in cultures. The philosophic dimension of this practical dilemma is the inability to relate novelties in their multiplicity to what is constant and common in them—the novelties of the discoveries and principles of successive and contemporary philosophers, the novelties of the discoveries and values of successive and coexistent communities, and the novelties of the discoveries and methods of successive and interdependent sciences.

The philosophic problem of discovery is, in the retrospect of history no less than in the contemporaneous societies of men and the interrelations of knowledge, an old problem which has been discussed under many guises—it is the problem of the one and the many, or the problem of the impact of external influence or change on knowledge and values, or the problem of the application of science to the study of man, society, and human behavior. All of these aspects are present in any instance of philosophic discovery, and a place must be made for them in the execution of the modest task that has been assigned to me of analyzing the circumstances and content of the flash of insight which might be called a discovery in the development of my own philosophic attitude. The statement of the formal aspect of the problem of discovery in its numerous ramifications serves as a massive background against which to trace, and perhaps to lose, the peculiarities of one series of psychological occurrences. That background may be particularized to the stages of my own development by differentiating the four senses of philosophy, for the moment of discovery which I propose to describe is one which I would relate particularly with the emergence in my experience of philosophy in its fourth sense. I had evolved a complete philosophy in the first sense, as a personal expression, at the age of twenty. Indeed, I have never since been able to construct a scheme of solutions of problems, old and new, nearly so complete, certain, or systematic. It had several characteristics which seemed to me important in a philosophy: it made use of the latest advances in the sciences, and particularly in psychology and sociology; it was expressed in a technical language, elaborated at crucial points in a mathematical symbolism, part of which I had borrowed from respected sources and part of which I had invented; it was organized in a system in which the principles were clearly stated and the operations formalized; it had practical applications; and, what was most important, it could be applied to any field of philosophy or to any other subject matter without the need of much effort to become familiar with the intricacies of the subject matter or its problems.

The completeness and attraction of this philosophy as a mode of self-expression were badly damaged by contact with philosophy in its second sense, in which it serves as an instrument to treat problems in the specific forms which they assume in times, and places, and circumstances, and with philosophy in its third sense, in which it makes use of the methods and the accomplishments of science to adapt itself as a form of knowledge to its problems. I discovered, as one step of this transition, that a philosophy is not made practical by the enunciation or the analysis of values and the concomitant criticism of present practices and alternative doctrines: solutions of practical problems are grounded in the situation but are justified by the values they achieve rather than by the opportunity, and they are dependent on the analysis of values that realize actual potentialities. I made the second step by discovering that a philosophy is not made scientific by professing admiration for the scientific method and by aping the technicalities of scientific formulation: achievement and failure in science both share these accidental qualities, and the application of the scientific method consists rather in the attainment of new insights, the discovery of means of validating them, and the inventive exploration of consequences that follow from them. Accompanying these two steps, but scarcely distinguishable from them as a third step, was the discovery that I had read the great philosophers with something less than intellectual ingenuity or sensitive insight, as functions of my own limited point of view rather than as presentations of problems, to be considered in their own right before being dismantled to solve my problems, or as constructions of proof whose grounds and inferences might have criteria other than the commonplaces and rules of operation engrained in my habits and elaborated in my philosophic preferences.

I attached little importance to these steps at the time they were taken, if indeed I was aware of them. They coincided with, if they were not part of, my formal education in philosophy. They may have left traces in my examinations, essays, and theses, but they were not relevant to any of the questions that tested my knowledge or to the contribution to knowledge which I was certified to have made in satisfying the conditions for the doctorate. The problem of the one and the many took concrete form for me in the teaching of two men during my work at Columbia University, and the crossing of their influence was a greater educational force than the teaching of either alone could have been, even if I had been more attentive to what each had said and more conscious than I was, at the time, of its significance. Frederick J. E. Woodbridge stressed with subtle insight and ingenious dialectic the structure of intelligibility in the world. Ideas, he taught, are not inventions constructed by the mind, but discoveries forced upon us by compelling realities whose natures are basically intelligible. Being has intimate relations with being understood, and the fundamental problem of philosophy is not how something nonrational becomes intelligible but how mind is related to many minds. John Dewey, when he returned from China and Japan in 1920, applied his experience and his reflections to the construction of two courses—one on Types of Philosophic Thought, the other on Types of Logical Theory—which set forth the basis of his philosophy more fully than it has appeared in the many books that he was to write in the succeeding decades. In those courses he dwelled on the term which was to become so important in the development of his logic and his political and social philosophy, and explained his hesitations in choosing it. By "experience," he meant, not a psychological stage nor an epistemological category, but rather the context and diversified circumstances in which problems arise and ideas are developed. If he were to seek a single synonym for what he meant by "experience," he said, he would use the term, "culture." He set himself the task of exploring in nonhistorical but systematic fashion the contacts, shifts, alternations, and equivalences of the problems which had been presented to philosophers by experience in their times and of the means which they had devised to treat them. The solutions, like the problems, found their materials, their forms, and their criteria in the economic, social, and intellectual circumstances in which they were developed. In the teachings of Woodbridge and of Dewey the problem of the one and the many is restated in terms appropriate to the problems of our times—not as a problem of essence and existence, nor as a problem of reality and appearance, but as a problem of truth and modes of formulation. The richness and diversity required by the experience and the problems of our times and suggested by the ramifications and successes of scientific inquiry revealed the tenuousness and poverty of the philosophic principles with which I had been engaged and their inadequacy despite the fact that they required only elaboration and application to yield a fully articulated philosophy.

I have constructed this elaborate background of specifications concerning the nature of discovery in philosophy and concerning the situation in which I found myself in education and experience, not as a dodge by which to avoid the question which I have undertaken to answer—the analysis of the occasion of a sudden flash of insight in philosophy and of the uses to which I have put it—but as an essential preliminary to making any answer to that question intelligible. Graham Wallas, who has devoted a book, *The Art of Thought*, to examining the problem of discovery and related processes in the richer data available in the testimony of great thinkers, finds himself constrained to follow a pattern of four stages, first, the Preparation of materials; second, Incubation; third, Illumination or occurrence of the idea; and, finally, Verification. The testimony that Wallas is able to provide for that stage which is intermediate between the labor of preparatory analysis and the unexplained occurrence of a solution is singularly unenlightening. New ideas came to Helmholtz "particularly readily during the slow ascent of wooded hills on a sunny day." Poincaré made two of his great mathematical discoveries after periods of Incubation, due in one case to his military service as a reservist and in the other case to a journey. Old and familiar ideas which I have searched out or encountered at hazard and new ideas, which have led to the reorganization of familiar materials and to hypotheses that I have tried against the requirements of those materials, have both occurred to me under the same two circumstances—from reading books and from conferring, particularly during the period of my work with Unesco, with people of backgrounds, presuppositions, and cultures different than my own. The occasion which seems to me to have influenced my work in philosophy more than any other was an insight that occurred to me in reading. It was not an experience that led to my conversion to a doctrine expressed or to my elaboration of a belief adumbrated and, indeed, I am embarrassed by the fact that I am not sure, after candid examination of my memories, which of two passages furnished the occasion of the insight. I incline consequently to the hypothesis that it was the conjunction and opposition of the two.

The two passages are in the writings of Cicero and of Plato. I attached little importance to the statement of Cicero when I first read it in the *De Finibus,* since it was obviously false. "'My view then, Cato,' I proceeded, 'is this, that those old disciples of Plato, Speusippus, Aristotle, and Xenocrates, and afterwards their pupils Polemo and Theophrastus, had developed a body of doctrine that left nothing to be desired either in fullness or finish, so that Zeno [the Stoic] on becoming the pupil of Polemo had no reason for differing either from his master himself or from his master's predecessors.'" This is obviously false, since Aristotle, Plato's pupil, devotes so many arguments to the explicit refutation of his master; since the Academy, Plato's school, runs in its evolution through a whole range of possible doctrines from dogmatic idealism to pragmatic skepticism, and the record of the development of the school shows scarcely a master who agreed with the teachings of his predecessor;

since the later Peripatetics were unsubtle and unfaithful Aristotelians; and since the Stoics were engaged in controversies, which shifted front with the successive controversialists, against Peripatetics and against Academics, Old and New. Yet as I read Cicero I became more aware of the full import of his thesis—that all philosophies (except the Epicurean, which is, taken simply, false but which, in so far as it is not false, falls under the same thesis) are particular expressions of the same truth and that, in so far as they succeeded in expressing that truth, they differ only verbally. Similarly I attached little importance to the statement in Plato's *Protagoras* at first, since it was obviously a comic interlude to a serious, though inclusive, discussion. After Protagoras, wearied and numbed by Socrates' questions concerning the practicability of his undertaking to teach civic science, was ready to abandon the discussion, he was persuaded to resume by asking rather than answering questions. He chose to vary the approach to the theme by undertaking the interpretation of a poet, Simonides, who wrote a poem developing the theme that it is hard to be good. When Protagoras had completed his interpretation, Socrates appealed to Prodicus and with his approval employed Prodicus's verbal art of interpreting language to remove the contradictions Protagoras had expounded. Socrates then gave a third interpretation of the poem using the resources of his dialectical method to expose the insufficiencies of both Protagoras's sophistic and Prodicus's semantic interpretations. He reinforced his own conclusion by quoting another, unknown, poet—"the good are sometimes bad and sometimes good." This is a paradox employed humorously to introduce a good Socratic point, that the good have the capacity of becoming bad, but the bad have no capacity whatever for becoming but always remain what they are. Yet, as I read in the Platonic dialogues I found myself modifying the verse of the unknown poet and speculating on the evidence that Plato found in the questions of Socrates and in the doctrines of other philosophers—which he can alternately quote for his purposes or refute—that the true is sometimes false and sometimes true.

Discovery is not the simple fitting, or passive addition, of further items of information to a collection of data or to a structure of theory. The effect of a new insight is to modify the interpretation of facts previously known and to necessitate the adjustment or abandonment of theories previously held. It may be welcomed as a contributing cause to total change and revolution in doctrine and attitude; or it may be admitted reluctantly as a sufficient reason for alteration of the customary and accepted. Reading may lead to discovery when what is read is not at first sight, or fully, credible or when it affords grounds for crediting principles or conclusions at variance with those to which assent had been given. Discovery does not result from reading about facts or discourses which follow from or accord with one's basic beliefs; at most such reading leads to the accretion and substantiation of doctrines and the increase and solidification of schools and sects. I had no great admiration for the philosophy of Cicero, although I was convinced in 1921, when the reading of the *De Finibus* came into conjunction with the reading of the *Protagoras*, that his importance as transmitter of Greek culture to the modern world was underrated today and that, under the influence of distaste for his utilitarian verbalism, the similarity of our own philosophic tendencies to his was overlooked. Plato's influence is more frequently acknowledged by modern philosophers, not always for reasons as good or as eloquently expressed as Whitehead's, but the effect of Platonic doctrines and dialectic is usually rendered in a truncated schema which reduces them to a cautious skepticism, like Cicero's Academicism, or a mystical science, like the organic philosophies of Nicholas of Cusa or Whitehead. I had come to see the merits that could be attributed to pragmatisms and to dialectics, but only by a kind of external and intellectual recognition, for I have never felt attracted to the use of pragmatic principles or dialectical methods, preferring to treat theoretic and practical questions separately rather than to assimilate theory to practice or practice to theory.

The recognition, therefore, that there is a sense in which truth, though one, has no single expression and a sense in which truth, though changeless, is rendered false in the uses to which it is put, was attractive in spite of the fact that it ran counter to my most fundamental convictions at the time. I should have preferred to think of the development of philosophy, as knowledge, as a progressive evolution in which errors were detected and discarded and truths were accumulated and interrelated. I should have preferred to think of the applications of philosophy, in practice, as the use of truths administered as specifics to cure evils and operating in constant fashion in conjunction with constant laws of nature and human nature.

Yet philosophic problems seemed to me to have taken on a new form from the new social, political, and moral problems of our times, and both problems, the philosophic and the practical, required a new philosophic approach. Our philosophic problems have centered, for the decades that have passed since I read Cicero and Plato together, in relativism and anti-intellectualism. In its simple form, relativism is a denial of over-all criteria of values, including truth, apart from the particular circumstances in which particular things are in fact valued; there is, however, a second dimension of relativism, which takes its frame of reference not in the different things men call good because they desire them, but in the different principles of partially developed and partially recognized philosophies which guide men's preferences and actions. The first is a relativism of values, based on the conviction that there is no reason why your good should be my good; the second is a relativism of schools and parties, based on the conviction that no reason is adequate to convince you, whatever its cogency and whatever its pertinence to the good, and errors must be extirpated, therefore, and truth must be advanced, by means other than reason—by propaganda, sophistic, indirection, deceit, slander, fear, and if necessary, suppression, force, and liquidation. In its simple form, anti-intellectualism is a confidence, accompanied by a distrust of analytic statement and rational proof, that sensitivity and good intentions are enough; there is, however, a second stage of anti-intellectualism, in which the distrust of reason, buttressed by reasons, becomes a roundly expressed and argued distress at other men's reasons in the oppositions and intolerances of schools, parties, and sects. The change in these narrowly philosophic problems, which gives them greater importance beyond philosophy than they have ever had before, results from changes in the world situation which makes the relations of peoples, nations, classes, and in general all associations, profoundly philosophic problems. Men of all cultures, of all nations, and of all philosophies have been brought into contacts that affect every aspect of their lives. The values which motivate them are different. Either their different values are different expressions of the same values, in which case values can be differentiated from pseudo-values and truths from errors; or they are irreducibly relative, in which case conflicts among value structures result from, and are resolved by, oppositions of power, and men would prefer to remain neutral to any such conflict unless they are involved, not by reason or conviction, but by interest or force. The statement of this conflict employs reasons and ideals; to judge by the arguments that have been employed to make it clear, the whole tradition of Western thought culminates in the oppositions which now tend to divide all men, and any philosopher may be blamed in those oppositions for the errors to be resisted, or, alternatively, may be praised as a source of truth or a guide for action. Philosophy has entered into a new importance in the ideological conflict, but the use of philosophy is so clouded by ambiguities that the practical relevance of principles and arguments is itself thrown into doubt. We are losing hold of truth because of the variety of ways in which it is expressed, and we are losing confidence in truth because of the degradations to which concepts, which were conceived to express ideals, and statements, which were thought to express truths, are put in their practical uses and manipulations.

I have gone ahead of the story of the flash of insight that came from Cicero and Plato some thirty years ago in order to indicate the significance I was later to attach to it. The steps by which the insight was bodied forth to this broad interpretation from the situation which followed World War I to the situation which developed from World War II were slow and meticulous. If it is true that there is no single statement of the single truth and that any statement of truth, however well articulated and painstakingly verified, is subject to degradation, misinterpretation, and misapplication, it becomes important to distinguish the aspects by which the forms of expression and proof may be differentiated and by which the criteria of continuing validity and value may be applied. Philosophies may be distinguished with respect to four basic differences: philosophers talk about different subject matters; they employ different methods in their treatment of the same or different matters; they base their methods on different assumptions and principles; and they direct their philosophic constructions and speculations to different ends. Once these differences have been elaborated, it is easy to recognize

Aristotle's four causes in them; and since Aristotle has been able to find no more than four causes, there was some ground for the presumption that I should encounter no more in the writings of another two thousand years of philosophers. But whereas inquiry into the operation of causes led Aristotle to examine the first principles of being and to develop what was later to be called a metaphysics, inquiry into the operation of causes had apparently started me on an examination of first principles of philosophic discourse and to develop a form of what is now called semantics. If I had unconsciously borrowed the principles of my inquiry from Aristotle, I was committed to using them on a different subject matter.

The changes in the subject matter which philosophers treat supply the most immediately apparent differences among philosophies. It is the source of most of the revolutions proclaimed by philosophers—such as Kant's and Dewey's Copernican revolutions—and it gives to the history of philosophy the appearance of periodization which lead philosophers and historians of some philosophic schools to discover that ages have their characteristic "spirits" or "climates" or "philosophies" and that the history of philosophy follows a cyclical or a cumulative or a rising and falling development. During any given period, philosophers treat in their theories and discussions what may be conceived broadly as the same subject matter, and they differ in the methods they employ, in the principles in which the method is grounded, and in the ends to which it is directed. For all the differences of philosophies, there is a homogeneity in the discussion inasmuch as they raise the same or comparable questions and give different answers to them. When the subject matter changes, due to external influences or to the revolutions of philosophers, the fundamental questions are changed and the problems that were basic and difficult in the previous period become derived and relatively easy to treat as simple consequences or as unreal puzzles, and philosophers in the new tradition may either underline their originality and independence of previous philosophic traditions or their fidelity to the old methods, perennial principles, and traditional purposes which are put to new uses in application to the new problems.

The broad philosophic sense in which philosophers for a time concentrate their attention on the same subject matter is apparent in the distinctions which they make in subject matters at each stage of the discussion. For a time they treat the nature of things as their fundamental concern and make problems of knowledge, action, and expression depend on basic principles of being and becoming, essence and existence, matter and motion. Differences concerning the nature of being lead eventually to such subtle differentiations, such complex interrelations, such massive consequences that philosophers turn in the search for prior questions to an examination of the grounds on which such differences can be simplified and the nature of things can be known and verified. For a time philosophers then seek criteria of knowledge which permit them to treat questions of the nature of things as well as questions of action and expression as consequences of these basic distinctions. But again differences concerning the nature and grounds of knowledge become subtle, massive, and polar, and philosophers turn in an effort to find prior questions to an examination of the means of simplifying such differences and of testing knowledge by the practical consequences to which it leads or by the form of language—scientific proof, practical communication, esthetic construction, spiritual preachment—in which they are set forth. The criteria of the practical and the techniques of verbal analysis, in turn, become involved in ambiguities, uncertainties, and antithetical formalisms, which return philosophers to the expectation that the ends of actions and the meanings and values of symbols must be grounded in the nature of things, and that the fundamental analysis for philosophy must be sought in being, not in knowledge, or action, or statement.

Recognition of the sequence in which philosophers have gone through these stages of reaction a number of times in the history of Western thought does not lead necessarily to a *Geistesgeschichte* or a dialectic according to which ages follow a necessary order of growth and decline, although it does reveal, as would be proper in the inquiry in which I proposed to engage, the grounds on which dialectical philosophies might allege such an order. The richness and diversity of approaches and methods can be distinguished, nonetheless, within each age and can be related to comparable methods, principles, and purposes across the dividing lines of subject matter and problems which separate ages.

Plato, Democritus, Aristotle, and the Sophists, whose lives overlapped, found their philosophic principles in the nature of things: Plato sought the fundamental reality in Ideas; Democritus explained all processes, including the processes of thought, by the motion of atoms; Aristotle professed to avoid reducing things to thoughts or thoughts to things, and constructed a system of sciences adjusted to differences of problems; and Isocrates reduced all theoretic problems to their practical terms and found the true philosophic method in rhetoric. The deaths of Alexander, Aristotle, and Demosthenes within a period of little more than a year marked the end of an epoch. Philosophers for a time thereafter sought their basic principles in the criteria of knowledge, yet Stoics and Epicureans, Academics and Skeptics derived inspiration for this new task in the earlier philosophies. Epicurus modified the doctrine of Democritus in the construction of his Canon to set forth and employ the criteria of knowledge and to make clear the inadequacies and irrelevancies of formal logic; the Academics professed to follow Plato in the sequences of their skeptical and dogmatic schools; the Stoics adapted something of the method and terminology of Aristotle to what they conceived to be the true development of Plato in the elaboration of a propositional logic; and the Peripatetics became scholars and technical scientists. Under the spreading Roman rule, philosophers took their beginnings in the consideration of how men talk and how men act, yet they appropriated to that analysis the doctrines of Stoics, Epicureans, Academics, and Skeptics. Cicero constructed a practical philosophy under the inspiration of Socrates and Isocrates by wedding wisdom and eloquence and by reconciling the differences of schools; Sextus Empiricus attacked dogmatism in all the sciences by analysis of the signs employed in constructing the sciences; rhetoric developed in many forms culminating under the Empire in a New Sophistic; and Platonism emerged under the same circumstances in a New Platonism.

Theory and practice, principles and experience, values and circumstances, all contributed to these successive changes of subject matter and to the modification which the oppositions of philosophers underwent in successive applications. The coming of Christianity affected the subject matter of philosophy in all these respects: it supplied new data and new tidings relevant to the nature, origin, and destiny of man; it suggested new principles for the organization of these and like data and provided new ends to which to orient life and knowledge; it first opposed and resisted and then appropriated and modified the methods of the philosophers. In the East, the development of a Christian philosophy took a theoretic turn in dogmatic disputes concerning the true doctrine; in the West, under the influence of Cyprian, Ambrose, and Augustine, it took a practical turn in the organization of the Church and in its establishment in the context of the Empire. Western Christianity found in the writings of St. Augustine a complete philosophy which was to continue to influence the whole course of Christian thought; Boethius professed to depart in no respect from the doctrine of Augustine, but he found it desirable to restate its arguments to bring forth the grounds and criteria on which it is established, and he furnished the basic texts which set Christians discussing the problem of the universal and the consolations of philosophy; Cassiodorus restated the liberal arts, treating the arts of the trivium as verbal, in relation to Christian doctrine, and Isidore of Seville reduced knowledge to an encyclopedic compendium organized according to the etymologies of the basic terms employed in stating it.

Philosophy took new life and a new subject matter from the practical problems of politics treated in terms of the liberal arts in the court of Charlemagne and from the practical problems of canon law treated in like terms in the court of Charles the Bald. These led to problems of criteria and sources of knowledge and action which threatened during the tenth and eleventh centuries to set theology and philosophy in opposition, but the method which was to be called the "Scholastic method" and which moved from canon law to theology and thence to philosophy provided a means for their reconciliation by assembling the opposed answers to common questions and by examining their differences and, in so doing, it set men discussing once more the problem of the universal. John of Salisbury, in the twelfth century, sought escape from these problems in a humanistic pragmatic philosophy, modeled on the Ciceronean Academicism and constructed in the light of the difficulties which his master, Pierre Abelard, encountered in the construction of a nominalistic dialectic. The translation of the works of Aristotle during the twelfth and early thirteenth century created a sharp break in the development of Christian philosophy by providing a new subject matter organized in a vast scientific corpus and a new method used in the treatment of that subject matter and expounded in Aristotle's treatises on logic. Roger Bacon, Alexander of Hales, Albertus Magnus, Bonaventura, and Thomas Aquinas, among many other writers, labored to reconcile this material to the doctrines of Christianity and to extricate the doctrines of Augustine from the consequences of its similarities and antitheses to Arabic Aristotelianism. All the varieties of methods found development and application during the thirteenth century, and the earlier fourteenth century turned, under the influence of Duns Scotus, from the complexities of metaphysics and theology to questions of criteria of knowledge by which to mediate those differences. The latter half of the fourteenth century and the Renaissance, in turn, abandoned epistemology to construct terminalistic logics, such as occupied Ockham, rhetorical and literary philosophies in forms as different as those of Ramus and Nizolius, practical philosophies such as Machiavelli elaborated, and in the interplay of methods and principles new interpretations of man's end and of the means by which to achieve it were sought in the Reformation and Counter-Reformation.

The development of modern science again provided a new subject matter for philosophy. Even before the seventeenth century, writers like Telesio and Campanella found the bases for their philosophies in the new science; and the philosophies of Bacon, Hobbes, Descartes, Spinoza, Leibnitz, Locke, Berkeley, and Hume are inseparable from efforts to state and develop the new methods of science and to apply them to philosophic problems and to speculations concerning man. Although many of these philosophers developed their methods by tracing the origin and relations of ideas, by distinguishing simple ideas, complex ideas, and modes, or by seeking clear, distinct, and adequate ideas, Kant was correct in recognizing that their philosophies were oriented to the nature of things—to God, nature, and the self, to thought and extension, to space and the motions of things—and in claiming the distinction for himself of having reoriented philosophy to man and to the forms of thought. The nineteenth century labored with the criteria and limits of thought and with the ramifications of philosophical anthropology and epistemology; and we have rounded the turn, once more in the twentieth century, by reacting against idealisms to seek the subject matter of philosophy in action, experience, and the patterns of cultures and in symbols, communication, and the demonstrations of science.

Even so cursory a view of the history of subject matters of philosophic discussion throws some light on the nature of the discovery that came to me from the pages of Cicero and Plato, for it explains the uneasy similarities of our own philosophic preoccupations to those of the Roman, the Carolingian, and the Renaissance periods. Cicero was engaged on a similar subject matter when he found a single truth differently expressed in the different philosophies, and Socrates's interlude with the Sophists in explanation of the poetic insight, that the good are sometimes bad and sometimes good, is closer to the doctrine of the New Academy, which Cicero professed, than to the loftier reaches of the Platonic doctrine of Ideas. Moreover, it explains why any application that I might seek to make of Aristotle's four causes would lead me, if I was sensitive to subject matter of my contemporaries in philosophy, to the development of a semantics as a propaedeutic to metaphysical or epistemological inquiries.

The differences of the methods employed by philosophers are apparent in the differentiation of the subject matters which they treat in successive periods. These differences are stated in a vast variety of ways, usually in polemical discussions in which all other methods are contrasted to the one employed in the statement. It early became apparent to me that some schematism must be developed which would permit the comparison of methods without distortion by the peculiarities of any one method, if the sense and the extent to which different philosophies express an identical or similar truth and the sense and the extent to which they slip into error and perversion were to be revealed objectively and neutrally. In the course of searching for such a schematism I became convinced that a formal structure would have to be found which would at one and the same time guarantee that the methods distinguished were mutually exclusive, exhaustive of the possibilities of methodological difference, and the source of all the subdivisions and secondary variations of method, and also that they were subject to statement, in the schematism, indifferently in equivalent though different forms according to all the methods. The basis for such a schematism must have some relation to the large structures which appear as philosophies are developed according to their appropriate methods. I found in a classification of these structures under four heads the beginnings of a schematism which satisfied the criteria I had set up.

There are, in the first place, philosophies which begin with the conviction that the whole, however the "whole" is conceived—the universe, the whole of knowledge or experience, the whole man, the whole of civilization, the whole of values, of modes of expression, or of means and potentialities of being, thought, action, and statement—cannot be treated adequately in terms of its parts. No independent entities, ideas, values, or actions are conceivable or possible in these philosophies, but the problem of philosophy is to trace the lines by which everything is related to everything else in being and operation, in knowledge and impulse, in value and implication. Philosophers who develop this conviction in varying ways frequently profess to use the dialectical method, and I decided to examine the method common to all such philosophies under the rubric "dialectic." There are, in the second place, and at the opposite extreme, philosophies which undertake the enterprise of seeking least parts from which to construct those portions of knowledge or reality that are now accessible to man, while postponing the delineation of the whole, except in so far as its nature is predetermined by the assumption that it can be treated by such construction, until knowledge is available for such reformulation. The least parts are sometimes sought in things (such as atoms whose characteristics, motions, and combinations will then explain all phenomena), sometimes in thought (such as simple ideas, whose characteristics, modifications, and combinations will then provide the criteria of certainty and probability and the method by which to proceed by least steps through the long chains of reasoning that constitute science), and sometimes in symbols or signs (such as the undefined terms and rules of combination which serve to construct languages and which provide the method by which ultimately to deduce all sciences from a single set of principles). In the phase in which these philosophies sought their principles in material atoms, they were criticized by dialecticians as "logistic," and in the phase in which they used symbols as principles, their proponents tended to describe the method as logistic, and I therefore decided to use that "logistic" as the rubric under which to study all such methods. There are, in the third place, philosophies which are midway between these two extreme assumptions, inasmuch as the philosophers who engage in philosophic speculation of this kind are equally dubious of the possibility and desirability of basing a philosophy on knowledge of the whole or of the least part, and they engage instead in the construction of a variety of sciences adapted to a variety of problems, subject matters, and purposes. These philosophers are inclined to treat philosophic method as "inquiry" and to orient philosophic inquiry to "problems," and I therefore studied the methods they employed in order to characterize the "problematic" method. In addition to philosophies oriented to the whole and to internal relations within it, and philosophies oriented to the part and to combinations and constructions which they make possible or explain, and philosophies oriented to problems and their resolution without reference to holistic or atomic principles, there are, in the fourth place, philosophies which oppose to all types of theoretic construction the conviction that philosophy and knowledge should seek criteria in particular and practical consequences in action. The names historically used by the proponents of this method have all taken on pejorative senses as a result of the attacks of more theoretic philosophers—as "sophistic" retains the sense Plato and Aristotle gave it and "academic" (apart from the new layer of meaning derived from association with modern schools) retains the sense Augustine and Duns Scotus gave it—and I therefore used the term, "operationalism," which is somewhat broader in its common use, to designate this method the "operational method."

The broad characteristics of these four methods and their adaptation to the subject matters discussed by philosophers in successive ages are apparent throughout the history of philosophy despite the great variety of forms which each of the methods assumes. The dialectical method is analogical: terms properly assume a variety of meanings in the course of their use even in scientific demonstration, and the development of dialectic has an apparent unity which permits later dialecticians to recognize earlier uses of dialectic, and indeed of any other method, as preparations for, and dialectically explained antecedents to, the forms of dialectic later practiced.

Moreover, the differences of subject matter which separate the ages, from the point of view of other methods, are only apparent, not real, from the point of view of dialectic, for the processes of things and the processes of thoughts, and *a fortiori* the processes of action and statement, all reflect the same dialectical pattern, and history is intimately related to, if not identical with, proof. The logistic method, on the contrary, is literal and univocal: terms should be defined unambiguously and should retain, throughout proof and communication, the same meanings. The changes of subject matter which separate the ages separate the successive uses of the logistic method by sharp differences, for the philosopher must decide, since the method depends on the combination of least parts, whether his least parts are to be atoms, simple ideas, or symbols and, once he has chosen one, he can state and explain phenomena relative to the others in its basic terms, and his method consists in one of the many forms of the "combinatory art." The problematic method depends, like the logistic method, on the establishment of univocal terms and literal meanings; but, since there are many problems and many sciences, any important term has many meanings which must be distinguished before the proper meaning is used in the proper place, while the interrelations among these meanings is established in basic sciences, like metaphysics, by means of analogies among meanings reminiscent of the dialectic method. The differences of subject matter discussed is reflected in the problematic method by differences of the analyses and the sciences taken to be "architectonic" in determining the spread and interrelation of meanings—sometimes metaphysics or epistemology, sometimes "politics" or semantics, sometimes sociology or the study of humanistic aspects of cultures and arts. The operational method, like dialectic, is not constrained to literal or single meanings in its use of terms, but unlike dialectic its meanings are imposed either by arbitrary decision of the user of the method or by irrational determination of the operation of circumstances: for the agent who has power to control what is done, meanings are what he decides they should be; otherwise, they are determined by chance or fortune to which the practitioner of the operational method learns to adapt his actions and meanings.

Not only may philosophic methods be described in terms of their use of symbols in application to the changes of subject matter in philosophy, which had early forced themselves on my attention as one of the means by which philosophies are differentiated from each other, but methods are also distinct from each other in the relations between science and action, theory and practice, which they entail. The relation of knowledge to action had seemed to me to be one of the outstanding problems of our times, and it was one of the problems which had led me to the inquiry concerning the relations among philosophies. There are four possible relations between theory and practice, and the fact that one of these relations followed from each of the methods I had sketched seemed to me partial confirmation of the soundness and relevance of my schematism. If, with the dialectician all things are to be explained in their mutual relations in a single whole, there is no difference between theory and practice. Dialecticians have repeatedly urged that identity and have criticized practice separated from theory and theory separated from practice throughout the history of dialectic. This at least is common, among all the important differences that separate them, between Plato's use of Socrates's principle that virtue is knowledge and the Marxist use of the science of the history of society as the prototype of all science and the source of all action. The operationalist's conviction that theory should be tested by practice and that theories without consequences in action are trivial has a similar effect of identifying theory and practice but for opposite reasons, since theory is then reduced to practice whereas practice reaches its fullest possibilities and clearest explanations on the background of an over-all theory in dialectic. The other two methods distinguish knowledge and action, theory and practice, but in two different ways. For the logistic method, theory is established in science while action finds its motive and cause in some impulse, nonrational in foundation and noncognitive in operation. Science and action are therefore mutually exclusive: it is possible to have a science of all varieties of processes, including the operations and actions of men, but the motives which lead a man to action, even the action of engaging in scientific inquiry, are found in passion, habituation, accident, as well as in reason. One modern form of this distinction has become popular among philosophers who practice the logistic method in the distinction between the language of science, which is cognitive, and the language of ethics or esthetics, which is noncognitive, inasmuch as it is persuasive or emotive. For the problematic method, on the other hand, the distinction between theory and practice does not lead to the conclusion that demonstration is scientific and action nonscientific, but rather to the conclusion that, since methods vary with the variation of problems, the method of the theoretic sciences is distinct from the method of the practical sciences. Both methods, the logistic and the problematic, lead to the conclusion that the scientific method should be employed more than it is in the treatment of the problems of human action; but in the logistic method, that conviction leads to the search for a science—like psychology, sociology, or anthropology—which uses the same scientific method as the natural sciences, to cure the tensions, fears, misapprehensions, and mental illnesses which prevent men from acting as they should, whereas in the problematic method, the same conviction leads to the search, avoiding the dangerous analogy of the natural sciences, for a science which will effect communication among men as the necessary preliminary to agreement concerning the use of the technical processes of engineering and the applied sciences and the application of the conclusions of the pure sciences.

These distinctions in the field of the practical brought to my attention a homogeneity between the dialectical and the operational methods, on the one hand, and the logistic and the problematic methods, on the other, which goes beyond questions of the relation of theory and practice to questions of "scientific method" in the various senses proper to each approach. To signify these similarities I found it desirable to invent two terms: "holoscopic" to indicate the respects in which dialectical and operational methods "view" problems in their relation to some "whole," and "meroscopic" to signify the two ways in which the logistic and problematic methods "view" problems relative to the "parts" from which the whole is constructed or to the circumstances which determine the occurrence and the character of the problem.

Two more differences—differences of principles or assumptions and differences of ends or purposes—enter into the differentiation of the vast number of philosophies which have been developed in the course of the history of thought. What I have said concerning the differences of subject matters and methods is sufficient to indicate the character of the inquiry in which I engaged as a result of the discovery to which I was led by Cicero and Plato, and whereas the additional differences of principles and ends are essential to account for the relations and oppositions among philosophies in their theoretic development and in their practical application, to set forth still more differences at this point would needlessly complicate the exposition of what is involved in a moment of discovery. One question which occurs at almost any stage of the elaboration of that discovery, however, must be answered if what I have said is not to be reduced to an obvious and simple-minded parologism. If the basic problem of this semantic investigation of the relation of meanings in different philosophies involves the classification of all possible methods, what method is used in that classification? If the classification is exhaustive of all methods, must not the method of classification be one of the methods classified, and is not the inquiry itself, therefore, involved in the relativities and distortions it seeks to avoid and to resolve?

The criteria which I set forth to govern the construction of the schematism of methods supplies the answer to these questions. The schematism must be neutral, not in the sense of being conceived and stated apart from the methods it treats, but in the sense of being susceptible of statement without distortion in each of the methods. The use of the method in the formulation of the schematism will, therefore, differ from the use of the method in the resolution of practical and philosophic problems. It is possible to examine the problem of the relation of methods dialectically, operationally, logistically, and problematically, taking as data the doctrines of philosophers—professional philosophers and also that much larger group of philosophers who simply relate what they think, say, and do to contexts larger than the immediate consequences they anticipate or encounter. This is a problem in what I came to call "historical" semantics, and there is no reason why the differences of meanings encountered in the course of discussion or history should not be subject to such statement in any of the methods. Once attention is turned from the varieties of philosophies as the subject matter of inquiry and once one of the methods is employed on the subject matter of philosophy adapted to the times and the preferences of the philosopher, the use of the method results in the development of a particular philosophy and in that philosophy particular meanings are determined and assigned to terms, which are to be preferred over other possible meanings. This is a problem in what I came to call "philosophical" semantics. The course of inquiry which I followed and the exposition which I have just given of it, thus, employ the problematic method. There is no reason why one should not be led from this problematic statement of the differences of method to the choice of the dialectical, the operational, or the logistic method as best adapted to the solution of some problems or as the preferable method for philosophy in general. There is likewise no reason why the schematic differences of method might not be restated dialectically, operationally, or logistically with no more pre-judgment or distortion, than in the statement I have given, in which, for example, prior to commitment to a philosophy which fixes its meaning, each of the four meanings of the "practical" is equally defensible and equally fruitful of consequences. I have made such a translation of the schematism into the other methods elsewhere, but, for our purposes today, indication of its possibility is sufficient to clarify the assumptions on which my analysis proceeded. Once the choice of the method is made, after the propaedeutic analysis of meanings in "historical" semantics, one is constrained by the "philosophic" semantics determined by one's assumptions to one set of meanings for all fundamental terms—for "cause" or "democracy" or "imagination"—and even the fullest tolerance of intellectual differences is no justification for restraining the impulse to demonstrate that other meanings are absurd or impractical in the treatment of problems to which the method is committed.

I have explained the discovery to which I was led from reading in Cicero and Plato by setting forth, in perhaps excessive detail, distinctions in the subject matters and methods of philosophers, and insights concerning these distinctions, to which the discovery led. I have explained the mechanisms in which I later encased the insight, not the insight itself, and since I sought those mechanisms in formal distinctions among philosophies and among sciences, I am afraid that I have given the discovery itself a formalistic and historical turn. The data on which the insight was employed were the statements, preferably the well ordered or scientific statements made by different men and in different circumstances, but form and history tend to conceal the purpose of the inquiry, which was philosophic, and to leave wholly out of account the novelty which the method introduces into the problems and applications of philosophy. "Historical" semantics derives its distinctions from history and provides means by which to read intellectual history more intelligently and more profitably; it leads from history to insight into the nature and the interrelations of the sciences and into the effectiveness and varieties of expressions of values. But the characteristic result of historical semantics, to which my attention was turned from my first efforts to treat the problem of varying meanings and varying proofs, is to be found in application to new problems of philosophy, which are the mark and product of our times.

Philosophy is not only a form of knowledge; it is also an expression of cultures. In a world in which many distinct and divergent cultures are in unavoidable contact as a result of the progress of science, the temptation is natural to seek solutions to the resulting tensions among peoples by the construction and use of another science. The application of any form of science chosen for this purpose conceals one form of philosophy, and the opposition to any such program is not an opposition to science, but the mark and indication of a whole range of philosophic problems which are prior to commitment to action or to grounds for action. They involve a preliminary study of the relations of cultures as expressions of values, divergent in form but possibly identical with each other in fundamental character, which reproduce, when they are stated formally, differences on which philosophers have been engaged ever since Socrates brought philosophy down from the skies. In those relations—whether they are stated theoretically or evolved practically in the course of action—real differences are confounded with differences which are only in expression and in approach. In the emerging community of the world the first problem of philosophy—the new metaphysics or at least the new prolegomenon to all future metaphysics—will expound the sense in which what is on some grounds or in some circumstances true is at other times false and dangerous.